"This is desperately serious work, an exacting memoir that excavates, with compassion for all involved, the harrowingly repetitive patterns of abuse as well as moments of something like hope, crushable and delicate, thwarted, and yet renewable. An agonized, beautiful, unflinching account."

——LEE UPTON, author of *Visitations: Stories*

"Kim Adrian's *The Twenty-Seventh Letter of the Alphabet* is an intimate portrait of the chaos and confusion of her mother's mental illness. It's also a deep meditation on storytelling itself—our desire to impose order, discover meaning, heal what is broken in us, and find a way to live with what can't be fixed. Innovative in form and comprised of razor-sharp vignettes, Adrian summons a rare, hard-won compassion for both her mother and herself."

——STEVE EDWARDS, author of *Breaking into the Backcountry*

"Out of a fragmented, deeply moving, and dazzling narrative, the author pieces together a hard-won love, made possible by her refusal to give up. Many books are described as 'brave'—this one really is."

——SUE WILLIAM SILVERMAN, author of *The Pat Boone Fan Club: My Life as a White Anglo-Saxon Jew*

"*The Twenty-Seventh Letter of the Alphabet* astonishes from 'A' all the way to the end. Funny, sad, unassuming, wise—exquisitely written—it will make you laugh, cry, wonder, and hope. You (and your vocabulary) will be the better for reading this beautiful book."

——DINAH LENNEY, author of *The Object Parade*

D1114389

"Kim Adrian's portrait of her mother—a woman who inflicts considerable damage, having had plenty done to her—is darkly comic, probing, and full of compassion. This memoir unfolds in the startling form of a glossary: an A-to-Z of key words that have shaped Adrian's coming-to-terms with family and its mysteries. *The Twenty-Seventh Letter of the Alphabet* is altogether remarkable."

— MARTHA COOLEY, author of *Guesswork: A Reckoning With Loss*

"Adrian has written the logical, not chronological, order of her family's treasures and skeletons. These snippets, snapshots, and sequences are the ABCs of answering those age-old family questions—who are we and what have we become? With compassion, humor, and heartrending love, Adrian uses the alphabet to compose redemption's glossary."

— AMY WALLEN, author of *When We Were Ghouls*

The Twenty-Seventh Letter of the Alphabet

AMERICAN LIVES / Series editor: Tobias Wolff

The Twenty-Seventh Letter of the Alphabet

A Memoir

Kim Adrian

University of Nebraska Press / Lincoln and London

Publication of this volume was assisted by the
Virginia Faulkner Fund, established in memory of
Virginia Faulkner, editor in chief of the University
of Nebraska Press.

Library of Congress Cataloging-in-Publication Data
Names: Adrian, Kim, author.
Title: The twenty-seventh letter of the alphabet: a
memoir / Kim Adrian.
Description: Lincoln: University of Nebraska Press,
[2018] | Series: American lives
   Identifiers: LCCN 2017057646
   ISBN 9781496201973 (pbk.: alk. paper)
   ISBN 9781496210265 (epub)
   ISBN 9781496210272 (mobi)
   ISBN 9781496210289 (pdf)
Subjects: LCSH: Adrian, Kim. | Mothers and
daughters—United States—Biography. | Children of
mentally ill mothers—United States—Biography. |
Adult children of dysfunctional families—Biography.
Classification: LCC HQ755.86 .A37 2018 |
DDC 306.87—dc23 LC record available at
https://lccn.loc.gov/2017057646

Set in ITC New Baskerville by Mikala R. Kolander

To my family

Contents

Author's Note

In the interest of privacy, the names of all the
people mentioned in this book have been changed.

The Twenty-Seventh Letter of the Alphabet

A

Abecedarian

One day as a child of eight or nine I went to school, sat down in my plastic chair, and proceeded to forget how to write. We'd been assigned a simple penmanship exercise, asked to transcribe a passage from a book into longhand script. I was the teacher's pet that year, and until that bright morning, when my mind seemed suddenly to empty itself out, my cursive exercises had been held up by her as examples of what the other children should be working toward. I took pride in copying the letters almost exactly as they were drawn on the green paper band above the blackboard, albeit with a unique twist or two of my own. I was especially proud of the bold proportions of my capital *P*'s, capital *L*'s, and small *g*'s, *b*'s, and *d*'s. In fact longhand was one of my favorite topics that year, allowing, as it seemed to, a back alley passage to the more adult realm of communication—where style and quickness were practical matters. But suddenly I was at a loss as to what exactly was supposed to happen between the pencil, the paper, and my hand, and I sat staring at the page for several minutes as a silent panic took root inside of me, somewhere behind my lungs, and grew.

After a while the teacher came over to my desk.

"What's the matter?" she asked, and in attempting to respond to what I knew was a perfectly simple question, I found it was not only my fingers but my mouth as well that could not form words.

"Come on, kiddo. You tired or something?" She left without waiting for an answer and walked back to her desk, the tweedy chafing of her slacks, the flat clack-clack of her sensible heels the only noises in the classroom aside from the steady ticking of the enormous clock above the door and the busy hoarseness of cheap paper eating the soft graphite cores of twenty-five No. 2 pencils.

Eventually, something inside of me clicked—freed up, just a little, just enough—and I began to write, copying the typed text from the book onto the sheet of paper in front of me, my pencil racing across its lemony expanse, filling its blue lines with shimmering threads of silver-black arabesques. Amazed that such a ridiculously easy task had only moments earlier seemed so impossible, I drew a breath of relief and looked at my page. It seemed off somehow, but I couldn't put my finger on what was wrong. The words on my paper seemed weirdly empty, as empty as their typeset cousins had been a few minutes earlier, staring at me from the pages of the book. They signified something, surely, to someone—but not to me. Besides, my work clearly ended before it should have, stopping halfway down the page while the other children were already toiling at the bottom edges of their papers. My words looked bizarre—I knew that, but I couldn't understand why. Still, I figured I'd completed the exercise as best I could and began reading for the next lesson. Glancing up at the teacher, I received a subtle wink as if to say, "That's my girl."

A few minutes later, when she came to collect our papers, she stood for a long time at my desk, staring at my page as if it were not a penmanship exercise at all but some kind of strange animal she'd never laid eyes on.

"What's this?" she said. "You've run all the words together! How can I read this? You've forgotten to put spaces between the words." She laughed then and said, "Or is this a little joke?"

Ab Ovo

A Latin term meaning, literally, "from the egg," and, less literally, "from the beginning," "from the very start," or "from the origin." But I've found that such things are often impossible to pinpoint.

I could, of course, begin with my own birth, which took place in M——, New Jersey, 1966: a typical midcentury hospital affair, complete with a spinal block for my mother and, at first feeding, a bottle of man-made formula for me. Or I could start with my mother's birth, a mere eighteen years earlier, since I'm never quite sure whose story this is anyway—hers or mine. It might even make sense to begin with my grandma Ellen's entrance into this world in 1916 somewhere in Upstate New York because my mother's mother was a tragic but fascinating woman, and many of the tragic but fascinating elements of her character informed the equally tragic and fascinating elements of my mother's character, and those elements have informed if not exactly my own character (I'm more of an ordinary type), then at least my deepest narrative urges. In the end, however, the real start, the true egg of this story, probably lies with the first time my grandfather sexually molested my mother, which, according to what she's told me, would have been around 1953, when she was five years old. Or maybe something cracked open and hatched roughly two decades later, the first time she picked me up and threw me down, which for a while was a bad habit of hers, one I sometimes think may have shaken something important out of me—perhaps the ability to decide where stories begin?

Then again, it's possible that the richest and most reliable place from which to begin this endeavor rests, instead, in a happy event— I'm thinking about the first time I met my husband, when we were both in college and he still had all that hair. Or maybe this story begins with the birth of our first child, a girl who's now thirteen years old and likes to paint each of her fingernails a different color. Or maybe, instead, this elusive *ovo* is actually hidden in the birth of our second child, a little boy who just two days ago lost his first tooth. Yes, something did shift in me then, when Isaac was born—I remember it distinctly. I don't know what to call it, this thing that started giving way (but has never completely gone) right around his birth, though I think it has something to do with being a daughter—with being my mother's daughter.

In those first few days following my son's birth, six years ago now, I spent most of my time simply watching the newness stream off of him. I'd had a C-section, so he and I spent four days in the hospital while things healed. My mother, Linda, visited toward the end of that period, and the first thing she said when she walked into the room was that I looked weird. She refused to hold Isaac because she was afraid of giving him one of her infections, but she scrutinized me, as she always does, very carefully and at the same time from behind a thick pane of distortion, and what she said was: "Kimmy, you look so weird! *So* weird! Are you all right?" I wanted to tell her that I'd just had a baby and a not insignificant surgery. I wanted to point out that we were in a hospital room with a brand-new human being—my son—and that he was all there was to talk about, think about, or look at. But she seemed almost oblivious to her grandson's presence and hardly glanced at him. Instead, what she did was explain, at some length and very high volume without the briefest of pauses (see *pressure of speech*), why it had taken her so long to visit—something about her car. And then she told me about my sister's birth, which, although it took place, of course, a long time ago, still seemed quite vivid in her mind as she described the protracted eighteen-hour labor that had resulted in the *grinding away of the posterior wall* of her vagina as well as *portions of the anterior wall* of her colon.

As she spoke I watched my son, who was lying in his hospital bassinet with its tall plastic sides, staring intently into the mid-distance while poking first one foot and then the other into the air as if he were testing some kind of invisible, semiviscous surface, the whole time thoughtfully pressing his lips together and then, just as thoughtfully, unpressing them. It made me so happy just to watch him. Actually, all those days in the hospital had been for me inde-scribably happy. I wanted to tell my mother this, but she was still talking, now explaining how for many months after my sister's birth, she'd *leaked fecal matter* from her vagina. So I didn't tell her that I was happy. Instead, I watched my son, and even though my mother con-tinued to talk, I no longer listened. I know that doesn't sound like much, but what I'm saying is, it was, because I'd always been the kind of daughter who listened very closely to her mother. Very closely.

Acceptance

A good idea, although quite often the very presence of this word in one's everyday vocabulary indicates conditions under which such an act (of acceptance) may prove difficult to implement. In my experience meditation and yoga are of tremendous use, as are homemade baked goods, luxury bath products, and the presence of young children. (See also *embarrassingly large collection of self-help books.*)

Adamant

"I just remember the Dairy Queen," says Tracy. We try to talk every weekend, long-distance: Boston to Chicago. Sunlight rakes through the openwork of the lace shawl I've draped across the bedroom window. Irregular polka dots of light scatter over the bed I share with my husband.

"What do you mean, the Dairy Queen?"

"Before we went to the bakery on Sunday mornings. Dad and I used to stop to get ice cream. That's why it took so long."

"It did take a long time."

"Oreo Blizzards. I just remember those. I don't know how you keep all that other crap in your head. All those memories."

"I don't know how you don't."

It's something we often discuss, my sister and I—the different ways we remember our childhoods. "There are worse," says Tracy, and she would know, having taught in a Chicago high school for nearly two decades to students who sometimes have crack addicts for mothers and convicts for fathers, to kids who sometimes get pregnant or shot dead before they're halfway through freshman year. But I, for whatever reason, have always been clear about this: that time, those years—our childhoods—sucked. On this I am adamant.

Of course, we had different childhoods, as siblings invariably do. For example, Tracy was my father's favorite. I was my mother's. Tracy was barely a year old at the time of our mother's first suicide attempt, while I was three and saw the blood, the razor blade, and the paramedics firsthand. Tracy wasn't quite two when our mother left us, and when she returned, Tracy was four, while I was already six. Beyond that, our natural temperaments are in many ways almost opposite. Those temperaments were often parsed by our mother, who liked to say that Tracy was athletic and I was artistic; Tracy good at math, I at English; Tracy practical and happy-go-lucky, I dreamy and oversensitive. Tracy, she often said, was easy-going, but I was incredibly stubborn. If Tracy wanted a lollipop, she'd joke, you could promise to get it for her the next day and never hear about it again. But I have always had (as my mother still occasionally puts it) "the memory of an elephant."

Agoraphobia

On one of her many cell phones, my mother calls to inform me that I am now her *only link to the outside world.* This is why, she says, I must do her grocery shopping.

"I can't do your grocery shopping, Mom. I have my own life. Remember? I have things to do."

"You don't understand," she says. "I can't go out of my apartment anymore. I don't know why, but as soon as I step foot out of this place, everything I do gets *immediately* fucked up. Everything I touch turns into a *disaster.* I don't know if I just have really crappy karma or what, but everyone I meet seems to get angry at me, and it just works a whole lot better when I don't leave the house."

Albatross

I've wanted to tell this story for as long as I can remember wanting anything at all. That may sound like an exaggeration, but it's not. I clearly remember waves of that rousing sensation—a kind of primitive narrative impulse—washing over me as far back as early childhood. But this story is complicated in the same way that mental illness is complicated. It has no *boundaries. There's no up or down to it. No right or left.

Amygdalae

Rooted etymologically in Greek words meaning "almond ton-sils," referring to their tapered and somewhat pendulant shape, the amygdalae are a paired set of ganglia located at the base of the brain. Considered part of the limbic system, they control, in concert with the hippocampus, the processing of both memory and emotion and for this reason are considered the seat of our fight-flight-or-freeze impulses. In people with post-traumatic stress disorder, the amygdalae tend to be enlarged. According to my mother, who has a remarkable but perhaps distorted knowledge of brain anatomy (and whose amygdalae are "big as grapefruits"), people with PTSD often experience even the smallest decisions and most innocuous encounters as fight-flight-or-freeze situations, as a result of which their amygdalae are enaged in near constant activity. Hence the enlargement.

Anger

To be avoided and/or maturely processed whenever possible. When not possible, best used, as per the suggestion of John Lydon (aka Johnny Rotten), as a kind of "energy."

Assholes

"All dentists, as I'm sure you know, are *vicious psycho-assholes.*" She describes her dental and medical problems to me over and over, in great detail. David says he doesn't know why I listen. I don't either, except that I sometimes imagine it might help. Imagine that by talking about my mother's "medical" issues, I'm really helping her talk about what her father did to her when she was a child. I'm pretty sure, though, that she doesn't think of it that way.

Avoidance

Tracy keeps buying them for her, so that by now my mother owns five, maybe six, cell phones. But at the moment only one of them works because in attempting to disable their tracking devices, she broke the others. On my own phone I've assigned my mother a distinctive ring tone. It sounds like a duck, and I rarely pick up when my phone starts quacking. In fact, I almost never touch my own cell phone because on it I frequently find text messages from my mother, and these often contain photographs I don't want to see. Occasionally, these photographs are innocuous—the sky outside her living room window or a flower near her parking space—but mostly she sends me selfies. My mother has always been fond of photographing herself, and the pictures she texts are often dramatically lit shots orchestrated to emphasize her high cheekbones or her large green eyes. I find them spooky. Also, she sometimes sends me photos documenting some of her more mysterious health problems. For example, one night when she was supposed to come over for dinner (she lives just one town away, in a subsidized apartment), she called our home phone a few hours after we'd already done the dishes and put the kids to bed to ask if I'd gotten the pictures she'd sent. "Check your cell phone," she said.

I did, and on it found a series of photographs she'd taken of her mouth. The accompanying text explained: *Driving to yr place this happened. Some kind of reaction. Had to turn home. Srry.*

In the photos her lips were three or four times their normal size, pink, nearly red, and completely smooth. They looked like enormous clown lips attached to her otherwise gaunt face. Seeing these images, I felt, as I so often do when dealing with my mother, an instant unraveling. Like vertigo, only backward. Instead of a sensation of falling through space, I feel space collapsing inside of me, something shutting down with incredible speed, telescoping, evaporating. I showed the pictures to David, who said, "Don't look at those," but it was too late.

B

B——, Massachusetts

The handsome Boston suburb where I live with my husband and our two children has excellent libraries, exemplary schools, a lot of very pretty public parks, and two good bookstores. There are also a few decent restaurants, a yarn store, three great bakeries, and a responsive police force. The children in B—— are generally well behaved. Some of the adults look sour, but this is a problem everywhere. Unfortunately, B—— is barely affordable on my husband's and my combined salaries (David is an architect, while I cobble together a patchwork of teaching gigs and freelance graphic design work).

We rent an apartment off the back of a large house on a busy street. To get to our place, you have to walk down a narrow concrete pathway that's crowded, in the summertime, with azaleas, hydrangeas, pale roses, leggy cherry tomato plants, struggling squash plants, and a raggedy box hedge. At the end of this path is a wooden gate—crooked but functional—and once you pass through this, the street almost completely falls away: everything is suddenly quieter thanks to the towering white maples that surround our yard and absorb the city's noise. Chipmunks, squirrels, rabbits, skunks, and even, occasionally, a wild turkey or two wander through both day and night. Just past the sculpture of awkward concrete pilings (made by our landlord in his grad school days) is our porch, crowded with a grill, a table and chairs, potted plants, various rackets, balls, bats, gardening tools, bikes, shoes, and scooters.

Though small and on the ground level, our apartment is very bright. When people first see it, they often say, "What a great space." It has concrete floors, which years ago I stained and stenciled to look like marble tiles but which are now scratched in those areas that get the most traffic, and there are dark patches under each one of our dining room chairs. Instead of walls, we put up bookshelves (often crammed two layers deep) that also serve as room partitions. There's a wood-burning stove and a big white ceiling fan to circulate its heat, three skylights (two of which leak), and a bank of seven tall windows that look out onto the yard—a space that now, in late October, is still green and lush, boasting jubilant displays of mahogany-colored dahlias, white chrysanthemums, pink geraniums, and countless orange rosehips. The four of us sleep in lofts suspended above the main living area, which, with a ceiling height of eighteen feet, is the apartment's real glory. The height of this space manages to make everything feel light and airy, at least when things are tidy—though to be honest, that's not often because our home is cluttered most of the time by an ever-changing, overflowing mix of bills and paperwork; bowls of bananas, apples, tomatoes, lemons, and other fruits in various states of ripeness; children's art projects; yarn and knitting needles; computer chargers; yoga props; Legos; baking pans; library books; blankets; shoes; board games; coats; hats; and always, for some reason, a sock or two that didn't quite make it into the hamper.

Sometimes I worry that our unconventional living space and cramped quarters create an odd burden for our children, whose friends—many of them—live in the large, beautifully appointed homes that are the pride of B——. But at other times it seems fine, even good, to live like this. The other day, for example, when Isaac found me clicking through old photos on my computer, he stopped me at an image of him and Isabella playing dress-up. In this photo, taken about three years ago, he wears a plastic crown and a pink-and-white chenille bedspread draped like a king's cloak over his small shoulders. It trails after him in a luxurious swirl. Isabella is dancing, laughing, her teeth softly illuminated by a ray of sunlight. She wears a pair of shorts, a T-shirt, and a black straw hat inherited from my mother that's pure glamour: its disklike brim is more than two feet across. Looped around her neck is a lavender feather boa and on her feet a pair of my high heels. Behind the children tower the seven windows, and beyond the windows there is nothing but green: a wall of overgrown grass and sun-shot leaves from the forsythia bush, the rose of Sharon, the bittersweet vines, the little blackthorn tree, and the white maples. These seven windows and the ever-shifting but essentially constant view they frame create the stage set of our lives. All the goings-on in our small apartment happen against this backdrop. "Stop!" said Isaac, putting his hand on top of mine, which was hovering over the trackpad. He put his face up very close to the computer screen, peered a little longer at the image on it, then said, "Everything about that picture is perfect."

Black Oxalis

My mother sometimes signs off her friendlier text messages as "LuLu LaBloom." There are many variations on this name. For instance, sometimes she's "Mere Lulu," and sometimes she's simply "LaBloom." Occasionally, she is also "Gleimug Czysvlos," but I don't what that means.

> Look at how fabulous the black Oxalis U gave me is doing! Next I'll kick your African Violet ass! LuLu LaBloom (qui est soulement le jardinière le plus formidable de le monde!)

> How would you like it if I moved a little closer 2 U? <Lulu La BLooM! >

> Punkins, please text me your recipe 4 lime/ginger/honey salad dressing ASAP. Have a huge freshsalad mix losing freshness vit! Thanx, Lulu la B!

Kimmy: Be on safe side & empty Fiji water bottle I left on porch—vit vit—B4 one of kids takes swig! Luv ya. ~ Gleimug Czysvlos

Hey kids, Thelma & Louise is on right now channel 7. Ta ta, LuLu.

Hi kabimps! Had GREAT time & hope U R glad I made it. I know my screwed up hearing/balance is a drag & must thank U 4 rolling w/it. Mere Gleimug.

Blanket

There was a time when my mother wasn't yet addicted to prescription drugs. When she was already broken but the cracks didn't show—unless, perhaps, you looked very closely. But my father didn't. He saw only the pretty face, the long legs, the green eyes, and the shiny, chestnut-colored hair. At least I don't know how else to explain it.

They went to the same high school. He was two years older. They dated a couple of times, but when he made a comment about her being "broad in the beam," she refused to see him for several months. When she eventually agreed to another date, he borrowed a friend's convertible to pick her up. Because she was ashamed of her house, she walked down the road to meet him. I know this story because my mother once told it to me and it burned itself into my brain. My grandma Ellen had just bought a white blanket that day, and my mother had taken it with her, wrapped around her shoulders, because it was the nicest thing she could find to wear. I grew up with this blanket, took it to college, still have it in fact. Made of some kind of super-sturdy synthetic material, it remains a blanket, though just barely: frayed and dingy, the weave has so expanded with age, you can fit your fingers through it. But back then, on the night I was conceived, it was still new—still fluffy and soft—and my mother wore it over her shoulders as she walked toward my father because, she told me so many years later, it made her feel *pure*.

Blocked

By "blocked" she means blocked from going about her life. Blocked from working, blocked from making friends, blocked from happiness, blocked from normalcy. There are people behind this blocking. Sometimes they talk to her directly, over the television. Other times they answer the phone when she dials 911—only it's not the "real" 911; it's the "fake" 911 because she's blocked from the real 911. The police block her, and store owners block her; the post office and AT&T and her local Peapod delivery service all block her. Dentists and doctors and the Department of Mental Health block her, the internet blocks her, also the Department of Motor Vehicles and Medicaid—they all, she insists, work hard and ceaselessly over the phone lines, through cables, and sometimes even on late night TV ads, to block her.

Blue Tea-Length Dress

In the jumbled box of family photographs my mother once gave me, there is an ancient, yellowed clipping from a local newspaper announcing my parents' wedding. Illustrated with a half-tone reproduction of her high school portrait, the title of the blurb reads, "Student Is Bride Elect." Technically speaking this is incorrect because by the time of their wedding my mother was already four months pregnant with me and had dropped out of high school. There are no surviving photographs of the event itself, but she once told me that it was a "modest affair" and that she wore a pale-blue, "tea-length" dress.

From my father I learned much more recently that after the ceremony, his parents invited his new wife's family over for a celebratory meal. We were making stuffed peppers (my grandma Bella's recipe) when he told me this story. He'd come up for a visit from New York City, where he's lived ever since he stopped drinking. He was mincing garlic, and I was cutting lengthwise slits into each of the peppers.

"Wait. You met her father? What was he like?"

"Strange."

"Strange like what?"

"Just strange."

"Dad! Details."

He looked up from the cutting board and said: "Not like the mother. I mean, it wasn't like you could tell right away that something was wrong just by looking at him. He was almost charming. Friendly. Joking around. But he gave off a cold vibe. I don't know what else to call it. He just seemed sort of sneaky."

Blur

I——, New Jersey, May 1966

The trees are just starting to come into leaf—it's early May. The sky is construction paper blue, the clouds at the horizon lofty and bright as meringue. The border of this photograph has yellowed, and there's a large fingerprint—a closed-loop type—in the upper left corner. There seems a quiet stateliness to the scene, although I realize this is just the way time translates the glossy finish of old photos. Standing in my grandparents' driveway, between two taupe-colored sedans, my mother, in checked pants and a dark sleeveless turtleneck, holds a newborn me. My face is a pink blur, her arm a white bar.

Big-Time Fraud

It's complicated. I don't understand the intricacies. But basically, Medicaid has something to do with the bank, which is stealing *millions of dollars* in her name. *Big-time fraud* is how she puts it. Also, the FBI is involved. So she doesn't want Medicaid anymore. She wants Medicare because Medicaid won't let her see doctors out of state, but Medicare will, which is obviously a *necessity* if she's ever going to find *proper treatment.* This is why she's unenrolled herself from Medicaid. When I tell her this worries me, when I say that I don't think she should be walking around uninsured, she says it's called *strategy* and asks if I've ever heard of it.

Bogeyman

I never met my mother's father, have seen only a single photograph of him, and heard his voice just once, fleetingly, over the telephone when I was fourteen: his oddly singsong Swedish accent ("Izyur muh-der-dare?"). For these reasons he has always been a kind of bogeyman to me, an almost mythological figure.

Although long dead by now, my grandfather still manages to occupy an enormous amount of real estate in my imagination, so I suppose it's not surprising that occasionally I dream about him. In these dreams he is always very short and dark, his skin curiously taut, and he almost invariably appears in the same setting: an enormous public lavatory full of clogged and overflowing toilets—dozens, sometimes hundreds or even thousands of broken and doorless bathroom stalls arranged in a senseless labyrinth. These dreams tend to last a long time, although my quest in them is simple and never varies: I am searching for a non-filthy stall, either for myself or for one of my children. At some point I stumble across my grandfather crouched in a dark puddle or perched on top of a black steaming heap—a tiny, nearly dwarfish creature, mocking me without even raising an eyebrow, without even looking at me.

Boots

Recently I told David about the heavy boots and he nodded. He said he knew what I was talking about. Then he said that actually, he thought they were kind of a cliché. But my husband doesn't own a pair of heavy boots, so he's no judge. Invisible yet weighty, the heavy boots work this way: you put them on in your childhood and drag them around with you for the rest of your life. Unless, that is, you find some ingenious way of kicking them off.

Borderline Personality Disorder

One of the more frequently cited of my mother's many psychiatric diagnoses (others of which include bipolar disorder, psychosis, hypomania, PTSD, paranoia, Narcissistic personality disorder, conversion disorder, and Munchausen syndrome). According to the Mayo Clinic website: "With borderline personality disorder, you may have a severely distorted self-image and feel worthless and fundamentally flawed. Anger, impulsiveness and frequent mood swings may push others away, even though you may desire to have loving and lasting relationships. If you have borderline personality disorder, don't get discouraged. Many people with this disorder get better with treatment and can live satisfying lives."

Or not.

Boundaries

A word my mother puts in air quotes.

Bright Vermilion

For the first few years of my life we lived in a small apartment in the basement of my paternal grandparents' house, a split ranch at the end of a quasi-rural road in I——, New Jersey. My father worked in a gravel pit (his first job out of high school), and my mother studied for her GED, helped her mother-in-law keep house, and took care of me. As a family, we spent much of our time upstairs, with my grandparents and my father's two teenaged sisters. We ate most of our meals up there, and watched television upstairs too. But I still retain a few memories of our apartment in the basement. For example, I remember that the linoleum floor tiles were tan imprinted with a design of thick black lines meant to look like wood grain. I also recall a large, futuristic-seeming bottle sterilization machine that took up most of the kitchen counter. In the living room there was a striped couch, a shag rug, a small television with a battered antenna, and a reading lamp made of stainless steel. Though I slept upstairs in my grandmother's sewing room (which had been converted into a nursery), my parents' bedroom was in the basement. I can still remember their room—a gloomy space with north-facing windows that looked directly into a dense yew hedge. It was only the kitchen of that apartment that was a little more cheerful, illuminated as it was by two large sliding glass doors near the fridge.

Beyond those doors lay the world: first the concrete patio and, beyond the patio, Grandpa Joe's garden, which, in summertime, was full of tomatoes, eggplants, shell peas, enormous zucchini, and other somewhat less absorbing vegetables, like chard and spinach. There were, of course, worms in the earth and, despite my grandfather's best efforts, snails in the garden. There were tiny, almost invisible mites—bright vermilion—crawling everywhere if you looked closely enough: on the tomato vines, on the chipped concrete of the patio, over the pine-green shingles of the house, on acorns and chard leaves and yew berries and even individual blades of grass. There were sparrows and blue jays, cardinals and robins, ladybugs and daddy longlegs and two German shepherds— Jackie and Flicka—who let me ride on their backs. There was a tricycle, a tea set, a bouncy ball with a handle. I had two feet and two legs, two knees, two hands, a large collection of Richard Scarry books, and at a certain point I even had a sister. It was, in short, all a child my age and disposition could possibly want.

Buttons

I don't let my mother into our house anymore because it's too hard to get her out again and also because she often talks about things (child molesters, gynecological exams gone awry, parasites thriving in her body) that I don't want my children to hear. But when I did let her into the house—when, for instance, we used to have her over for dinner every so often—she would usually arrive about an hour late, then spend much of her visit in the bathroom. One night, shortly after Isaac was born, I asked her over for a spaghetti dinner. The table was set, the sauce long done cooking, the pasta water boiling, the salad in bowls on the table, when she called from her car to say that she was parked on our street and, though she had looked and looked, she couldn't find our place. So I ran outside to search for her. It was raining as I walked up and down the sidewalk. A man with a newspaper over his head gave me a funny look, because of my slippers, I guess, but I ignored him. Eventually I found her sitting in her car about a block and a half away. The interior lights were on. I could see that she was wearing a white tank top, had one arm raised over her head, and seemed to be washing her armpit. I crossed our street, which tends to be busy, and stood well out in front of her car so that I wouldn't frighten her.

"Mom!" I yelled. There was a bottle of mouthwash and a hairbrush on the dashboard. "It's cold," I said. "Come on."

As we ate that night, I noticed some marks on her neck—three or four dark, shiny spots about the size of dimes, running down each side. These spots, she explained, had just appeared on their own. I knew this wasn't true but for simplicity's sake pretended to believe her. She told us the spots were right over her salivary glands, which were clearly *ossifying* because they were *hard as rocks*. At one point Isabella stood next to her grandmother's chair and touched each of the spots on her neck, one by one, and my mother said: "See? See how hard they are?" I had to resist the urge to jump up and wash my daughter's hands.

After dinner, while David was putting the kids to bed, I started telling my mother a story. This is always a very interesting proposition—trying to tell my mother a story. It rarely works. At first, though, I was encouraged because she said she was interested in this story. "I really want to hear this," she said, "I just have to pee." Then she went to the bathroom for about twenty minutes. When she came out, she asked for a bottle of cleanser. "Just something to scrub out the sink. Then I really want to hear your story." She said she needed to disinfect the sink because she'd rinsed out her mouth and she was worried about leaving germs behind. I told her to forget about it. I'd do it later. But she insisted, so I found a rag and some powder and started cleaning the sink myself, and as I scrubbed, I attempted to pick up my story where I'd left off, but my mother interrupted to say she wanted to clean the sink herself and took the rag from me. She worked, then, for about five minutes, really throwing herself into the job, getting every nook and cranny—the gaps under the parts of the faucet that turn, the curved edge of the overflow valve, the stem of the stopper. "I know you think I'm crazy," she said as I stood there watching.

"No, I don't."

"Yes, you do."

"I just worry," I said, uncrossing my arms.

Still bent over the sink, she turned to look at me. She had to tilt her head because her glasses had slid halfway down the narrow bridge of her nose. "I just want you to know, I'd do exactly the same thing if I were you," she said. "I mean, if I had a mother who I thought didn't have all her buttons, I wouldn't let my children get too close either."

C

Cahoots

One of my mother's favorite words, as in "in cahoots," a phrase she frequently employs in sentences such as: "Medicaid is *obviously* in cahoots with *DMH!" Or: "DMH is *obviously* in cahoots with my landlord!"

Cedar

Many of the most important events of my childhood were unexperienced. Unfortunately, when things are unexperienced, they cannot be told or retold—they can barely be remembered. Technically, this is called "dissociation," a straightforward enough term meaning that you disassociate from your surroundings. Pull out. Shut down. Close up shop. Oddly, I've found, the off-center focal point of many a dissociative episode can be recalled even decades later with almost perfect clarity. Memory clings to such a point with at least as much tenacity as it rejects the primary event. For example, when I was three years old, I saw my parents argue while standing in the doorway between the kitchen and their bedroom in our tiny apartment in the basement of my grandparents' house. My father seemed both immovable and towering, also much too close to my mother, who for her part kept clawing at his face—as if she were daring him to hit her. This, eventually, he did, although I cannot actually see, through the thick haze of static, the blow. Nor can I see myself clamping onto his leg. I cannot see him peeling me off either, or throwing me across the room, but this is what happened, according to my mother, who years later would often recount this string of events like a weird mantra. All I remember for myself is the foot of my parents' bureau on the other side of the room: a curved knob of reddish wood covered lightly in dust.

Colic

Isaac's crib was arranged at the foot of our bed. This was back when I still let my mother into our apartment, back when David and I were sleeping downstairs in an alcove off the living room to be near the baby. She'd stopped by without calling ahead. I'd put on some water for tea, then showed her her grandson, fast asleep in his crib. His tiny, knobby legs were sticking out of his diaper, which was printed with images of a famous cartoon character based on a sponge. My mother shook her head and said: "You are so lucky. He's so good. You've been lucky with both of them. They're both such calm, happy, cheerful kids."

Then she told me a story I'd heard many times before. It was about Tracy as a baby and how she'd been allergic to formula, hungry and colicky all the time. She told me again about the terrifying weight loss, the frequent doctors' visits, the constant crying. And then she told me something I didn't know.

"Sometimes I couldn't handle it. I really couldn't. I was *so* young. You have to remember. I didn't have any role models. I didn't know what to do. Sometimes I'd put her in her crib and leave her there. Your grandmother worked in the factory three or four days a week back then, and when she was gone, I didn't have any help. So I just put her in her crib and pulled the shades and shut the door and left her there. For hours she used to cry. Sometimes she'd cry all day long!" My mother's mouth was stretched into an upside-down *U*, her brow collapsed. Her fingers, resting on the crib railing, shook slightly. I said something about postpartum depression and rubbed her back. But these were empty gestures. If she'd been a friend, I might have understood, but she was my mother, and Tracy was my sister, and my gestures were bogus. What I wanted was for her to leave. I wanted to lie down. And when I was done lying down, I wanted to call my sister—not to tell her what I'd just learned but to send something through the phone line, time-traveling magic that doesn't really exist (I know that!), but I wanted to send it anyway.

Comme des Garçons

Isaac has a friend over after school, a boy in his first grade class. The two of them are busy making dinosaurs out of Legos when my mother knocks at the door. I'm not expecting her, but she never calls ahead because she thinks her phones are being tapped and she doesn't want DMH to know when she's leaving her apartment because she's worried they'll send someone over to search through her paperwork.

Isaac's friend's mother and sister have both come along as well, and the three of us—the mother, the sister, and I—are sitting on the living room floor. I am trying to teach the girl how to knit because her Game Boy has run out of batteries and she is bored. We've gotten through the process of casting on and she's working on her second row when my mother knocks. I excuse myself and step out onto our porch, careful to shut the door behind me.

"Did he give you my *message?*"

"What message?"

"I thought so!"

She is wearing an enormous white nylon jacket. It is square shaped, and it hangs down to her knees. I'm not sure if that's the way it's supposed to fit, but the effect is kind of preppy and vaguely Comme des Garçons at the same time. Underneath the jacket she has on a pair of white jeans that I gave her a while back and some white platform sneakers.

"Mom, I have company. Isaac has a friend over. I can't talk."

"You never want to talk, but we have to talk. I don't expect you to believe this, Kimberli, but I am very, *very* ill. Things are happening quickly. We need to discuss certain technicalities. You have to come over and spend a few hours with me so that we can discuss certain extremely important, *factual* items."

"Like what?"

"Like *life insurance.*" She purses her lips then, to make sure I understand that these words are code for *I'm going to die soon, you know.*

"Mom, I don't have time for this."

"You don't have time for your own mother?"

"I don't have time for your endless problems, your imagined illnesses, your supposedly impending death, your paranoia."

She takes a step backward, as if she'd been literally stunned by an actual electrical shock, puts her hand on her chest, and says: "What are you saying? You think I'm paranoid? *Me?* Kimberli, this is not *child's play.* When are you finally going to get it? When it's too late?"

I'm feeling pretty uncomfortable at this point because I know that Isaac's friend's mother and sister are in a perfect position to see me as our front door has a large glass panel in the middle of it, and beyond me they can also no doubt make out my old, frail, crazy mother in her huge white nylon jacket. And even though the door is shut, it's also likely that they can hear us because our voices are raised. Things are heated.

"How long is this going to last?" she asks, "all this anger, all these *boundaries?*" Then she begins to cry, and says, "Oh, Kimmy, if you only knew how much I miss you loving me."

I pause to consider the unusual construction of this sentence. Then the phone starts ringing. I tell her I have to go, but when I turn to open the door, she grabs my arm. I pull away. "That's probably Isabella calling. I have to go."

"Don't you dare!"

"I have to. It's Isabella!"

"Don't!" my mother shouts. I go inside anyway, shutting the door behind me, leaving her standing alone on the porch as I am now in the habit of doing. She stands there with her arms at her sides staring down at something. Her feet? The doorknob? As I run for the phone, I flash what I'm pretty sure is a shit-eating grin at my son's friend's mother, then pick up the receiver. Just as I'd predicted, it's Isabella. She's called to tell me that her play rehearsal is over and she's coming straight home because she has to work on a science project that's due tomorrow. I somehow hear her say these things even as my mother pushes the door open, not all the way but wide enough to shout inside: "Your *shrink* is destroying your mind, you know. She's *destroying your mind!*"

Concentration

I'm not sure this counts as a memory at all. I know only that we're eating something, my mother and I. Toast perhaps. Something that takes a bit of concentration. We're sitting at our kitchen table downstairs, in the basement apartment, and for some reason I see us, all these years later, bathed in sunlight. But who knows? It was so long ago. It might have been raining. It might have been carrot sticks or cookies. The only thing I remember with anything approaching certainty is the act of chewing. Doggedly, doggedly chewing. And somewhere nearby, yet very far away, a baby is making complicated noises: ragged strings of spit and air.

Confabulation

My mother wore a fuchsia pink peignoir—layer upon layer of semitransparent chiffon trimmed with matching ostrich feathers—the morning she sliced her left wrist with my father's razor blade. She was twenty-one years old. I was three and a half. Tracy was just learning to walk. I remember the peignoir most of all but also many legs—a whole forest of adult legs through which I battled my way toward the bathroom door. My father, his parents, his sisters—they were all crowded there, shouting, pounding. At one point my father threw himself against the door, but this did nothing, so Grandpa Joe threw himself against it. Over and over the two of them ran at the door until it finally splintered in its frame and someone reached inside to undo the lock. My mother stood there in her beautiful peignoir, holding her arm away from her body as the blood leapt in spurts. On the floor, near her feet, it ran along the right angles of grout in between the tiles. Later there were two paramedics who tied her arm off above her wrist with a tourniquet so the blood would stop jumping. But it was all wrong! They'd tied the wrong arm! I kept shouting at them to put the tourniquet on the other arm. One of them was young and kind. The other old and gruff. "Please!" I screamed, hopping from foot to foot. "It's the wrong arm!"

"Shhhhh!" said the older one. "This is how you do it."

Confusion

The dominant emotion I hold in my heart (or whatever somatic port emotions actually reside in) for my mother is a complex thing: tender and livid, destructive, oppressive. To consider my feelings for her—even fleetingly—late at night is to experience brief but richly nauseating pulses of something like hopelessness, only more deathy.

Connoisseur

She buys cleaning products the way I buy luxury bath products, which is to say enthusiastically but with the discretion of a connoisseur. She collects them in large numbers, often in the largest sizes available, sizes you didn't even know existed, sizes that are cartoonishly, industrially enormous, in containers you might be surprised to find even in a city hospital. She likes all the basics—bleach, ammonia, scrubbing powders—but also enjoys experimenting with more unusual products, such as ionized dust wipes or gels that claim to draw out deeply engrained mildew. My mother doesn't simply amass these things but actually uses them because she really loves to clean and maintains a strict philosophy of cleaning, which boils down to one essential idea: it's of utmost importance to clean *deeply*. Surface cleaning, she has told me I don't know how many times, is next to *pointless* because anything can look clean on top but be absolutely filthy just beneath.

Constellations

Cabbage is a cheap and useful vegetable. I like the homey, simple taste of it in nearly every form—boiled, braised, fermented, and pickled. However, I cannot eat or buy or prepare cabbage without the certain visitation of a very old memory. In it Grandma Bella stands at the kitchen counter. She is about to cut up a large, pale head of green cabbage. The sun streams in through the window above the sink. I know this because my father stands over his mother, screaming, and tiny spheres of spit fly from his mouth, and these are illuminated by the sunlight. His face is red, his mouth huge, his black Buddy Holly–style eyeglasses wildly askew. His mother is much shorter than he. She is small and round, and she is also, at this point, the person I trust and love most in the world. On her olive-skinned arms are constellations of smooth white dots from the wax she handles in the munitions factory she works at three days a week. The dots are not technically part of this memory (I just thought I'd mention them), but my grandmother's smallness and her roundness are because she seems especially these things with my father towering over her.

I am in this memory too, at least physically—or maybe I should say proprioceptively, by which I mean that I feel myself to be exceedingly tiny, to be, in essence, all eyes—a low perspective gazing up at the scene. The emotions that fill me as I look on the adults and the sun and the cabbage and the knife are a fluctuating combination of dread and something like wonder. For instance, when my father grabs the cabbage his mother is about to chop and hurls it against the kitchen floor, I am completely awestruck. The act makes no sense at all to me. I doubt I could have been more surprised had he removed his own head and thrown it at the floor, had it been his head that smacked against the linoleum, then spun crazily around the room, his head that my grandmother eventually retrieved, shaking slightly, and put back in its place.

Constitution

My mother has always described her father as a "Black Swede," meaning dark, short, and wiry, like the so-called Black Irish. But my grandmother, when she first met her future husband in New Orleans, refused to believe he was Swedish at all until she saw his papers. His hair was too curly, too dark, his skin too brown, his Portuguese (he'd joined that country's merchant marines when he was fourteen) too fluent.

It's odd—really odd, I think—but in our family Swedishness is infused with an almost mystical quality. For instance, the other night on the phone (my ear sweats she talks so much, so nonstop, for so long; it aches when I finally hang up), after telling me about the parasites she's been massaging out of her gums, my mother exclaimed: "All I can say is, thank God for my Swedish constitution! If not for that, I'd be dead!"

Conversion Disorder

In people with conversion disorder, difficult, painful, or entirely unbearable emotions are sublimated or even transformed into mysterious physical ailments. For example, my mother's systemic bacterial infection, her concerns about worms living in her left eye, sperm-like organisms proliferating in the glands all over her body, her vestibular issues and deafness in one ear, unusual funguses in her mucus membranes, strange objects nested in the roots of her teeth, and so on and so forth, all seem to me the likely manifestations of a hefty case of conversion disorder.

Cookies

Before I came to understand a couple of interesting facts about gratitude—for instance, that it's a remarkably good tool for getting calm and feeling okay about a wide range of emotions, experiences, and realities, and also that it can be practiced just as good posture or effective joke delivery can be practiced—I relied on baked goods to accomplish roughly the same thing. Indeed, baked goods remain a hardcore habit of mine. I am particularly fond of making and eating cookies but also love to make and eat fruit pies and, on occasion, simple, old-fashioned cakes: devil's food, coconut, burnt sugar, buttermilk, poppy seed. Call me retro, but being a good baker makes me feel like a good mother, and being a good mother makes me feel like a worthwhile human being. It's my hope and sincere desire that my children, as they grow older, will not view my at times rather frenzied activities in the kitchen as a more or less neurotic emotional construction but instead will cherish memories of me at the oven, spatula in hand, with scents of chocolate, vanilla, mace, lemon, cinnamon, and honey redolent in the air, and with tastes and textures that they might, at some much later date in their lives, recall as incomparably sweet and yielding—tastes of childhoods safe, unhindered, and essentially happy.

Crazy

When I ask how she knows there are worms in her left eye, she says: "I *know* because I have actually *pulled* a worm out of my eye. It was super long and super skinny, and it just kept coming." When I try, delicately, to suggest that maybe what she pulled from her eye wasn't a worm but something else, I leave the "something else" unstated because she'd be insulted by the word *imaginary*, and the word *capillary* (which is the only other possibility to occur to me) seems too gruesome to verbalize.

"Why?" sighs my mother. "Why are you so invested in this idea I'm just this crazy, *crazy* lady? I'm telling you, this thing was *alive*, and it was *moving*, and it came out with hardly any tugging *at all*."

Criminal

Tap-tap-tap. She knocks very lightly on the screen door because she's still afraid of waking up Isaac even though he stopped taking naps years ago and in any case he's out of the house since it's a school day and only lunchtime. Because it's impossible to get her to stop talking once she gets going, I don't answer right away but instead rush to fill a laundry basket with a load of damp clothes from the machine. I might as well hang up some laundry while she talks my ear off, is my reasoning.

When I open the door, laundry basket in hand, neither of us makes any mention of her previous visit. Instead, she says: "Oh, that's perfect, Kimmy. Those will dry in a jiffy on a day like this. I just *love* the smell of clothes that have been hung outside to dry. There's nothing like it! So fresh and sweet."

We walk over to the clothesline stretched across our backyard, and I begin clipping things to it as she speaks. It's not that I don't listen. I do. Sort of. But in the same way I might listen to a buzz saw or a leaf blower. I hear certain words, certain all-too-familiar words—*teeth, doctors, landlord*, DMH—and these alert me to the fact that nothing new is being said. But at a certain point my mother starts talking about something that piques my interest, something I haven't heard before concerning the psych ward she was committed to after her first suicide attempt.

"God, I hated that place so much," she says. She is helpfully holding out a pair of Isaac's shorts for me to hang on the line, but she's gripping them kind of hard, so I have to tug them out of her hand. "I was so stupid! So young! I didn't understand that the only way I was ever going to get out of that place was to lie. My doctor—he was such a pathetic little man, such a short little *itty-bitty* man, *classic* Napoleon complex!—he used to ask me every day the same stupid, meaningless question. *Are you ready to go home and be a good wife and a loving mother, Linda?* And every day, I refused to answer him. I had no idea what he was doing. His treatment of me was *absurdly* minimal. Criminal, really. It consisted of just two things. Two! Tranquilizers and that same stupid question, over and over." Making her voice go comically deep and adding what I think might be a German accent she says, "*Are you ready to go home and be a good wife and a loving mother, Linda?*"

"So what happened?"

"Well, one day I finally—*finally*—got another patient to tell me what I had to do. She set me straight. Said the bastard just needed me to say it for his form or something. And so the next day, when he asked if I was ready to go home and be a good wife and a loving mother, I said yes. He said he wanted to hear me *say* the words, so I said, 'Yes-I-am-ready-to-go-home-and-be-a-good-wife-and-a-loving-mother.' And boom—what do you know—the next day I was released."

Crux

The small two-bedroom apartment my parents rented after my mother was released from the hospital was part of a large brick complex of similar apartments arranged around a central lawn divided by half a dozen concrete walkways littered with children's toys—balls and dolls and chalk and bikes. I spent a lot of time watching my mother clean in this apartment, which she did with formidable energy and an impressive array of tools. For instance, to mop the kitchen floor, she used a gigantic super-absorbent sponge that looked like a massive chunk of caramel-flavored cake, a thick rubber mat to protect her knees, rubber gloves that reached to her elbows, a kerchief to hold back her hair, and, of course, a bucket filled with soapy, sharp-smelling water. I often begged her to let me help with this chore, but she said I was too small, I'd just get in the way. I was allowed to watch, but this, obviously, was a tremendous disappointment. After all, watching someone mop the floor, no matter how secretly relieved you might be simply to keep an eye on them so as to make sure they're not about to kill themselves, is not exactly a three-year-old's idea of fun. I had given up hope of ever getting to participate in this fascinating operation when one day my mother came home with a bag full of wonderful surprises: a miniature bucket, a miniature sponge, a miniature rubber mat, a miniature pair of gloves, and a miniature kerchief. The kerchief I remember as being especially beautiful, made of a fine-wale blue corduroy and dotted with white flowers.

That day we mopped the kitchen floor together, and even now, when I recall that ancient afternoon, I feel something molten—something golden, warm. Maybe this is happiness. Or maybe it's sunlight because in fact the sun was shining that day, glittering on the soap bubbles that floated in the air then settled in quivering half-domes on the countertops and the linoleum tiles and the sides of the bucket. The kitchen was full of this rambunctious light. It ricocheted off everything, exploding in white stars on the spotless windows, in the watery streaks on the floor, in the lenses of mother's glasses, and on her straight white teeth whenever she smiled her slightly crooked smile.

Crystalline

S——, New Jersey, May 6, 1970

A photograph of my fourth birthday reveals a listless gathering of three children and two young women—presumably mothers. There are few strips of crepe paper strung above our dining room table and, stuck to the wall, a single red balloon. I perch at the edge of my chair, ready to blow out the candles on a store-bought cake, but I might just as well be in a doctor's office waiting to get a shot. No one is smiling.

That morning I'd received a new pair of Buster Brown shoes—sturdy little oxfords made of brown leather with bright red laces. I liked them very much, mostly because of the laces because I was interested in all things red. Red was a song around me—a mysterious pattern. Red was the round rug in our living room, red were my sister's bow-shaped plastic barrettes, red was the charm at the end of my mother's favorite necklace, red were the stripes on my father's athletic socks, red was my velvet jumper, and red were the buttons on my soft white winter coat. To this day I feel certain there's some good thing hidden in red, though I've never discovered exactly what it might be or why it chooses red.

Later that afternoon, after the party, while Tracy was napping, I played with my second favorite gift: a musical jewelry box with a pop-up ballerina hidden inside. I can still see this tiny plastic figure perfectly, chiseled in every particular. Standing next to my bureau, I repeatedly opened and shut the lid of the music box to watch her pop into view. I was mesmerized by her uncanny spinning, the tinny music, and the mechanism hidden in the base of the box that generated that music: a studded brass cylinder that also spun and, in spinning, resisted a stiff row of plinking metal tines. The ballerina's red lips were printed slightly off-center from her plastic mouth, and I was preoccupied by the question of whether she would be prettier with her lips centered or less pretty. I remember this as well: when I heard my father come home from work, I slammed the box shut and ran like hell to hide.

Culmination

The next day my mother was gone. Aunt Inga had picked her up in the middle of the night, while the rest of us were asleep, and driven her to the airport, only we didn't know this—at least I didn't. All I knew was that something had made a huge crashing noise in the living room very early in the morning, when it was still barely light outside. When I got up to investigate, I found my father standing near a hole in the wall. He was wearing pajama bottoms, and in one hand he held a piece of paper.

"Your mother's gone," he said. He was breathing heavily.

"What do you mean gone?"

The man terrified me, but the question had to be asked.

"Gone!" he screamed, and I booked it back to my bed as fast as I could.

D

Dappled

Although I count them as the happiest years of my childhood, I possess very few memories from the time we lived with my grandparents, when my mother was in Florida. What memories I do own seem oddly random. My grandfather putting ketchup on his scrambled eggs, for instance. Why do I remember that? Or my grandmother getting into the passenger seat of their taupe-colored Buick, sliding her bottom across the vinyl seat sideways before swinging her legs around and shutting the door. Why that? The smell of garlic on her hands. Or that of cigarette smoke and something spicier (nutmeg?) in her hair. The set of my grandfather's mouth—a thoughtful frown—when he read the paper at breakfast. The jagged salt-and-pepper static of the TV. The itchy wool weave of the couch. The olive-green nubs of the living room rug. The dim, slightly dank coolness of the garage. The metal rack full of curvaceous green Coke bottles at the base of the stairs. The dappled shadows—sunlight fractured by pine needles—flitting across my bed at naptime. The heavy cut glass ashtrays, one amber colored, one amethyst colored, both spotted with gummy stains of nicotine. The oily, slightly iridescent jostle of black coffee in milk glass mugs. The soft, slightly pillowy give of the orange vinyl placemats under my elbows. The dusky finish on the black and green plastic grapes heaped in a dimpled pressed glass bowl in the middle of the kitchen table.

Decoy

The day I lost my first tooth I took it out of my pocket to study it on the bus ride home from school: its glossy planes, its bloody ridge. A kid in front of me hung over the back of his seat to inform me that the tooth fairy didn't actually exist. "It's really just your mother." My mother had been in Florida for nearly a year at that point, only I didn't know that. I didn't know if she was dead or alive. My father, my grandparents: nobody spoke of her. I knew only that I didn't have a mother anymore, so that's what I said. What I remember next seems too cinematic: a busload of children pointing, chanting: "Doesn't have a mother! Doesn't have a mother! Doesn't have a mother!" The idea that not having a mother was something to be ashamed of was news to me, but I slid right into it.

My grandmother was waiting for me at the top of the hill, a block away from our house. When the bus opened its door, I stumbled down the black rubber steps and into her arms, crying. She asked the driver what had happened, and he said something about "damn kids," then pulled away. But by that point it wasn't the damn kids I was upset about—it was my tooth, which had fallen out of my hand as I'd gotten off the bus. When I was finally calm enough to communicate this to my grandmother, she told me not to worry because the tooth fairy would come anyway.

"The tooth fairy doesn't care about the tooth, really!"

I said I cared about the tooth, and she said, "Don't worry, we'll find it!"

This, clearly, was impossible, but she squatted down at the side of the road and began to run her fingers through the dirt and gravel, and I squatted next to her. After a while she picked up a small white pebble and announced: "Here it is! I found your tooth!"

"Grandma, I think that's a pebble."

"Maybe you're right."

She crouched again. We searched for a long time, side by side, running our fingers through the fine dirt and the larger pebbles.

Even after it started drizzling, we kept searching. The rain was tiny, cold, prickling. My grandmother showed me another pebble, smaller and whiter than the first.

"That's not my tooth either."

"No. Look. I think it is." It was obvious that this was just another pebble, but I felt bad for her, so I agreed it could be my tooth. As we walked home, she pulled the side of her cardigan around my shoulders to keep the rain off.

Deer

Stretching behind my grandparents' house were several flat acres of swampy forest, and most days after work, still wearing his navy-blue factory uniform, my grandfather would walk his dogs along a network of narrow paths through those woods. Often I went with him. On these excursions we were generally quiet, but every once in a while he would point out something of interest: a cardinal flashing through the trees, a circling hawk. There were massive skunk cabbages—much taller than I—and bogs filled with snapping turtles, which my grandfather sternly assured me would bite my finger "clean off" if I got too close. There were animal prints in the mud and leaves rotting in puddles and scat everywhere—rabbit, coyote, raccoon, deer. Once he showed me a misshapen ball of gray toilet paper high up in a pine tree and told me it was an abandoned wasp nest. Another time he gave me a tiny, softly brittle fragment of shell the color of the sky, only slightly more acid, and said a baby bird had come out of it. Another time he held out a pair of shimmering pale brown wings attached to each other by white filaments and topped by fine antennae and explained that this arrangement had once been a moth but that someone—a bird or maybe a bat—had eaten its body. And once, he quietly lifted me above the brambles so I could see a deer standing a short distance away on an icy carpet of dead leaves. A fine-grained, saltlike snow fell from the sky and bounced on the ground. All around us—the faintest clattering.

Deft

At some point somebody used the term *half-orphans* to describe Tracy and me. This may have been one of my grandmother's friends, probably one of her neighbors—maybe Nancy, who baby-sat us a few days a week when my grandmother was at the factory. In any case the kitchen suggests itself as a setting. The term struck me as tragic and therefore intriguing but not really applicable because if I were a half-orphan, wouldn't I feel tragic? But I didn't. I felt fine. In fact, ever since I was old enough to achieve any sort of retrospective distance on my childhood, I have always considered the two years that my mother was in Florida, which is to say the two years that Tracy and I lived with our grandparents, as the happiest part of it. The easiest, the most plump with affection. And yet there's very little left of that time, memory-wise. This, I know, is only to be expected. But it smarts.

Many of my most vivid memories are food based: lasagna and pizza and fried eggs and pans of crispy scrapple, whole roast chickens with gravy, meatballs with spaghetti, chocolate pie with whipped cream . . . Even more than the food, though, I remember my grandmother's hands: strong, soft, dark, quick, deft. Uncanny, almost as if they were independent beings, separate animals. They flew over vegetables, reducing them to chips and dice and chunks and strips. They dug into sugar and flour, cubed sticks of butter, measured spoonfuls of molasses, honey, lard. They scattered salt and herbs, dimpled pizza dough, whipped cream, squeezed oranges, stirred custards, junkets, sauces, all with such careless precision. She often let me help, but it was hopeless—my hands were slow and small. Flour exploded. Milk spattered. But now, as an adult, I sometimes watch my own hands, in my own kitchen, as I'm making something—macaroons, say, or my grandmother's meatballs or birthday cake—and I think they look something like hers.

Delivery

For my fifth birthday my grandparents bought me an Easy-Bake Oven. Two friends came over, plus there was Tracy. We sat in my grandmother's kitchen at a child-size table and drank weak tea out of tiny red plastic teacups and made little cakes—hardly bigger than an adult's palm—from miniature boxes of cake mix: chocolate and marble and "cherry." Even then, I loved baking. We were eating the red-flecked cherry cake when the doorbell rang, and my grandmother hurriedly ushered our party into her sewing room and ordered us to stay there. "Promise not to come out," she said.

Huddled in the sewing room—which was crowded with bolts of fabric, an ironing board, a spare bed—we wondered what was going on. It was my birthday. I think that must have emboldened me. Because even though I'd promised not to, I snuck out of the room, crept down the hall, and poked my head around the corner. Like an expert spy. From there I could see, at the base of the stairs, my mother and her sister, my aunt Inga, standing at the front door. They both held large presents wrapped in silver paper, tied with long, curly ribbons, and these, needless to say, seemed to promise great things. But something was wrong. My grandmother kept pushing the younger women out of the doorway. And they kept pushing back at her. Although of course I recognized my mother, she struck me as strangely unfamiliar. Almost too real. Aunt Inga was strange too: her hair was frosted nearly white and her lips were covered in metallic lipstick. The three of them whispered angrily at each other. I couldn't hear what they were saying, but it was clear that my grandmother wouldn't let the two younger women into the house and refused even to take the presents.

Part of me understood that I should run downstairs and embrace the tall, young stranger standing in the door, but another part of me bristled at this idea. Although I wanted the presents, what I recognized at that moment, without having the words to name it, was a sense of my own will. It was exhilarating. Over my mother I chose my grandmother. Over emotion, I chose self-control. I chose choice itself.

Deny

My mother insists that her many wide-ranging physical problems would simply disappear if only she could find a doctor willing to give her high doses of intravenous super-strength antibiotics delivered nonstop for six months to a year. *Whatever it takes!* However, as she has never succeeded in convincing any of her many, many doctors of the existence of the *systemic bacterial infection* she believes has inhabited her body for several decades now, she is invariably denied this treatment.

Detective

It's like I'm the detective but the case is impossible. Still, I'm stubborn, so I keep at it. In fact, this is secretly how I think of myself: the stubbornest detective alive. Because despite the dismal prospects, I've been working on this case for as long as I can remember. I know it's stupid, but deep down I subscribe to an elaborate form of magical thinking in which words—and words alone—possess the secret ability to travel through time, which explains why, on some level, some part of me actually believes I can get back there, to the past. It's just a matter of finding exactly the right words and putting them in exactly the right order. Not the almost words in the almost order but the exact ones in the exact order. Like a code. Once I get everything in just the right place, I'll simply tunnel my way back. Back and back and back and back—decades before my own birth if necessary. The irony, of course, is that once I got there (I've thought this all through), the whole idea of solving the case would become instantly moot because if I ever actually made it, I'd finally be able to give up this fucking *albatross*—just toss it, close the case, chuck the evidence—because at that point I could simply concentrate my efforts on saving certain people, and punishing others.

DMH

The central villain in my mother's increasingly involved, debilitating, and weirdly self-fulfilling delusions is the Massachusetts

Department of Mental Health, or, as she usually refers to it, DMH. DMH wants her *out of the way* because she *knows too much.* She knows, for instance, that certain doctors are *criminally incompetent.* Also that *criminal abuses* have taken place. Somehow this knowledge is worth *millions of dollars,* which is why DMH goes to such extraordinary, indeed almost unimaginable, pains to narrow her world. Their ultimate goal, she tells me over and over, is to land her permanently in a locked ward in a long-term psychiatric institution, at which point they will, she is sure, force-administer enormous doses of psychopharmaceutical drugs so as to render her beyond any capacity for logic, speech, self-defense, or legal action.

Domesticity

A kind of faith, in my experience.

Don Juan

Miami, Florida, 1971

A hypothetical thought: what if she hadn't come back? What if she'd stayed there, working as a secretary, dating men like the one in this photograph: older, handsome, apparently wealthy. She looks pleased, if not exactly happy, posing in front of a large white yacht with this guy—this oily, self-satisfied guy. Smiling into the sun, she has one arm around his shoulders. Her other hand rests lightly on his deeply tanned, slightly flabby belly. He's a bit icky: slick in a middle-aged, rich-boy sort of way, with graying chest hair and a smirk that says he's in it for the short run. But even so, she might have been happier. We all might have been.

Doppelgängers

Whenever I see my mother by chance in cafés and gift shops, at the grocery store, or just walking along the street, I think: "She looks better than I thought! She looks fine!" I think, "She's still beautiful!" I always slow my pace to study her in detail, though at the same time I am careful not to let her see me. She is always tall and thin with gray, shoulder-length hair, high cheekbones, and long limbs. All of which makes sense. But there are other details that don't quite fit, which is why I study her so carefully. For instance, my mother, when I see her by chance, here or there, around town, is always very well dressed, wearing, perhaps, a stylish raincoat or pleated slacks and expensive loafers. Her hair is professionally cut, not riddled with bald spots. Also, she doesn't hide her teeth behind her hand when she speaks, and when she does speak, she doesn't do so nervously or for much too long. I notice all these details, and while I recognize the fact that they do not quite make sense, the illusion remains.

Sometimes, if he's with me, I'll grab David's arm and say, "Is that my mother?"

"Are you joking?" he once asked.

Another time, not long ago, I was walking with my children in the little commercial center of our town when I spotted my mother in a gourmet ice cream shop. She was sitting with her back to the window, reading a Nadine Gordimer novel, slowly picking at a cup of chocolate ice cream. I stopped to study the slope of this woman's shoulders, the nape of her neck, and the beautiful hand-woven shawl loosely draped around what appeared to be a fine, hand-knit sweater. Isabella asked me what was wrong, and I said, "I think that might be *Mormor." She said, "That is not Mormor." I asked my daughter if she was sure, and she said, "Do you really think that, if that were Mormor, she'd just be sitting there all calm, reading a book and eating an ice cream?" I said no, probably she wouldn't be doing those things. But I was still reluctant to leave and remained planted in front of the window until Isabella said, "Mama, it's not her," and pulled me along.

Dos and Don'ts

Do not lose yourself in the past. Do not lose yourself in the future. Do not get caught in your anger, worries, or fears. Come back to the present moment, and touch life deeply.

—*Thich Nhat Hanh*

Don't regret what's happened. If it's in the past, let it go. Don't even remember it!

—*Rumi*

Dote

Tracy and I shared the room my father's sisters had slept in when they were young, with its two matching brass beds, two white chenille bedspreads. Our father slept in the room he'd had in high school: a spartan space that just barely fit a single bed, a dresser, and a small wheeled table on which he kept a typewriter.

We didn't see him much during the years we lived with our grandparents. He was working a lot of the time—no longer in the gravel pit, though at the same business (a large computer company), only now he was a gofer in the accounting department. But even at night he wasn't around much. That didn't matter because my grandfather was, and my grandfather read books to me and showed me how magnets worked and tape measures and the garage door. He let me peel back the soft yellow paper from the red wax marker he kept in his shirt pocket and doodle with the chunky carpenter's pencil he kept next to it (both of these being objects of supreme fascination to me). He taught me how to tell when a tomato is ripe by its smell and how to approach a dog so it doesn't get nervous (offer your hand below the level of its snout). At night, after Tracy was in bed, I'd watch TV with him, sprawled on the living room rug, while he sat in his armchair, smoking a cigar. I was happy to watch whatever was on—the news mostly. Normally, he didn't talk much, and he laughed even less. But when *All in the Family* was on, he chuckled a lot, and so did I, not because I got the jokes (I didn't) but because I listened to the laugh track for my cues.

Drenched

It's not my memory—it's my mother's, and it is very dim. I see it as if from behind a Vaseline-coated lens, drenched in sepia. But still, it's part of my experience, if only because I've heard the story so many times. The image annoys me, no doubt because every time my mother evokes it, she cries (even to this day). It goes like this: the first time I saw her after she returned from Florida, I was six years old. She was twenty-four. For some reason we were very far away from one another on the gravel road by my grandmother's house—my other grandmother's house. My mother was walking in one direction, and I was charging toward her from the other, as fast as I could. The sepia tones are so deep, I can hardly make out a thing, but I know (because she has told me) that when I reached her, I leapt onto her and hugged her with my arms and my legs, *like a little monkey*, and didn't let go for a long time.

DUI

My mother's 2004 steel-gray Honda Accord is sitting in her parking spot in the lot in front of her apartment complex with four flat tires. It's been like this for six months because she decided not to renew her license. When I ask why, she says, "I don't expect you to understand."

Dulce de Leche

It's only early December, but they're forecasting a huge blizzard to hit Boston tonight, so David and I decide to run some groceries over to my mother. Neither of us is looking forward to the visit, which is why we promise each other we'll stay no more than five minutes. We've bought most everything on the list she gave us, including a bunch of cleaning products (dust wipes, tissues, paper towels, disinfectant spray, rubbing alcohol, cotton balls, oven cleaner), as well as a bag of gorp (cashew–banana–white chocolate chip), two frozen pizzas, a loaf of sourdough bread, a half-gallon of milk, two gallons of water, frozen mushroom lasagna, a pack of English muffins, an extra large jar of honey, extra chunky peanut butter, a microwavable bag of rice pilaf, a pint of Dulche de Leche ice cream, and one phone card.

Although it's late afternoon, my mother answers the door in her bathrobe. This isn't surprising. What is surprising is how small and frail she looks, even though she's looked this way for a while now, and probably what I should really be surprised by is the fact that I'm still surprised. Her left eye is deeply bloodshot and noticeably smaller than the right, but it still seems in slightly better condition than the last time I saw her, although the iris itself looks weirdly mineralized, and the skin surrounding the eye is loose and very chapped.

"I don't know what's wrong with it," she says when she catches me looking. David and I sidle into her crowded kitchen, past the movable butcher-block counter piled high with cleaning supplies and overstuffed boxes of ancient paperwork, and she starts talking the way she usually does—without pause or grammatical contour. "I can't see out of it at all, and sometimes it just drifts over to the side for no reason. And when I squirt saline up inside the lid really, really forcefully, all these little tumors fall out, all these little white tumors—I can't tell you how much I appreciate this, oh, gorp, I love gorp, water, great."

"Here's the phone card," says David, digging it out of his coat pocket.

"Thank you *so* much. *This* I really need. *This* is crucial. Jerry came over to try to fix my phone last night and he says it's all clear but he doesn't know what he's talking about." Jerry is her landlord. "Now, Kimberli, please I just need to ask you one thing when you talk on the phone." Here she gestures to the door, which we left open, and asks David, in a whisper, to shut it, presumably so that no one can hear what she is about to tell us. "I know what it's like, I used to complain about my mother to my sisters on the phone all the time, but please, please, *please*, I'm asking you to *please* refrain from doing anything like that, from talking about me on the phone to anyone at all in any context whatsoever because they're listening and you never know when they're going to pick up. I got a phone call just last night from the fake 911, not the real one, I could tell because it had the 508 area code, and it was a man and a woman and they were mocking me and laughing, so nasty—you wouldn't believe how nasty people can be. The woman was just *cackling* and they were saying *Even your daughter hates you even your daughter thinks you're crazy, you're so far gone everyone knows you should be in the hospital!* Now you know that's not right—911 shouldn't be calling me! I'm telling you they're all in on it. I can't tell which line is safe and which isn't, and now even the television is affected—I don't know how they do it, but the ads late at night, I don't know why anyone would go to the trouble, but they're directed at me. I *know* that sounds crazy, but you'd have to see them, and then you'd know. But only late, late, late at night. These crazy ads. At least the local police finally cleared my computer line, but AT&T is relentless, I mean they are re-*lent*-less. It's a no-good company. I'm telling you, they're rotten to the core, but they're working on it now. They're investigating so you know it's the truth because they wouldn't spend good government money researching this if there wasn't something to it. So now do you believe me?"

I am, as is usually the case during such exchanges with my mother, transfixed, you could even say hypnotized, by her words, some part of my brain trying to make sense of the complicated technical terms she keeps trotting out, city codes and even some sort of statute at one point. There are also many more observations about her hometown police force and how helpful they can be on occasion as well as references to vague governmental agencies that I'm not sure actually exist. I feel rooted to the spot, just trying to take it in, searching—as I suppose I'll do for the rest of my life—for a thread of logic, no matter how tenuous, but David is doing what he always does when my mother talks like this, which is to say getting itchy and impatient and increasingly determined to get us out of there.

"Linda," he says, speaking over my mother in a loud voice. "Linda, we have to go." My husband is very good at saying these words and can say them steadily over and over, which I have trouble doing. He can also say the related and equally helpful sentence, "Linda, you have to go," in precisely the same manner on those occasions that demand it. Four or five times, he repeats this sentence about us having to go, but she doesn't seem to hear him.

When she starts telling us for the third time about the man and the woman who called her from the *fake 911* to say that her daughter hates her, David tugs the sleeve of my coat and I begin walking backward. And that's how we leave her apartment, walking backward with my mother still talking at us. Even when we are out on the front stoop, and then when we are in parking lot and she is on the front stoop, she continues talking, only louder, in fact, now she's shouting to be sure we hear. The snow has started to fall in soft, ragged, nearly golf ball–sized clumps, and this strikes me as magical and beautiful but also mysterious and sad. David and I walk through these tumbling clumps across the parking lot and get into our car, and still my mother keeps talking. Arms crossed over her chest, she's talking about her all her favorite subjects in quickening spirals—phones, police, doctors, infections. Her words make faint clouds in front of her. It's only when David starts the engine that she says anything resembling goodbye.

"Okay, okay, okay," she says. "Okay, thank you for all this. Thank you for the gorp and the water and the paper towels and the ice cream and *especially* thank you for the phone card because I need that more than anything else and say hi to the kids or at least say hi to Isabella because probably Isaac doesn't even remember me anymore but say hi anyway and drive safely." Then she blows us a kiss, and I blow one back, but it's lame because my face won't move.

E

Edelweiss

After she came back from Florida, my mother lived for several months with the Aunts (see *German, *hair ribbons) in New York City. Every couple of weeks or so, my father would drive Tracy and me into Manhattan for a visit. I remember these encounters as being vaguely stressful in the sense that our mother was almost a stranger to us by that point and at the same time extremely keen on impressing us, which, as every child knows, can be terribly exhausting. On one of these visits we made an Easter Bunny cake covered in coconut flakes, with jellybean eyes and black licorice whiskers. On another, she took us to the Empire State Building and bought us tiny paper bags stuffed with roast chestnuts—cottony, smoky, and sweet. Another time we climbed the Statue of Liberty, and once when I came into the city alone, without Tracy, she took me to get my hair cut and curled at a fancy salon. Afterward we went to dinner at Maxwell's Plum. I had a hamburger, she had a salad. There remains one photograph from this outing. We are on the sidewalk, in the sun. I wear a green sundress embroidered with small white flowers. My hair is softly curled around my face. I'm studying something inside a bag I'm holding. My mother wears linen slacks and a raw silk blouse. Her dark hair falls in front of her face as she bends to hug me. She smells like Jean Naté.

Effective

On our fifth or sixth visit, Tracy and I brought matching calico-covered suitcases. The plan was for us to sleep over. But our father had no sooner dropped us off than our mother led us right back to the elevator and outside again, then onto the street and up to a rusty brown car I'd never seen before. It was crammed with boxes, suitcases, blankets, pillows, and clothing. She told us to climb in, then piled more things on top of us—dresses and blouses covered with slippery plastic sleeves. "The three of us are going on a great adventure," she said. "We're going to live in a wonderful little house. It's perfect—you'll see. It's on an *adorable* street full of children *exactly* your age! Won't that be fun?"

"Where will Grandma and Grandpa live?" I wanted to know.

"We don't need them, the old fuddy-duddies! We're going to have so much more fun on our own, just us three girls. It'll be like a party all the time!"

Another sheaf of clothes wrapped in filmy plastic was draped over the seat in front of me, and still more clothing hung from a hook above the window to my right, blocking the view. Tracy was not quite four years old. As we drove, she chewed her nails and craned her neck to peer avidly out the front window. At some point on our journey, we came to an unmanned tollbooth. Such things are practically nonexistent nowadays, but they were common back then: tollbooths equipped with white plastic buckets into which drivers tossed their coins. Exact change only. The coins funneled down into a mechanism where something clicked that made the gate lift. That day my mother tossed her change into the bucket, but nothing happened. The gate didn't lift. She reached out to give it a shake, but this accomplished nothing, so she put in more coins, but still the gate didn't lift, so she leaned on her horn for a long time. When no one came, she tried backing up, but the driver behind us honked his horn.

"Moron," she said, then floored it. The white and orange barrier exploded against our windshield with a crunching sound. Useless shards of wood tumbled off the hood of our car. It felt impossible. Like backwards time. Like anti-gravity.

After that we drove with the radio on loud, over unfamiliar highways, down wide avenues, into a town I didn't recognize, and finally onto a dead-end street crowded with small houses, chock full, it was true, of children just our age. My mother pulled into the driveway of a modest white house with pink shutters and said: "*Ta-da!* We're home! How do you like it?" Tracy was sleeping, her cheek pressed against a cardboard box. I said it was beautiful. Pink was my favorite color.

"Aren't we going to have fun?" she asked, hugging me hard into her collarbones.

"Yes," I said. "It will be like a party every day."

Effing Idiot

Somewhere on the Jersey Shore, 1972

Aunt Becky must have taken this picture of my mother, Tracy, and me posing in front of the ocean on a stretch of hard-packed sand. Our shadows are dark pools at our feet. My mother has one arm around my sister and one arm around me. I lean into her side as the wind whips my hair across my face. Tracy looks beside herself with excitement—a grin full of tiny white teeth, short, exuberant tufts of hair sticking out of her head. My mother wears a white-and-black-checked bikini bottom and a Dr. Pepper baseball shirt. Also a pair of violet-tinted aviator glasses. She has arranged her legs in a casual movie star stance, knees gracefully knocked together, one foot angled sideways.

After a lunch of bologna sandwiches and lemonade that tasted musty from the old thermos we'd poured it from, my mother said, "Let's do it!" She took my hand, and the two of us marched into the ocean together. I was afraid, but because I have never wanted anybody's love and approval the way I wanted my mother's when I was a child, I pretended to be brave. She taught me how to ride the waves that day, giving me instructions as we treaded water. I remember these instructions as being pithy but at the same time exactly right because all I had to do was follow them and I was suddenly able to climb onto the back of a wave just as it swelled beneath me. We did this over and over again, dozens of times—gliding on top of the waves as they rose and rushed toward the shore.

But then there were no more waves. We'd gone out too far. And out there the water seemed much darker, much colder, and somehow denser. There were only long, low swells, like a sheet being smoothed in slow motion. Sunlight shimmered across the water, breaking into millions of reflections that looked like coins, so exactly like coins that I couldn't quite believe they weren't and tried to balance my mind for as long as possible on that fragile line—the one between imagination (coins) and knowledge (light)—because I wanted to decide, once and for all, if they were gold or silver.

I was getting tired. My knees kept knocking into one another. My legs felt blocky, numb. My teeth were chattering, and they, too, felt oddly insensate in my head, like wood. My mother said, "Oh, your lips are turning blue." I asked to hold her hand, but she said she wanted to practice her backstroke, so I dog-paddled in place as I watched her swim, the water quietly splashing around me. My jaw ached. When she came back, we searched the beach for Tracy and Aunt Becky, but the people there looked so far away—as tiny as beads. Actually, the word that occurred to me at the time was *sprinkles*. Eventually, we became aware of a faint whistle, and when we realized this sound was coming from a lifeguard as he swam in our direction, we laughed. How absurd! He was so angry, blasting on that whistle. So mad yet so tiny! We laughed and laughed. When he finally reached us, he asked my mother if she was crazy, then put his arm around me and explained how I was to hold onto him. I had to put my arms around his neck but grip my own forearms so that I wouldn't choke him as he swam. His body curved and bumped under mine as we made our way back to shore, and yet something about the motion must have relaxed me because I remember waking with a jolt when he finally swung me around and stood up to carry me out of the water.

Sitting on the beach, plastering her feet with wet sand, Tracy squinted at us but said nothing. Aunt Becky rushed up and wrapped me in a towel. She thanked the lifeguard, then looked at my mother and said, "Jesus H. Christ, Linda, are you insane?" My mother said,

"Don't start, Beck, don't even start," and marched off with her shoulders thrown back, her arms and legs stiff and goosefleshed.

"That dope," said Aunt Becky. "That effing idiot. She doesn't even know where she's going."

Elaborate

I'm adamant, not obdurate. There were good moments, too, and I remember those as well. For example, the first Easter after she took us back, my mother was so broke that the Easter Bunny's offerings were decidedly spartan. Rattling around at the bottom of our baskets were a handful of jellybeans, a few marshmallow chicks, and some rectangles of chocolate cut from a larger bar. But this is just how my mother describes things. What I remember is different. I remember that every piece of chocolate was individually wrapped in tinfoil, shiny side out, and tinfoil, as far as I was concerned, was a kind of silver. On top of this, every glittering square was tied with a bit of lavender ribbon and each marshmallow chick was carefully swaddled in a paper doily.

Elegance

Our Backyard, G——, New Jersey, 1972

My grandmother, in bell-bottoms and a tank top, stands with her left hand on her hip. In her right hand she holds a glass printed with the American flag. She has the kind of old lady belly children get confused about—she looks solidly second trimester. I'm seven years old, wearing a shirred pink top and blue shorts, seated at the foot of my mother's chaise lounge, fussing with something in both hands, my shoulders up by my ears. Aunt Elsa, wearing a bold, floral print shirt, sits in a lawn chair and gestures with one hand. Legs bent, bare feet tucked under the straps of her chaise, my mother is very tan and dressed entirely in white—a slim halter top and fitted slacks. Her lush dark hair falls around her shoulders; she wears sunglasses and a single gold bangle. Even at this scale it gleams. She is thin, her limbs almost extravagantly long. She inspects her sister with characteristic stiffness, chin high. In those days my mother's siblings often accused her of arrogance, though she claimed they just resented the fact that she had *class*.

Elderly

Character is a favorite word of my mother, who is fond of referring to herself as a "real" one. In fact, I can clearly recall, even now, the first time I heard her do so. I was six years old. We had recently moved into the two-bedroom apartment on the top floor of the white house with the pink shutters. I don't know where Tracy was on this particular afternoon, maybe napping, maybe playing with some of the kids in the neighborhood; the memory includes only my mother, me, and our new sandals—two pairs of Dr. Scholl's. My mother's were in the adult style, with a raised foot bed curvaceously sculpted from birch wood, while mine, meant for a child, had low, pancake-flat soles.

She was at that time in the habit of wearing luxurious clothes, clothes I have since come to suspect were bought for her by the men she dated in Florida. Her belts, earrings, shoes, slacks, and blouses all transfixed me with a certain quality I now recognize *as* quality but back then could only identify as a mysterious sort of density. I felt extremely proud to be walking along our new street in my new sandals with my, in a sense, new mother, who seemed to me, after her lengthy absence, almost a kind of goddess—beautiful, exciting, and above all, glamorous. I adored her to an almost physically painful degree.

Holding my hand very tightly, speaking almost incessantly, without space for dialogue, I remember that she painted a picture of herself as an old lady that day: "I'm always going to wear Dr. Scholl's, you know that?" she said. "When I'm an old lady, I'll still be wearing Dr. Scholl's. Won't I be a funky old lady? Can't you just see it? *A real character!* And you—sweetie—you'll never leave me, will you? When I'm an old lady, you'll never put me in an old folks' home, will you? Promise me. Do you promise? You'll practically be an old lady yourself then, and we can be old ladies together. And I'll be the funky one."

David, Isabella, Isaac, and I had gone to the beach. Also, two of our three dogs—the two who were still alive, Inky and Chimmi. It was an extremely hot day, which is why Isaac (just a few weeks old) and I stayed out of the sun under a makeshift tent while David, Isabella, and the dogs chased one another back and forth along a thin crescent of sand bracketed by red boulders. Watching them, I felt jealous and a little abandoned. I also missed our third dog, Oscar, who had died just a few days before Isaac was born.

Though I usually found nursing a pleasure, that day it was sandy, sticky, sweaty. Tiny heat blisters bloomed on my son's cheeks. His gums, I thought, looked dark. I told David that we should leave, but he and Isabella and the dogs were having such a good time that I was gently ignored, once, twice, three times. Finally, I made him look at the bumps on Isaac's cheeks, which he said weren't really that bumpy, and the darkness of his gums, which he said weren't that dark. Still, he agreed we could leave, though not exactly with enthusiasm.

When I feel guilty, it feels like my bones are rotting. It's totally disabling. I think that's what happened that day. Everything inside me broke because I'd insisted on going home when everyone else was having such a good time, and I felt guilty about it. Or maybe it was postpartum depression. It's hard to say. I just remember that as we started packing up our things and loading them into the car, I had the sense that I was detaching from my normal life, from my own self—playacting somehow. I knew what I looked like to anyone else: I looked like a woman who'd gone to the beach with her husband and children and who was now packing up the car while holding her beautiful, sleepy newborn on one hip. But the feeling of dissonance between the woman I appeared to be and the disorder I felt on the inside was expanding at a frightening rate. This is a feeling I usually experience only in the company of my mother: a deep panic—a sense that there's no escape. Only that day the thing I couldn't escape was myself.

On the way home we stopped at an old-fashioned corner store that also sold gas and had an ice cream stand. At the ice cream stand I ordered something odd, a flavor I'd never heard of—butter crunch. This is, of course, a well-known type of donut but not of ice cream—for good reason, it turns out. Isabella got a scoop of chocolate. And David, as he always does, ordered mocha chip. The butter crunch flavor was sweet and gummy, so much so that I started to cry. David offered to buy me a new cone, but I said it was too late. I said the line was too long, we had to get home, and I didn't want to spend the money. He said that was silly, and I said it wasn't. He said it was, and I said it fucking was not. Finally, he offered to switch cones with me. The mocha chip flavor was really much, much better, but I felt guilty for taking it, so I offered him a bite. He happily accepted, only the thing of it was, he took a really big bite. I mean, it truly was a very large bite.

There's a difference, of course, between yelling and scream-ing, and I screamed when I saw how big a bite he took. We were still in the parking lot near the ice cream stand, and I screamed, not caring who heard me—the flirting teenagers, the other mom standing with her kids in the sun, the girl working in slow motion behind the ice cream counter, my own children. Suddenly I hated everything—my husband, summer, ice cream, myself. I hated all the crap that I, for whatever reason, insist on carrying around inside me. I hated my childhood and everything it lacked, which is to say things I don't even know the names of, which is seriously unhelpful. Most of all, I hated my own failures and frustrations and thwarted ambitions, of which I have many, although I usually pretend otherwise. This feeling of hatred was multiplying inside of me, like some kind of grotesque psychological cancer, kalei-doscopically expanding into a boundless field of self-loathing. I didn't say any of this, of course—I couldn't have at the time—but some version of it was streaming out of me anyway in the form of weirdly high-pitched sentences concerning what was and wasn't fair about ice cream and beaches and babies. Isabella made the pithy observation that I was being "pathetic," and while, mentally,

I couldn't have agreed more, I did not do so verbally. Instead, I threw the mocha chip ice cream cone out the car window and cried, silently, the entire fifty-minute drive home.

That night, after a couple of quick Google searches, I found a book called *Anger* by a Buddhist monk named Thich Nhat Hanh, and the next day I checked out a copy of it from our neighborhood library. Over the next couple of weeks, I read *Anger* three times in a row, once quickly, like a drowning woman, and twice more slowly. Later I ordered my own copy so I could make notes in the margins. And then I ordered other books by Thich Nhat Hanh, who happens to be quite prolific. Eventually, I ordered more books by the same New Age press that published *Anger*, and then I ordered still more books by other New Age presses and other Buddhist monks. In fact, over the last several years, I've bought and read many, many books by many Buddhist monks as well as ancient and contemporary yogis, experts on meditation, and psychologists who offer wise words about the plight of our inner child, not to mention a few mindful eating experts, child rearing experts, and marriage experts, even—in one especially pointless instance—a book about how improving your handwriting can change your life. In fact, for three or four years following that day at the beach, I read little besides books of this sort, which means that at this point my collection of self-help books has grown so large as to be frankly embarrassing, for which reason I keep it upstairs, in the sleeping loft I share with David, where it's more or less out of sight but at the same time within easy reach.

Endeavor

When you touch the present moment, you touch the past
and the future. When you touch time, you touch space.
When you touch space, you touch time. When you touch
the lemon tree in early spring, you touch the lemons that
will be there in three or four months. You can do that
because the lemons are already there. You can touch the

lemon tree in the historical dimension or the ultimate dimension; it is up to you.

—*Thich Nhat Hanh*

Erase

I asked my mother when I would get to see my grandmother again, and she sighed, sat on the arm of the couch, and pulled me onto her lap. Tucking my hair behind my ear, she said, "You really love your grandma, don't you?" Her voice sounded complicated, so I didn't say anything. She asked if I loved my grandmother as much as I loved her, and again I couldn't bring myself to say anything because the way I missed my grandmother at that point was physical. It felt like salt or acid. It was making me sick.

"Do you love her more than you love me?" she asked, and here, at last, was a question I could answer.

"No!"

"That's good," she said, "because your grandmother isn't what she appears to be."

She then told me a strange story.

"For three days and three nights," she said, "when we were still living in the basement, your grandmother locked me in the dog room."

I knew the dog room: it was the small, windowless space off the garage where my grandfather kept his dogs at night. Perhaps one hundred feet square, the ceiling of the dog room was slanted because it was tucked underneath the stairs. The floor was concrete and always covered with fresh newspapers to keep the dogs from getting a chill when they lay down.

"Your grandparents would come twice a day to toss food at me—bones and crusts of bread—and every day they beat me, *like a dog*. For three days and three nights they did this. They stripped me to my underwear. I had to sleep on the newspapers, like the dogs, who were my only friends."

My mother's words were too warm, too plosive. They made my ear itch, and the itch was like a contagion because as she spoke

I could feel something growing in me. Of course, it's easy to say now that this was a story told by a mentally ill young woman and for this reason was full of helpless lies and unintentional cruelty, but at the time I thought it was a true story about true things, and as my mother whispered it to me, everything I knew became unknown and everything I trusted became untrusted. The world as I had always understood it began to disappear, as if a corrosive fog were gobbling it up. I didn't think she was lying, though I did ask if what she said was true.

"Of course it's true. Would I *ever* lie to you?"

Then she told me the whole story all over again, and when she was done, she brushed a few strands of my hair away from my face and asked if I still missed my grandmother. When I said no, I understood for the first time how, with just a single word, it is possible to erase a part of yourself. Then she asked if I hated my grandmother, and after some hesitation I said yes. I said I hated my grandmother, and again I understood how easy, how nearly effortless, it can be to erase vast portions of yourself.

Errand

Usually complicated and pointless and hard to explain, often time-consuming and embarrassing, not to mention necessitating my complicity—no matter how passive—in some form of deceit, the errands my mother asks me to run for her are nothing but trouble, which is why I usually say no. No! No! No! But her most recent request involves something so perfectly simple that I can't refuse. All I have to do is hand-deliver a thick manila envelope to the municipal office that's in charge of her Section 8 housing. This office happens to be right on my street—just a few hundred feet away, literally a three-minute walk, door to door, so the whole thing, she assures me, won't take more than ten minutes, tops. Because I am extremely concerned that my mother never, ever, lose her Section 8 housing voucher and because she tells me that keeping this voucher depends directly on dropping off this thick manila envelope, I say okay, even though I don't understand why she can't do it herself. After all, she just handed the envelope to me, and I'm practically across the street. Why the extra step?

"Trust me. It will make a *world* of difference if they see this coming from you. They think *I'm* crazy!"

No matter how disastrous they usually are, running errands for my mother is like putting money in the guilt bank, where I'm so massively in debt, and I figure this particular errand is an easy way to pay down at least a small fraction of my outstanding balance, so the next time I have a bit of spare time, I walk over to the Municipal Housing Office, where I tell the woman behind the desk that I am dropping off some papers for my mother. When I say her name, the woman purses her lips.

"Oh. Hold on."

"Can't I just leave this with you? She said I could just drop it off. She said you would know what this is about."

"You're going to have to hold on. Just wait right there. Those have to be hand-delivered." She goes behind a partition, where I can hear her talking to another woman with a deeper, more annoyed-sounding voice. There is a big sigh, and then a middle-aged lady dressed in a burgundy-colored pantsuit emerges from the back offices and pumps her fingers at me, like, *Give me the envelope.* She peeks inside it and says, "So, they're here."

"What are?"

"Does your mother have some kind of death wish? How self-destructive can one person get?"

I suddenly feel like an idiot for not checking to see what was inside the envelope.

"It's like that woman's *trying* to get evicted," she says as she turns to go back behind the partition.

"Wait!" I yell. "What's in there? She's my mother. I don't want her to get evicted."

"It's out of your hands. It's out of all our hands. Your mama just loves trouble. Most folks feel thankful to have a landlord like that. But not your mother. No, she just has to stir things up, that one."

F

Facade

G——, *New Jersey, 1974*

I'm in the kitchen in the house with the pink shutters—there's the brown stove, the Revere Ware pots and pans with the black plastic handles, the stainless steel teakettle, the enamel butterfly chimes dangling above the sink. And there's *Fannie Farmer* open on the counter, still newish. I'm putting something very small—a peanut, a jellybean?—into my mouth. Seven years old, I wear an oversized pair of purple-tinted sunglasses and lean toward the camera in an uncharacteristically punky sort of way. No doubt it's because of the sunglasses, because of the kind of psychic protection they provide, but I'm projecting something kind of spiky. It almost looks like defiance.

Fantasy

My mother's teeth are small and broken and yellow. Several are missing. When she talks, she often hides her mouth behind her hand. But this was not always the case. There was a time when her teeth were large, white, straight. Yet even then there were problems—alignment issues, muscle tension, mysterious needles of pain. These things required prescription drugs and long periods of rest spent in silence and darkness. When I was a kid, I used to fantasize about fixing her teeth. The first time the idea occurred to me, I was sitting on the lid of a large wooden toy chest in the bedroom I shared with Tracy, looking out onto the street, onto the bleak suburban landscape—white sky, black tree branches, empty sidewalks—when I suddenly found myself buoyed up by an incredible vision: one day, when I was grown-up, I would become very rich, so rich I'd be able to rescue my mother's mouth, alleviate her pain, fix her "bite."

Father

Even at the time I felt it was a grave tactical mistake on my mother's part, my father coming to live with us. But soon enough— maybe eight or nine months after she'd put Tracy and me into her overcrowded hatchback and taken us to live in the little house on the dead-end street full of kids our own age—we were a family of four again. For a while I didn't recognize him. This, clearly, is a deformed memory. It hadn't been that long since I'd last seen him. All the same, this was my genuine experience—it's how I remember it, in any case. *Who is this guy?* Once I even asked him, "Who are you?"

"I'm your father," he said and gave me a Tootsie Roll, as if to prove it. But I still didn't trust him.

Fedora

A Party Somewhere in New Jersey or Perhaps New York, 1974

I think of this as a picture of the man my father might have been, of the man I think he wanted to be, at least for a while. He is twenty-eight years old and still lean, clean-shaven. Sitting on a couch in front of a picture window hung with apricot-colored drapes, he wears a brown fedora pushed far back on his head and a beautiful shirt of shimmering white-on-white checks. His gaze is directed downward at something in his lap, so that all you see behind his gold-rimmed glasses are his eyelashes and, above them, the dramatic sweep of his eyebrows. His face—every angle of it—is an elegant contradiction, masculine yet delicate: the long Sicilian nose, the nostrils slightly flared, the glossy black ringlets, the perfect skin. His cheeks are pink! He looks like a poet.

Feliz Navidad

In a Department Store, 1974

Santa's totally drunk or on drugs or something, nodding out. There's a placard hanging around his neck. I think this must be some kind of ID. It says "2–12324 Miles to the North Pole." I'm only eight, but already I seem completely unconvinced by the whole deal. Tracy, on Santa's other leg, appears deeply troubled by something. Maybe, on top of everything else (the closed eyes, the slipping beard, the sweaty face), Santa has bad breath—Tracy's upper lip is raised in just such a way as to suggest this. We wear matching beige tights and turtlenecks, matching plaid jumpers with intersecting bars of olive and brown. I remember those jumpers. They itched like hell. But they were very cute—our mother made them. She was (no doubt still would be, if she put her mind to it) a very talented seamstress.

Filthy

What we called "kneeling" in my family, psychological literature calls "self-soothing," other more familiar forms of which include head banging, nail biting, and thumb sucking. Although I started kneeling right after my mother's first suicide attempt, when I was three years old, I continued to do so long after her return. I knelt everywhere—in school, on buses, at restaurants, in friends' houses, on neighbors' lawns.

Isaac has a friend who masturbates in a similar way, only she doesn't kneel. She stretches her legs out straight in front of her and squeezes her thighs fiercely together. I've seen her do this at school, and what struck me most—beyond the fact that she appeared trapped in a quiet agony—was that no one else seemed to notice, not the other children, not the after-school science teacher, not the teacher's college-aged assistant. Or maybe they did. Maybe everyone in the room simply chose to let her do what she seemed so bent on doing by ignoring it. Perhaps they understood that she couldn't help what she was doing, just as I couldn't when I was her age. She wore, I suspect, the same expression I must have worn back then; and all these years later, watching her, I felt both sad and ashamed. A compulsion is so terribly private.

When my mother explained to me that what I was doing was sexual and therefore constituted a form of pleasure, I was not only mortified, I was confused. I was outraged. How could this act—so ugly, painful, and relentless—be called pleasure?

Like Isaac's friend, I sometimes knelt in very public settings, yet no one seemed to notice—at least no one but my mother. Unfortunately, she saw me all the time. In fact, during the two years we lived in the house with the pink shutters, it seemed to me that her primary objective in life was to cure me of what she called my "filthy habit."

She was always catching me in the act, no matter how carefully I hid or how quietly I went about my business. And when she caught me, she would pick me up and throw me down. Usually, she threw me onto a soft surface, such as a nearby couch or bed (two pieces of furniture I often hid behind), but occasionally she threw me to the floor, and at those times I became acutely aware of the bones in my own body. At a certain point I realized I could masturbate in the bathroom, and for a while this was a tremendous relief. I imagined the endless game of cat and mouse had finally come to a close. But it didn't take long for her to spy on me through the crack under the bathroom door, and when I came out, she still picked me up and threw me down. After that I started rolling up the bathmat and wedging it into the crack under the door, but this, obviously, was a shortsighted strategy. One day I emerged from the bathroom to find her standing in the hallway, arms crossed over her chest, eyes narrowed. She spoke very softly as she put her hand against my face and asked, "What did you just do?"

"Nothing."

"Do you want to change your mind about that? Because your face is bright red, and your cheeks are burning hot, and I know exactly what you've been doing, and it's a filthy, disgusting habit!"

I tried to run down the hall to the bedroom I shared with Tracy, but my mother was somehow attached to me. Her voice was a physical thing. It touched my brain directly. "You disgusting little brat," she whispered, her breath hot on my ear. "I can see right through you. I know everything you do. I can see you through doors and through walls. I can see you when you're at school. I know exactly what you're up to even when you're miles away. I know you better than you know yourself! Don't you *ever* forget that."

Float (1)

In yoga, to float is to execute a slow, controlled, seemingly magical transition between two dissimilar postures. For example, in the transition from *adho mukha svanasana* (downward-facing dog) to the one officially known as *dandasana* (stick pose, or seated at the front of your mat with your legs extended), the most graceful float is, in fact, a subtle handstand half-pike followed by a quick pelvic tuck, which allows you to slip your legs in a graceful arc between your hands and then out in front of you at exactly the same instant you settle your hips on the floor.

There is also, of course, a metaphorical sense to the idea of floating, which is more or less the same thing Buddhists call "being in the present." In this second sense it is entirely possible to float while doing the dishes or designing a website or driving in heavy traffic or even, theoretically speaking, while talking on the phone with one's mother about the worms in her eye (although this last example would, obviously, constitute a very advanced form of floating).

Although I practice yoga daily, I still cannot float physically, but every once in a while I find myself floating in the second sense. This happens most often in the company of Isaac, who is still young enough to float, himself, for long stretches at a time without even realizing he's doing so. For example, if we eat pistachios together or read *Asterix and Obelix* together or practice karate together, he usually floats while doing so, and sometimes it's contagious. Floating is easy around him. Even with Isabella, seven years older than her brother, I occasionally catch a little air time.

Float (2)

If I love yoga, and I do, it's because I studied ballet as a child, and yoga is to me an extension of that experience, which taught me many curious things about living in a human body, such as the fact that movement can sometimes travel through you as breath travels through a hollow reed and the related fact that vibratory sensation is the root impetus of all physical expression and the fact that if you point your toes, it is not merely your toe muscles that do the work, it is not even in your leg muscles, but something deep in your belly and even further than that, something—a vibration of sorts—in your mind.

I danced in three different ballet studios from the age of six to the age of thirteen. During that stretch of years my parents fought nearly constantly, moved house much too often, launched two fairly robust careers, made some excellent meals, went to night school, and became, in their own individual ways, increasingly unhinged. Through it all I danced. I wasn't talented, but I was hardworking, and in many ways ballet was the most constant, enjoyable, and reliable element of my childhood. I loved especially to leap, and I loved also, especially, to sweat.

Float (3)

The idea is that alcoholism hopscotches through the male line of my father's family. For example, my father's mother's brother was an alcoholic. So was my father's father's grandfather. Clearly, there's no genetic connection between these two examples, yet they are often cited—by my father, his sisters, even me—as a form of explanation.

But when I was a kid, I had no idea my father was an alcoholic. I only knew that he drank a lot of wine. So much wine, in fact, that when Tracy and I decided at some point to collect all the corks from all the wine bottles that came through our house, we filled an entire kitchen drawer inside of a year. After that we began filling a spare colander. After that our mother told us we either had to throw out the corks or do something useful with them, so we dumped them out on a blanket and contemplated. What could we make with so many corks? My father proposed the construction of a raft. "But what would we do with a raft?" "Float away," he said. I understood that he was joking, but at the same time something about his tone gave me pause.

Florist

My mother calls at 11:23 p.m. to say I need to come by and pick out anything of hers I want.

"I'm giving up my Section 8 voucher. I'm leaving the country. You can have anything. That nice little mahogany table."

"Where are you going?"

"You don't need to know the specifics."

"How are you going to afford it?"

"That's my concern, not yours. Now listen, I know how much you and your sister *love* DMH and do anything they want you to. But you *need* to not call them. You *need* to not tell them that I'm moving. I just have to get away from this hellhole. I've finally forgiven you for bringing me here, Kimberli, but as you know, *Massachusetts has been a living nightmare for me, and I just need the freedom to be happy—to go somewhere where I can just be *me*. A florist."

Flower

Have you ever seen somebody beat somebody else up? I mean in real life. It gets very slow after a certain point because the person who's winning has to do a lot of heavy, clumsy lifting simply in order to keep the fight going, organizing the basic physical bulk of the person who's losing so as to land another punch. I once watched my father beat my mother in this slow-motion way. The fight woke me up. At first it was just a lot of shouting and moving in and out of rooms, back and forth along the hallway of our apartment. My mother made dramatic gestures while saying things I couldn't understand except in the most general terms, by which I mean it was clear that she was mocking my father, while he, for his part, did that disturbing looming trick of his, breathing heavily through flared nostrils and leaning in very close to her face. It didn't take long before their legs and arms started going haywire, flying around in all the wrong places. Everything was getting mixed-up. I shouted at them, begging them to stop, but was ignored to such a degree that I remember actually wondering if I'd somehow become invisible.

I had, by that point, already witnessed a number of physical fights, not just between my parents but also between my mother's siblings (see *gods*). But something about this fight seemed different—harder to keep track of. It was as if the three of us were being swept down some secret, hidden vein of reality. As if we were getting siphoned quickly off, transported somewhere far away from the familiar world, someplace where the normal rules of existence had no bearing.

At a certain point my mother started moving very slowly, barely responding even when my father pounded her upper body—in particular, her head—against the corner of the kitchen doorway. In between hitting her head against the doorway, he pulled her body upright, as if to align her spine and in this way more accurately hit her head against the doorframe another time. And every time her head hit against the doorframe, a soft, almost prim sound came out of her, as if she were clearing her throat in her sleep. It was the smallness of this noise that worried me more than anything else, though at the moment I was of course almost entirely preoccupied with my father—all my energies bent on trying to pry him off of her.

What I didn't understand (and wouldn't for many years to come) was that despite all that was taking place around me, something else, also quite enormous, was happening inside of me. Inside of me something was growing with tremendous speed, racing through me, taking form, saturating my being on a cellular level. It would take decades for me to begin to recognize the character of this internal event, which I now understand to be the blossoming of rage, because I was, at the moment, so involved with the task at hand, and yet nothing I did—not even throwing my entire body at my father—had any effect on him. Or almost no effect, because I did get in his way eventually. I know because there is a blank spot, and then there is a hammered copper hinge. This hinge was part of the cabinet under the stove, and even now, in memory, it remains spectacularly in focus: tarnished and spade-like, it is full of tiny, shallow divots. A fine line of grime runs around its edge.

Frankly

I'm not sure why I bother with this. Except that the past calls to me so plaintively. As if I could help, all these years later. I feel like one of those avid old men who troll the beaches at odd hours, hunched over metal detectors, searching for something. But what?

Frantic

All that remains are a few random details, like the placement of the gray rectangle that was the television in the corner of the living room and the diffuse glare light from the streetlight seeping through the semitransparent curtains and the harsher trapezoid of fluorescent light spilling from the kitchen into the dining room.

I think of that night, now, as a kind of hinge. So many things depended on it, so many things fell out from it. Huge chunks of my personality, for example, were forged that night, despite the iffy quality of my memories, which are staticky and truncated. I know this: at some point my parents moved from a standing position in the kitchen doorway to a prone one in the middle of the living room floor. And there, in the center of this uncentered memory, is a mound. My father is sitting on top of it, and one arm is going up and then it's coming down. Then it goes up again, and then it comes back down. I am not in this picture at all. I am only a monkey-like presence, a scrawny frantically hopping shadow trying to pull him off of her. Years later my father told me over one of our weekly dinners (see *Osteria*) that if it hadn't been for my pulling and screaming, he might have killed her because he was in a "blackout," meaning so drunk that his senses had shut down.

"Nothing can get through when you're in a blackout," he explained, more than a decade later. "But for some reason, at some point, you did. That's when I stopped."

I remember his feet on the stairs: each step a slightly different sound.

I remember my mother's unmoving form. Her face was swollen and lumpy and smeared with things. It was a mental challenge to simply recognize her. Long dark strands of her hair were stuck to her cheeks and forehead. One eyelid and both lips were swollen and bright red. They looked like rubber. I decided she must be dead, and I started keening. I was just a kid in New Jersey, but I was keening my head off, rocking back and forth over my mother's still body. I see all this as if in a movie, more or less from above. In this way it's almost entirely false. What's real, the only detail that flares for me, is the shag carpet under my knees: it itched. Somehow it still does.

Freak

When she knocks on our door without warning, I step out onto our porch and tell her right off the bat that she can't do it anymore—come by whenever she feels like it and just expect me to stop everything I'm doing in order to talk to her.

"*Why*, Kimberli? Why do you hate me so much?"

"I don't hate you! I just have things to do. I have a whole life, you know."

It seems clear we're headed toward a fight, the same fight we always have, but suddenly she looks very concerned as she puts a hand on my forearm. "It's because of that time when you were seven, isn't it? I'm *so* sorry about that, Kimmy. You have no idea. I'll never forgive myself for what I did to you that day."

"I don't know what you're talking about."

"The day I threw you," she whispers.

"Mom. You threw me more than once."

"No! Don't make things worse than they were! It was bad enough. Even to do it once. I make no excuses. None. But you have to understand where I was coming from." There are creases on her forehead I've never noticed before. Her eyebrows are sparse and speckled gray. The skin of her face hangs listlessly from the beautiful old bones. I just wanted to protect you. I thought people would think you were a freak. You masturbated so much. It was scary."

Funky

M——, New Jersey, 1975

How'd she figure things, afterward? After half our block had stood outside in the middle of the night, bathed in the pulsing lights of police cars and the ambulance, watching as she was brought outside on a stretcher? After she returned home, so bruised and swollen that Tracy and I had to eat our meals at the next-door neighbor's house for half the week because she was too sore to get out of bed? What stubborn, sad, or twisted thing in her thought, *Sure! Let's give it another go?*

My father's hair is long in this photograph—it reaches almost to his shoulders. It is wavy and shiny and black. His aviator glasses are amber tinted, his shirt collar enormous, his woolen vest knit in a large-scale argyle pattern of green and red diamonds. The best descriptor for this outfit might be *funky*. He is just beginning to get fat, which is the way I remember him from my childhood. My mother, though, looks svelte and fashionable in her tilting white beret and gold hoop earrings. Her brow is high, her smile wide— every tooth still sound, still white.

This is the only photo I know of that shows the four of us together. It was taken on Christmas Eve at Grandma Ellen's house (my mother's mother). I can tell because of the holiday cards pinned to the wall behind our heads; the cards encircle a poster of wild horses kicking up dust in a bleached-out western landscape. This poster is duct-taped to the white wood paneling, and the four of us are sitting on the couch just beneath it. Sliding off my mother's lap, I hold two gingham-printed stuffed animals that have been sewn together in a permanent hug; their species is unclear, but one is blue and one is pink. On our father's lap, looking as if she might fall asleep at any second, Tracy holds a similar pair of animals, red and white, also locked in an eternal embrace.

Furphy

Drugs, according to David, are my mother's real, essential problem, not mental illness or childhood trauma. I find this take simplistic, but I do wonder if all those other things—the worms, the landlord problems, the paranoia, the endless issues with her teeth—wouldn't be half so bad without the drugs, which she gets from various doctors, whose prescriptions she fills at far-flung pharmacies, one of which is in Rhode Island and another in New Hampshire. These drugs she combines in ways I don't understand, ways that seem to essentially obliterate her. Yes, surely my mother is an addict, yet I find it hard to square this thought emotionally because she has always, for as long as I can remember, insisted that she hates drugs—she hates drugs and everybody who does drugs and all varieties of addicts because addicts are weak. Addicts are users. And they *lie, lie, lie, lie.* She often takes great relish in listing out the addicts in her life as examples of precisely the type of person she is not: "My brothers and sisters are addicts. My father was an addict. And your father is the *ultimate* addict. And nothing—*nothing*—makes me sicker than an addict!"

G

Gallberries

The most exciting thing I knew as a child was driving down the long dirt road that led to my grandmother's house. Why this was such a thrill, I can't say, but to this day I still occasionally dream about that road, and these dreams are always exhilarating, despite the fact that when I stop to examine the actual experience, there was hardly anything to it: gravel spitting up from our car wheels with a sound like heavy rain; thin blades of sunlight stretching through the birch tree branches; thickets of gallberry holly coated with gray dust; pollen so heavy that, in the summertime, our windows were yellow with it by the time we reached my grandmother's.

The house itself was small and dirty. Everything in it was amiss—broken, peeling, mildewed, crumbling, rotting, smelly (especially in the bathroom, as there was no running water and we flushed with a bucket, though only when absolutely necessary). Yet despite all of this, it was to me a place of wonder, almost part of another world, as if it had sprung from the pages of a half-forgotten fairy tale.

In the kitchen there was a pump at the sink and a cast-iron pot-bellied, coal-burning stove set on a platform of wobbling bricks. In the wintertime I liked to stare into the narrow slots of this stove, at the jagged chunks of coal inside that burned neon orange and emitted an icelike sound, a kind of tinkling or crinkling. There was also a "painting" over the table that depicted a jug of wine and two apples as well as an old-fashioned clock, the hands of which were real hands—made of metal with filigree tips—that stuck out from the surface of the painting and traced the hours of the day like any other clock. The stairs leading from the kitchen to the bedroom on the second floor were painted fire-engine red, and the wall in this stairwell was covered with several decades' worth of wallpaper. Tracy and I spent hours on those stairs, peeling away chips of chalky paper, revealing endless variations of plaids and florals and hunting scenes, yet we never got to the bottom of it.

When we slept over on the weekends, Grandma Ellen gave us her double bed upstairs and she slept on the couch in the living room. Under the slanted roof upstairs, there were two windows, dusty and busy with insects: large moths, angry flies, drunken-seeming bumblebees all noodled at the panes. Spiders fussed in the corners.

The smallest room in that three-room house was the living room, which was paneled with fake wood—white with gray striations—and crowded with potted plants and a large, staticky television with rabbit ear antennae. For some reason this room terrified me—maybe because it was dark and always felt cool or maybe because we sometimes watched scary movies in there with Aunt Elsa, our mother's youngest sister. In any case this room frightened me so much that I used to hold my breath as I ran through it whenever I had to use the bathroom. But it also contained an object I found almost unbearably beautiful: that poster of wild horses stampeding across a desert landscape at sunset. I loved this image not so much for how it looked as for how it sounded because every time I ran past it, I could just make out the faint thunder of distant hooves.

Gape

Grandma Ellen's forehead was high and elegantly rounded. Her jaw was dramatically angled, her cheekbones lofty but narrow. She might have been pretty if not for her pronounced underbite, which gave her a vaguely pugnacious look. Her nose was scooped and conspicuously small—a rarity in our family, so rare, in fact, that I have often wondered whether she hadn't at some point (perhaps in New Orleans—see *hair shirt*) gotten a nose job. But it was her eyes

that were her most striking feature—blue with a violet tinge, forever shadowed underneath by two dark, nearly purple semicircles.

Grandma Ellen was so perennially exhausted that whenever she
rode in the car with us, my mother at the wheel, she'd drop off
after a mere five minutes—her head thrown back against the passenger seat, mouth wide open in a helpless surrender to her own
bottomless fatigue. Amazed and a little disgusted by the gaping
black hole of her mouth and the snores that issued from it, Tracy
and I would spiral into hysterical fits of laughter in the back seat.
Now I wonder if maybe our grandmother wasn't tired because
of the coughing—she coughed all the time, every three or four
minutes because of the whooping cough she'd barely survived as
a child, which had scarred and weakened her lungs. The cough
itself always followed precisely the same trajectory: a hoarse, deep
rattle followed by an attenuated, almost musical wheeze.

She often served us canned soup with saltines for lunch and
cups of milky tea and slices of toast spread with deviled ham or
sprinkled with sugar for a snack. She sang us children's songs, like
"Pony Boy" and "Itsy Bitsy Spider" and "I'm a Little Teapot," as
well as an unorthodox version of "Miss Mary Mack" that I can't
quite remember now, outside of the fact that the silver buttons
played a slightly X-rated role. She loved animals and fed the hoards
of feral cats and dogs in her rural neighborhood with huge pots
of rice that she put outside for them (or if it was raining, inside)
and allowed all the pregnant cats and dogs to have their litters in
a hole at the back of her house, where part of the foundation had
caved in. She loved animals so much that there was a period of
time—a couple of weeks or maybe even longer—when she refused
to wash her hair because she insisted that there was a spider living
in it and she didn't want to hurt it.

Garlic

My father learned how to go stony—face red, nostrils flared, hands
clenched, still as a statue. But he never hit her again. My mother,
on the other hand, grew more and more wildly antagonistic. Often

her aggression manifested in unusual ways. For example, she occasionally sliced cloves of garlic paper thin and tucked the slivers into the pockets and linings of his suits before he left for work so that the stench rose up around him, a mystery of embarrassment that twice got him sent home from the office.

For years this memory seemed suspect to me—it's just so odd. Slivers of garlic? Hidden in suits? I figured I must have dreamed it: a baroque *confabulation* inspired by my father's Italian heritage. But once, in my thirties, I asked my mother if it was true. Had she actually put garlic in my father's suits?

"*You betcha!*" she said. Then she explained how she used to slice the cloves using a razor blade so as to make the slivers as *thin as possible*, so thin, in fact, as to be *nearly transparent* and in this way *practically impossible to detect.*

"But why?" I asked, and she looked at me for a moment with an expression I couldn't quite read. Then she said my name in this way she does sometimes, very quick, very boxy. All sharp angles. "*Kimberli.* You'll forgive that man anything. But me—a little garlic and you'd think it was the crime of the century!"

German

Grandma Ellen's father was English, but he disappeared just months after her birth, so whatever blood he contributed to that line of the family has always seemed to count for less. For next to nothing, in fact. Instead, I think of my grandmother as being mostly German because her maternal grandparents came from Germany around the turn of the century and settled in the Catskills, where my grandmother grew up.

In 1918 Grandma Ellen's mother died in the influenza pandemic, which left her essentially orphaned. Just two years old, she was raised from that point on by her teenaged aunts (or as my family has always called them, "the Aunts"—always with the definite article). This is why I think of Germany when I think of my grandmother—because the Aunts were practically German in every respect except birth, and in raising their young niece, they managed to shape her character almost completely. Which isn't to say *directly*, because Grandma Ellen would eventually build her entire adult life in opposition to everything her aunts stood for.

Some of the more stereotypically Germanic attributes of the Aunts included an emphasis on propriety, an adoration of all things solidly bourgeois, strict habits of diet and self-care, restrained facial expressions that often conveyed an apparent lack of emotion, a taciturn Protestantism, an uncomplaining work ethic, and an almost fetishistic habit of coupon cutting. All these, of course, are admirable qualities seen in a certain light, and the two old spinsters (when I knew them) in fact led a very comfortable life. But my grandmother inherited not a single one of these traits or habits.

As a child, I often compared and contrasted my grandmother with the Aunts. It seemed unthinkable that Millie and Gert, with their countless lace doilies, their white gloves, their fine china, their towers of hatboxes, could in fact, in real and actual life, no matter how many years earlier, have raised my grandmother, who lived in such a small and squalid house, with floors so saturated with coal dust that to walk around barefoot on them for even a few minutes turned the soles of Tracy's and my feet a shiny, silvery black. Not to put too fine a point on it, my grandmother was gossipy, coarse, and dead poor. I don't know if she was lazy or just uninterested in the "finer things" in life, but she didn't seem to care about how she looked or what sort of impression she made. Certainly she was not religious. If she dedicated herself to anything at all, it was to books, which she loved to read one right after another—fat, cheap paperbacks bought at the drugstore counter, half a dozen at a time. These she read by the dim light of her kitchen window, which was made not of glass but of a sheet of plastic that snapped in the frame when the wind was up.

Gestation

She said the spider had laid an egg in her hair and she wanted to give it time to hatch. It smelled mustardy in my grandmother's kitchen. Warm and sour and a little bit like piss. She looked not at me when she spoke, and not at Tracy, but above us, maybe at the clock painting on the wall or at the dim, speckled Budweiser mirror that hung next to it. I remember wondering if she actually believed this story or if she was just teasing us. Maybe she was telling us this story because she thought it would entertain us. Or was it some kind of a game? Or a test of some kind? If so, would I fail if I didn't believe her? Or if I did? Did she think the story would make us laugh? Enchant us? All of these possibilities ran through my mind, and this too: I didn't want to hurt her feelings. If she truly believed that a spider was living in her hair, I didn't want her to know I thought that was crazy. It was a lot to consider, but I was used to it. I had long ago perfected a strategy for such situations: I simply arranged my face in an expression of genial neutrality.

Gesture

M——, New Jersey, circa 1951

In the only photograph I've ever seen of my mother's father, he and my grandmother pose with the first four of their seven children in front of what appears to be a new black car, gleaming and voluptuous with silvery hubcaps and grill. Above the car is a clothesline with a dozen or so pins attached to it. The sky is white, and a gentle glare seems to press down on the scene. Things must have been good at this point. My grandparents are well-dressed: my grandfather in a double-breasted black suit, my grandmother in a long skirt, high heels, and a white ruffled blouse with a dainty bow at the neck. Her hair, softly curled, flows down both sides of her narrow, high-cheekboned face to her shoulders. She wears lipstick, an almost sultry expression, and nylons. Her shoes are half-hidden in the patchy grass. My grandfather looks to be about thirty years old. He's got a Jean-Paul Belmondo thing going on. A tough-guy vulnerability. A face crowded with its own dramatic features. His hair is brown and wavy, his skin a good two or three shades darker than my grandmother's. One of his hands rests on his eldest daughter's shoulder. This gesture could be protective, or it could be reminding her to stand still, or it could be a statement of possession. On his hip, encircled by his right arm, is my mother, chubby and towheaded. She is playing with his tie. About three years old, she looks very serious about the tie. My grandmother holds the baby, my aunt Becky, in both arms, cupping one of her tiny, curling feet in one hand. The oldest child, my uncle Thor, squints into the camera and grasps the dark folds of his mother's skirt with his fist. He can't be older than five or six, yet he wears exactly the same expression he will for the rest of his life. The best word for this might be *removed*.

Giant, Midget

Some weekends Tracy and I slept over at our grandmother's house, some we slept over with the Aunts in New York City. Technically speaking, the Aunts were Tracy's and my great-grandaunts, and not surprisingly, they were extremely old. They were also kind and boring and impossible to keep straight, probably on account of their wigs—identical steel-gray helmets. Tracy's and my confusion regarding which aunt was which forced us to construct sentences with enormous holes in them, holes where their names would normally have fit. But our troubles lifted one day when, sitting on a chalk-blue angora blanket spread across one of their twin beds (the smell of mothballs sifting up from underneath us), Tracy hit on a brilliant mnemonic: the short one, she said, had the name that started with *M*—Millie, which we could remember because *M* is also the first letter of the word *midget*. And *G* was the start of both *Gert* (who was tall and big-boned) and the word *giant*.

After that our time with the Aunts was a little easier, linguistically speaking, but those weekends still dragged. There just wasn't a lot to do besides eating the hearty meals Aunt Millie cranked out with remarkable energy (noodles with meatballs, potatoes and corned beef, chicken and rice in cream sauce, turkey pie, sardines smashed with mayonnaise, duck hash with poached eggs, stewed prunes, pickled watermelon rind, lemon pudding) and sitting on the Persian rug in the living room to "play" with the one toy in the entire apartment—a set of nesting Matryoshka dolls—while Aunt Gert thumbed through the pile of newspapers she kept on her damask footstool.

Being so distant from their own long-ago childhoods, the Aunts seemed to have lost any insider knowledge they once might have possessed about children, such as how to play with them or talk to them. On top of this, they were obsessed with propriety and discouraged whimsy of any kind, so in short our visits with them—irregular but numerous—remained sterile encounters.

Now, of course, at this much later point in my life, I really wish I'd been a different sort of child—more avid, more suspicious, less shy. For example, I wish I'd asked the Aunts questions, many questions. Such as, *What is wrong with my mother?* If I'd been less quiet, less fearfully polite, I might even have pressed them to reveal why the two of them had never married, and certainly I would have asked them the most interesting question of all—one I pondered often: how was it that the two of them lived in such decent, respectable comfort, while their niece, my grandmother, inhabited such a tiny, dirty, ramshackle house? Who knows—had I been more inquisitive, the Aunts might have enlightened me on these and many other points of interest, in which case my entire life may have unfolded in a completely different direction. Because if such mysteries had been explained early on, I might not find myself, as I do today, still struggling to solve them.

Gjetost

We called it the "Refrigerator Story," although it was just a description, not a story. When I was little, I couldn't hear it often enough. I used to beg my mother to tell it to me again and again. Like most of her stories about her own early life, the Refrigerator Story seemed like a fragment from a fairy tale: a glimpse into some other, much more intensely colored reality. At the very center of this story stood—yes—a refrigerator, and inside the refrigerator was a shelf that no one but my grandfather was allowed to touch. On this shelf he kept many exotic foods that reminded him of Sweden, his homeland. Some of these foods sounded woodsy and sweet, like limpa bread and lingonberries; others struck me as odd, like creamed herring or gjetost, a sweet brown goat cheese, which, I knew because my mother once bought a block to show me, looks and even tastes weirdly like caramel. But many of the foods she described seemed downright barbaric, such as the raw sirloin steaks she said her father chopped very fine, using two knives at once— chop-chop-chop-chop-chop-chop-chop—until the meat was soft and *silky as pudding*. He would then make a mound of this mush on a plate ("rabiff," he called it), cover it with raw onion (also very finely chopped), and over the whole, break a fresh egg. I had no idea, when I was young, what my grandfather did to my mother when she was a child, and yet I still understood him to be a kind of devil; the Refrigerator Story seemed proof of this. It was like being related to Rumplestiltskin or the Big Bad Wolf—some creature whose wickedness pushed right up against the brink of imagining— because it wasn't just the raw sirloin and blood sausage and black pudding that amazed me with their grotesque otherworldliness; it was the fact that, according to my mother and her siblings (who also told this story), there were times that my grandfather went about making and eating his elaborately chopped *rabiff* when the rest of the refrigerator was empty.

Glam

She often enlisted Tracy and me to help her quit. "Stop picking!" we'd say whenever we caught her. Sometimes she'd say "thank you" and put her hand down, but more often than not she'd just keep going.

Once she told me that she'd learned how to pick her hair during her two-month stay in the psychiatric hospital she was admitted to after her first suicide attempt. She was twenty-one years old at the time, and there was an older woman on her ward, a fellow patient, whom she found glamorous because she read thick, serious novels and had a Belgian accent and because she did something pretty and intricate with individual strands of her hair. My mother said she studied this woman's motions: the dainty picking, the airy twirling—not unlike a one-handed game of cat's cradle—and finally the subtle tug that resulted in the slow-motion sifting of a single strand of hair to the floor. She practiced all the moves. Got them down. By the time she came back from Florida, she was a bona fide trichotillomaniac. Her habit fascinated me as much as it had fascinated her when she'd watched the Belgian woman in the hospital. I thought it looked sophisticated, in a distracted sort of way, and tried to do it myself until she caught me at it and batted my hand away from my head. "Don't do that!" she said. "It makes you look crazy."

Glimpse

M——, New Jersey, circa 1952

Squinting into the sun, about four and five years old, respectively, my mother and her oldest sister, Inga, sit outside on a wooden chair. Inga wears a white pinafore, my mother a plaid gingham dress with a lacy bib and puffed sleeves. Things have been carefully arranged for this photograph; the chair's eyelet skirt, its placement out of doors, the bow in my aunt's hair all speak to this.

So, why is it that whoever took the photograph staged the scene in front of an abandoned bus, headed downhill, its front end hidden in some woods? Not far from the bus is a strange construction, about fifteen feet high. It looks like it might be a turbine or some kind of large generator, haphazardly boarded up with wooden planks. Whatever it is, it is not photogenic. My mother is eating something.

For years, whenever I looked at this photograph, I didn't see the bus or the weird whatever-it-is in the background, only the lace, the grass, the trees, the two tanned little girls—not exactly happy. Still, for some reason I assumed my mother was eating something delicious and that the deliciousness of whatever it was must have been the cause of her look of intense concentration. One day, studying the photograph more closely, I realized that she's in fact eating a potato, a raw one to judge from the tautness of its skin and her grip on it. She's chomping into it the way you would chomp into an apple.

I'm sure I'd still see an apple there, despite the oblong shape, the dusky skin, except that once, while cooking dinner with my mother, I noticed her pop a slice of raw potato into her mouth. I'd never seen anyone eat raw potato before and had the notion that uncooked potatoes were mildly poisonous, the way potato leaves are or potato skins if too green. She seemed flustered when I asked why she'd eaten it, and in the offhand, somewhat aggressive way she adopts whenever she feels the roots of her poverty showing, she told me she'd eaten raw potatoes the whole time she was growing up—that raw potatoes were often the only snack to be had, and sometimes they were dinner.

"Try it," she said. "It's not bad."

Gloom

Hairbrushes and leather belts and wooden spoons. Bare hands on occasion too. My mother was strong, but you wouldn't know it when she hit us. She held back, most of the time. Still, the spankings hurt, not least our pride. And generally speaking, they lowered the mood quite a bit. The internal weather could be negatively affected for days. Protests were met with sarcasm and statements to the effect that neither Tracy nor I had any idea what "real" physical abuse was and therefore no cause for complaint.

Glossary

A kind of door—this glossary is, anyway—a door I am in the midst of constructing, and when I am done with this door, I will shut it, and on the other side of it, I will leave my heavy boots, because I am pretty sure I will be more comfortable without them, and I suspect that if I am more comfortable, I will also be more useful, generally speaking—to my children, my husband, my community, my extended family, maybe even to my mother. Or not. Maybe I'm just talking through my nonexistent hat about my nonexistent boots, which are, of course, mere *metaphor*, just like the door I would never actually be able to shut—not all the way—even if this glossary were one.

Gods

On holidays my grandmother's house was crowded with my mother's six brothers and sisters, their romantic interests, and the four of us. Grandma Ellen was there too, needless to say, brittle and strange.

Those celebrations were crowded, warm, loud. But at the same time there was something wonderful about them, larger than life. This feeling had everything to do with my aunts and uncles, who, although they seemed at the time vaguely interchangeable (there were just so many of them), were as a group unlike anybody else I knew. Boisterous. Big-boned. Reckless. Even to this day, my aunt Elsa or uncle Lucas will suddenly come to mind whenever I am surprised by a shaft of pollen-lit sunlight or the sound of a single acoustic guitar played out of doors or the sight of young, bare, dirty feet.

There were times when the holidays we spent at my grandmother's house went the way holidays are supposed to go: nobody got too drunk or too mad or too mean, and at the end of the night everybody hugged everybody else goodbye before climbing into their respective cars and driving home. But at other times things unraveled well before that point.

How does experience blur? How do once-specific memories smear, over time, into the haze of general impressions? I can't say which gatherings at my grandmother's house ended with a drunken insult tossed recklessly into the conversation, an insult that created a chain reaction of speech and gesture until the whole room came alive in a special way, yet I still remember exactly how the volume zipped right up at those moments. How the laughter spiraled more loudly, more sourly, more quickly. How plosives became more plosive, sibilants more sibilant.

Yet when I search for concrete details, I can bring to mind only two fragile, bleached-out memories of actual physical fights.

One began outdoors, in my grandmother's front yard, near the driveway—first a shove, then another, then a fist grabbing a collar. I watched my father and my uncle go at it like this, as I stood near the lilac bush. The other argument was between two women—which two, I can't say. One of them might have been my mother. One of them might have been my aunt Becky. Or it could have been my aunts Inga and Elsa. In any case I was sitting on a folding chair at the kitchen table, mourning my sweet potatoes, which suddenly seemed much less appetizing. And I remember this: the two women—whoever they were—fought like children. Like Tracy and me: slappy and spastic, lifting their heads away from one another while using the same frantic pawing motions that my sister and I used when we fought, only they were, of course, grown women. They were gigantic. And although I recognized even at the time that there was something pathetic about this behavior, in another sense it felt like watching the gods fight.

Going Shit à la Ape

Tracy and I were sitting at the small, white, formica-topped table in our kitchen eating cereal—cornflakes or maybe Life, which was a favorite at the time. We'd moved earlier that year from the top floor of the house with the pink shutters to the top floor of a house with black shutters three towns over because my mother had gotten into an irreconcilable argument with the landlady in the house with the pink shutters. This apartment wouldn't last long either, for the same reason, but at the time Tracy and I were just eating our breakfast cereal and watching our parakeets, Greenie and Bluey, as they hopped around in their cage near the window, beyond which it was snowing—big soft clumps sifting slowly downward. My mother had recently started working at a new job—not as a secretary (which was what she'd always been before) but in a sales capacity at a large computer company. She was running late, so she called down the hall from the bathroom to ask our father to make her some toast.

"Sure," he said, and popped in two slices. Then he got busy with something else—maybe pouring orange juice for Tracy or lighting a cigarette for himself because both of my parents were still smoking at that point (despite the fact that Tracy and I went to great lengths every day to hide their cigarettes and break them or soak them or throw them out). When the toast popped up, Tracy and I kept eating our cereal and watching the birds and the snow. It took a while, but eventually my father retrieved the two slices, put them on a plate, and buttered them. Then he called down the hall to our mother to say her toast was ready.

Seconds later, she swept into the kitchen wearing a long, pleated skirt, dark nylons, and a special sort of silky top she called a "blouson," which had a big silk bow attached at the neck. Her hair was still up in heavy electric rollers.

"God, I'm starving!" she said as she rushed up to the counter, only once she got there, she didn't pick up the toast and start eating. Instead, she put both hands on either side of the plate, almost as if bracing herself, and suddenly that thing that terrified me more than anything else in the world began to fill the room.

"What the *fuck* is this?" she said. Her voice went incredibly high, nearly bleating. "What the *fucking* fuck is this?" She swept the plate off the counter. It flew across the room and hit a wall, exploding shards of china everywhere. Squawking madly, our parakeets flew around in their cage, corner to corner to corner to corner to corner: a crazy blur of blue and green wings. "You call that fucking toast! I asked you to make me fucking *toast*, and that's the best you can do?! Any retard knows you have to butter toast when it's hot. When it's *hot*! Otherwise, it's fucking *cement*!"

Goofy

M——, New Jersey, 1976

There was a time when this was my favorite joke, and this is a photograph of that time, that joke. I'm nearly ten years old (the date stamped on the back of the photo reads APRIL 1976) and wearing my favorite shirt. It was a slippery nylon thing, the weave of which had a texture of tiny grooves. On a pale heather-blue ground, dozens of fluffy white teddy bears float like almost-clouds. I loved that shirt, its cool, cheap silkiness, its sophisticated silver blue. I also wear bell-bottoms way too big for me—they cover my feet entirely. My hair, parted down the middle, falls straight around my face. My eyebrows are lifted, my smile broad and a bit gappy (not all of my adult teeth have grown in). I'm standing in Grandma Ellen's kitchen: there's the fruit cart wallpaper, the ochre-colored vinyl floor with patches of blackened plywood showing through, the card table set for what looks like a small buffet—a jug of wine, a cake, I think, maybe a casserole, some plates.

The joke is this: I'm a scrawny ten-year-old, thin as a poker with no hips; everything's small about me except my cheeks, which are very chubby, and my hands, which are amazingly, astoundingly large. In "my" right hand I hold a pair of John Lennon–style sunglasses and appear to be flipping them around with debonair nonchalance. With "my" left hand I gesture in a *Can-you-believe-it?* kind of way in the air near my hair. "My" hands are as big as my face, which is beaming, because I so love this joke. On her knees behind me, my mother crouches very carefully. I clasp my arms behind my back while she reaches up from underneath them, so that her hands seem to be mine. I don't talk in this joke, just add the appropriate facial expressions as she speaks and swings her hands here and there.

"Oh, I'm just so shocked!" she says, pressing a palm to my cheek. "Do you really think so?" Her index finger pensively touches my lower lip. "I have such a terrible itch!" she says, and scratches my scalp. "Do I look okay? Do I look all right?" Her fingers flutter all over my face. "Are you sure?"

Gordian Knot

We were in the hallway, near the kitchen, and I was having a hard time talking. This was so often the case when I was a kid. The words just wouldn't come out. I knew it seemed like I was hiding something, but she was making me nervous. She'd accused me of lying, and I got confused. Looking back on it now, it seems simple enough. I'd been invited out by a group of friends for pizza. My mother had insisted that a grown-up accompany us. It had taken forever, over the phone, to work out the logistics, but finally somebody's mother agreed to be there, only she was thinking two steps ahead, and she'd left to run some errands as soon as she'd dropped us off at the pizza parlor. Later she returned to pick us up. It was all pretty straightforward, I can see that now. But at the time my mother was impatient with my stuttering. Convinced that I was hiding something, that I was lying, she hit me. The bruise lasted for a while: a shiner under my left eye. The next week, when she was picking me up after school, another mother accused her of being a child abuser.

What made this incident stick for all these years wasn't the blow itself. It wasn't even my mother's violent reaction to what had been essentially a misunderstanding. Nor was it that another adult had accused her of abusing me. No, what really got me at the time was how she related her interaction with her accuser (she'd been alone with the woman) to the rest of us at the dinner table that night—with a kind of dainty sniffing, as if her dignity had been terribly bruised, yet somehow she was holding up . . . Then she turned to me, as if I'd said something.

"I didn't *hit* you, Kimberli! It was just a little slap. Maybe my hand slipped, or maybe you moved. But I didn't hit you." And at that instant reality—as it so often did—suddenly buckled and rearranged itself: the blow of a few days earlier was now a slap, the trajectory of which had simply been miscalculated. This was now the story, and any deviation from it, I knew, would be tantamount to lying.

Grab

M——, New Jersey, 1958

Hair unevenly chopped—there are wings and chunks and random wisps—my mother poses for her fifth grade portrait. There's a feline quality to her face. You find it in the upswept cheekbones, in the tapering eyes. Her gaze is direct. There is still some trust in it. This photograph is small and printed on especially thin paper. There's a cigarette burn at the right-hand edge and a tear running from the left, across her face to her shoulder. When I look at the girl in this photo, I feel like I'm trying to grab something in a dream.

Guess

Tracy and I shared a single bed for years, but even when we had our own rooms, we often climbed into bed with each other if one of us felt scared (usually me). We played a game then: pictures in the air. Car. Teddy. Mustache. Image after image etched into the darkness with our index fingers. How did we do it? How did one see what the other had drawn when it was nighttime, when we were tired, and the images, in any case, were nothing but currents of air and part of the game was to draw as quickly as possible? Just a swoosh, and there's your bike! It's a mystery. And yet we always guessed right. Grapes. Flower. Coffeepot. Shoe. It was almost as if we knew what the other one was thinking.

Guilt

I can feel it sometimes at the back of my neck or underneath my sternum. My mother's unhappiness is inside me. It's pain in my bones. Salt in my blood.

Gus

"Pop" is how my mother and her siblings referred to their father, although when I was young, I had no idea that the word *Pop* could be used in this way—to designate a father—and I assumed that the person my aunts and uncles spoke of so often in such high-pitched, even strident tones at those holiday gatherings, this Pop, must be a very special family friend, a colorful eccentric who had somehow inserted himself into all the family lore. Above all, I assumed Pop must be a man of deep magnetism because whenever his name came up, the air went high voltage.

One day when I was about eight or nine years old, at one of those crowded, loud, and raucous holiday meals at my grandmother's house, I asked, "Who's 'Pop' anyway?" and amid the enormous guffaws this question generated, I heard my mother's voice from the other side of the room, quiet but absolute: "He's dead to me."

My grandmother called him by a different name, which I learned the day a cop pulled her over when Tracy and I happened to be in the back seat.

"This vehicle belongs to Gustaf Forsgren," said the policeman. I could see only his belly, stretching the dark blue fabric of his uniform, and his hands, holding a pen and a small pad. "Can you tell me his whereabouts please, ma'am?"

My grandmother assured the officer that she hadn't seen her husband in almost a decade. "Gus left me years ago," she said, and then, gesturing toward me with her thumb, "I haven't heard from him since before this one was born."

H

Hair Ribbons

I've never met anybody who hates anybody as much as my grandmother hated the Aunts. Even deep into old age, she found ways to insert this hatred into the most unlikely conversations, wailing (always with fresh grief), "They gave me no love!"

I've often wondered what it was, exactly, that she meant by this. Did they never tell her stories? Or did they neglect to hug her? Or maybe, in their pale, almost ice-blue German eyes, she simply never found herself reflected, rosy and apple-like?

My mother invariably mentions hair ribbons when attempting to explain the animosity between the Aunts and their only niece. Her reasoning runs like this: *The Aunts were so young! Still just girls themselves when their sister died. The family had so little money to begin with, and then along comes little Ellen, so sick. She was always being taken to the doctor. There was no money left over for things like hair ribbons— the sorts of things young girls need in order to feel pretty, in order to go out in the world and be courted.* It's odd, but this explanation never seems to vary, even in inflection.

Hair Shirt

As a child—so the story goes—Grandma Ellen was bright, studious, and especially good at English. She did so well in high school, in fact, that she graduated two years early with a full scholarship to Hunter College in New York City. But instead of accepting this gift, this unheard-of opportunity (she was the only one in her family to make it through high school, let alone be admitted to college), she ran away from home. Why? My mother has always explained it this way: *She was just looking for love. Love was all she wanted!*

That my grandmother refused the scholarship is uncontested in family lore—I've heard the story dozens of times. But what she did next remains a mystery, mostly because she herself told two very different versions of what happened. In one version she took an eight-day train ride from New York City to New Orleans, where she worked for several years as a lonely secretary, saving money and occasionally going to the movies on weekends with her roommates, who were also lonely secretaries. The second version (which didn't surface until she was an old woman, at which point she told it frequently) follows the first up to a point: she still went to New Orleans, she still lived and worked with other women, but instead of taking a job as a secretary, she became a prostitute. And in this story it was as a prostitute that she eventually met her future husband.

I have often wondered how my grandmother settled on that particular man. Maybe she smelled it right away—his misanthropy. Maybe she could tell he liked to swim upstream, like her. Or maybe she thought he'd *be* her stream, her river of swill. Then again, maybe her calculations were far less complicated than that—maybe she just thought, with the shortsighted vengeance of a child or in any case an emotionally stunted young woman: *He's perfect! The Aunts will hate him!*

Halos

M——, New Jersey, circa 1961

Nine kids posing with popsicles in someone's backyard. This photo is black-and-white, but the fixer must have been off because everything is a tad pink. My uncle Nils and aunt Becky are easy to spot—they're the only ones who had dark hair as children. And there's one of the neighbors' kids: a toddler pixie with bows twisted into her hair. My aunt Elsa, about eight years old, sits in the front row with her legs bent under her—one hand clutching a popsicle, the other her crotch. At first I thought my mother must be one of the older girls with shiny bangs—all giggles, shoulders hunched—but according to the list of names on the back, she is the serious-looking one on the far left, wearing cat's-eye glasses, a sailor shirt, and polka-dot pants. All the other children are so completely in this moment—squinting, laughing, licking, frowning, crouching, biting, twisting . . . Certain things are made obvious by their expressions, their wiggly gestures. The grass, for instance, is clearly ticklish, the popsicles melting, the sun hot—it burns halos in their hair. But my mother is very still and holds her popsicle to her lips as if she were merely testing its temperature.

Hand

The party had something to do with the Unitarian church we'd for some mysterious reason started attending. Our religious days didn't last long. Just a few months. But in the thick of it, my parents hosted an afternoon gathering for their fellow parishioners. There were daiquiris for the grown-ups, lemonade for the kids. Watermelon. Potato chips. I forget the guests—they were strangers—but I do remember feeling mortified in front of them when my mother suggested that I touch a huge caterpillar I'd discovered sunning itself on a rock. As long as my hand, freakishly fat, murky grayish brown, it was dotted with tiny white nubs and covered in a fine, silvery fuzz.

"Don't be such a Goody Two-Shoes," said my mother. "It's just nature. Touch it!" Then she took my hand and put it on top of the caterpillar. "Hold it!" she said, and she pressed down on my hand. I felt the animal give under my palm. It was warm from the sun and incredibly soft, fleshy but resilient, silky and slightly prickly and dry. I sensed tiny muscular vibrations streaming through its body, and when I lifted my hand, its presence was imprinted there.

"That wasn't so bad, was it?"

"No."

"You shouldn't be so afraid of everything," she said. "She's afraid of her own shadow," she told a nearby guest.

After that I wandered around the yard for a few minutes, pretending to be interested in different things—grass, whatever. I knew she was watching me. I knew she was waiting. I didn't want to give her the satisfaction. But in the end I couldn't help myself, and I ran upstairs to scrub my hand.

Hannah Levinsky

We moved a lot when I was growing up. It was the drugs, I think. The Valium. That's my theory now. My mother's behavior must have raised a lot of eyebrows. Probably it worried people. Landlords. Once, as we were moving out of an apartment we'd rented for only a single year, my mother told me that the landlady was a witch. *A crazy drug addicted old witch.* That's a signal. I knew it even then. Externalizing her own most suspect behaviors and pinning them on someone else. Then again, it could have been my father's drinking that made our landlords think twice.

However, we did manage to rent one place for a stretch of almost five years. This was a comically ugly house, three stories tall, located on a two-lane turnpike in a modestly affluent, midsized suburban town in northern New Jersey. I have since searched for this address on Google Maps and found that in "Street View" it actually seems a rather handsome place. Since the time we lived there, someone has painted it a beautiful shade of light gray and trimmed it in slate blue. But back in the day its stucco slabs were scrambled egg yellow, its shutters brown, its front door a dull, depressing orange. Its only points of beauty as far as I was concerned were the Japanese maple in the front yard, the gravel driveway (full of quartz crystals if you looked closely), and the weedy field that stretched, it seemed, forever back behind the house (though Google Maps again proves me wrong).

During the first three years we lived at this address, I attended the Franklin Pierce Elementary School, and at the Franklin Pierce Elementary School I had one teacher who didn't know how to spell the word *freight* and one teacher who was dying of cancer and for this reason often posed existentially baffling questions and one teacher named Hannah Levinsky, who let me read under her desk, near her stockinged feet (she liked to kick off her loafers), every day for as long as I wanted—sometimes an hour, sometimes more, sometimes twice a day. In addition, Mrs. Levinsky spent a long time every week talking with me about the books I was reading—Nancy Drew mysteries, *Old Yeller*, *Tom Sawyer*, *One Is One*, *Mrs. Frisby and the Rats of NIMH*. I think it's fair to say that I never felt safer—more simply at ease—during the years we lived in the stucco house than when I was tucked under Mrs. Levinsky's desk, curled up near her bunioned, slightly sour-smelling feet, squinting into the dimness, reading as fast as I could, one book right after another.

Hatred

The phone rings, and I wish I'd let the machine get it because it's my aunt Becky. Even though she was my favorite when I was a kid, I haven't spoken to her in years because after Isabella was born, I decided to avoid my mother's family as much as possible. So, needless to say, things are awkward at first. The point of her call, my aunt tells me, is to see if I might be able to convince my mother to sign something—an insurance claim on the land my grandmother's house stood on before it burned down a couple of years ago. There is some money available, she explains, a few thousand dollars per sibling, but this money can only be dispersed if all the siblings sign the claim, and she's having trouble getting my mother on board.

"I thought you might have better luck."

"I doubt it. But I'll try."

After that we try to catch up. She asks about my kids, and I ask about my cousins and their kids, her grandchildren. She tells me she's playing a lot of bridge these days and that she is happy. I say I, too, am happy. And then for some reason—I'm not sure how we got here—we're talking about *mental illness.

"You do realize that nobody on either side of the family was ever mentally ill before your mother," she says in a way that strikes me as oddly preemptive. I ask if she's sure, and she says, "Of course I'm sure."

"But your fa-fa-fa-father." The word comes out of my mouth like that, as if spoken by a stuttering comic book character. "How do you explain the things he di-di-did to you guys?"

"Oh, he wasn't *crazy!*" says Aunt Becky, practically spitting the words into the phone. "He was just a *bastard.* I mean, he was just a really *mean* bastard. A goddamn bastard. And alcoholic, of course. And excuse me for saying so, but basically addicted to sex. But he wasn't *crazy.*" Okay, I think, so we have different definitions of crazy. Then I ask whether or not she thought my mother had seemed at all off-kilter as a kid.

"Oh, god, no! I mean, we were always saying things like, 'What are you, crazy, Linda?' But we didn't really mean *crazy.* Still, she was always doing these *crazy* things. I think it had something to do with . . . I don't know if you know this, but for some reason our father just *hated* your mother. I guess because she hated him. The rest of us, if he came home drunk, we'd all pretend to be asleep, but not your mother. She'd just get right up in his face and start yelling at him. I don't know why—it always ended the same way. He used to throw her across the room. I mean *throw.* Just pick her up and spin her around over his head and then throw her down, hard. Sometimes he threw her down the stairs. And I think—I think all those impacts. I'm not sure, but I've always thought—they must have done something. I mean to her brain."

Haywire

There have been at least a half-dozen official diagnoses, though none of them have ever truly fit the bill. I guess this is why Tracy sounds kind of excited when she tells me she thinks she's finally pegged it. We try to talk every weekend. Our conversations usually go this way: my sister tells me about her work; I tell her about mine; we talk about her dog, my kids, and what we're both making for dinner. Then we talk about our mother.

"My friend Mary found it on the web. It's called 'delusional disorder.' She matches all the symptoms."

"Like what?"

"Like paranoid but about non-impossible things. Things that could actually happen but that are extremely unlikely. That's why it's so confusing." I can hear her clacking away on her keyboard, then she reads from her computer screen, her voice going in and out of focus as she skims the page: "Delusions of inflated self-worth, power, or knowledge . . . Jealousy . . . Delusions of persecution . . . Convinced they're being malevolently treated . . . Somatic delusions including medical conditions."

"Sounds good," I say. "Sounds good." But to be honest, I don't actually care what it's called. As much as I understand Tracy's excitement, I stopped worrying about the official name for whatever's wrong with our mother a long time ago. In fact, at this point I almost prefer whatever she's "got" not to have a name or a clear set of conditions because the way I see it, she is what she is. An imagination gone haywire. A body of confusion. A wreck of a story. A mother. My mother.

Heart

It was the weekend. I know because we were all home, cleaning different parts of the house, and that was a Sunday ritual. Suddenly my mother called out, "Jake! Jake!" Her tone was interesting—frantic, even frightened. Tracy and I came running downstairs and watched as she showed our father something in the cramped half-bathroom off the foyer.

"Look at that!" she said, "What is that? I just threw up, and that's what came out."

She pointed to a hard, small piece of flesh—oddly shaped, brownish pink—bobbing in the toilet bowl. It looked smooth and tough and muscular and for all these reasons struck me as worrisome. But my father, unfazed by the mysterious chunk or perhaps even amused (it was always so hard to tell), just shrugged and said, "Maybe it's your heart."

Hedgehogs

Y——, New Jersey, circa 1976

We are completely out, lying next to each other in the twisted pink sheets of our parents' bed. Our forearms are intertwined, our fingers lightly laced, our heads tilted at the same angle. We both embrace the same type of stuffed animal. These look vaguely hedgehoggy. Tracy's is blue. Mine is yellow. We are just two sisters, asleep. Thoroughly unremarkable. Yet someone saw fit to pick up the camera.

Helens

A large group of us were visiting the Aunts in their apartment on Easter Sunday. Grandma Ellen was there, all my aunts and uncles were there, and so were "the Cousins." The Cousins, like the Aunts, were always referred to in this way—as a pair. I remember them as sweet, plump middle-aged women with short hair and soft bodies. We saw them once or twice a year. Only one of the Cousins was actually related to the family and then only by the most tenuous connection. Still, they were the Cousins. Oddly, both women were named Helen, which is why we also sometimes referred to them as "the Cousins Helen." In retrospect I suspect they were a couple, although no one ever spoke of them in those terms at the time.

For some reason the Cousins Helen took a special interest in Tracy and me. On this particular day the four of us sat across from each other at a card table that had been set up in the living room because there wasn't enough space for everyone in the Aunts' dining room. One of the Cousins asked me a question, then leaned across the card table to listen to my answer. This was the Helen with dark hair—the one who was related to us. She smiled as I spoke, and her smile made a river of words rush out of me. This river kept bubbling out of me—it was almost embarrassing. But my cousin, who wasn't actually my cousin, who was in her forties and who was probably gay although strictly silent about it, kept nodding and smiling—and not only with her mouth but with her eyes as well. I can't remember what I was talking about—maybe my excitement at being assigned the role of a cloud in an upcoming ballet recital or maybe the plot synopsis of the latest Nancy Drew mystery novel I was reading. I only know that this invisible river kept spilling out of me with more and more force, more and more enthusiasm, more and more words, until suddenly I sensed my mother at my side. Bending down, she put her face very close to mine, so close that I could feel her breath pulsing against my ear. Pinching the flesh of my upper arm and twisting it, she whispered, "Don't be so *goddamned cocky!*" then strode off toward the dining room. There was, of course, some awkwardness after that. I lost not only my train of thought but my voice. And even though both Helens urged me to continue, I couldn't because the shame I felt was doing something strange to my eyes; it was as if they were stuck, so that even when I tried, I simply couldn't wrench them away from the fake plastic weave covering the surface of the card table.

Hens' Teeth

It is not at all easy to get a Section 8 housing voucher in Massachusetts. As a rule, they are *rare as hens' teeth* (my mother's term—but accurate). In fact, Section 8 housing vouchers tend to be issued almost exclusively in cases of domestic violence, but that's the genius of my mother, of her resourceful nature, because she's good at working with what she has. And mostly what she has is imagination.

She got her Section 8 voucher by claiming that she was being domestically abused at the halfway house she was sent to after her last hospitalization. The abuser, she insisted, was DMH itself, and somebody, somewhere, believed her. Either that or somebody, somewhere, looked at her chopped hair and enormous eyes and broken teeth, and that somebody decided, in a moment of grace, that rules are for bending.

Here We Go Again

The day she chased him out of the house with a meat cleaver, Tracy and I screamed from the sidelines, begging them to stop. That was often our position. Even now I can see the cords sticking out from my sister's neck as she leaned over the banister, shouting, every bit of her straining, and for some reason I found this funny—found the cords in my sister's neck ridiculous and sweet but mostly pointless. She just seemed so earnest. We were standing at the top of the stairwell, looking down at the maniacs below us. My mother was thirty, maybe thirty-one, years old. At the time she had her hair done in a poodle perm. Rangy and thin, she might have been wearing, as she so often did in those days, some boldly striped item—an oversized rugby shirt perhaps. A pair of large, peach-colored, plastic-framed eyeglasses would have sat perched on her narrow, perfectly proportioned nose. But these are details dredged from the dim swamp of general impressions created over long years. Much more in focus are my sister's corded neck and the musky smell of the stairwell itself, down which our father's fat limbs went spiraling as he shouted: "You're crazy! Are you crazy! You're crazy!" And our mother, with her skinny arms, her pointy elbows, her kinky hair, went spiraling after him.

Hershey's Kiss

Somewhere in New Jersey, 1978

I look like any kid in this picture, any kid wearing overalls and a black T-shirt with a giant Hershey's Kiss printed on it. Any kid with braces and straight brown hair squinting into the sun. Behind me a white, glare-filled sky hovers over the tarpaper roof of a stable. I stand next to a friend named Mikki. She sports designer jeans and flipped-back hair. My arm is slung around her shoulders. Nearby are four horses, all chestnut brown, and a slouchy guy. My hair is pulled back from my face, white plastic barrettes at both temples. My shoulders are scrawny. Although I've recently turned twelve years old, there's still a trace of a much younger child in me—it's in my cheeks, which hint at the chipmunk, and in my eyes, which are soft and unguarded in the way it seems only children's eyes can be. On the back of this photograph, in slightly smudged blue ink, in my mother's hand, is a single word: *Punkins.*

Hidden Contexts

The "booger board" hung over the washing machine in the basement. One of more disturbing documents of my mother's arrested development, this was a canvas-covered tackboard, perhaps twenty-four by twenty-four inches square, covered with a thick layer of glossy white paint and, as the name indicates, mucus excretions of a nasal variety. I mean, how else can I put it? My sister and I both avoided even remote visual contact with this object whenever possible, were careful to take friends, when heading into the yard, the long way around (i.e., through the front door, not the back, which was off the laundry room), and to this day share a somewhat wild and uneasy laughter whenever one or the other of us invokes this old "inside joke."

I say it counts as evidence of my mother's arrested development, and while this is true (in many ways it often seems to me that she is emotionally no older than a child of six or seven), there were other contributing factors—chief among them, her need to be constantly purging herself of one thing or another. Over the years this purging obsession has involved digging into her ears with bobby pins, attempting to pull out her own teeth with pliers, aggressively expressing all the glands in her body, and most recently, removing what she has described as foot-long, threadlike worms from her left eye. These activities (the list goes on—the list is long) always bring to mind, to my mind anyway, the roots of the word *incest*, which in Latin means "impure" or "unclean." If etymology can offer in this case, as it so often seems able to, any instruction as to latent realities and hidden contexts, I think it's safe to assume that whatever my maternal grandfather did to my mother on those nights when he sat by the side of the bed she shared with her three sisters (one bed, four girls) made her feel so contaminated inside that to this day she remains determined to work the filth out of her system by whatever means necessary.

Hide-and-Seek

During those years we lived in the stucco house, my father must have been chronically sleep-deprived because not only did he work full-time as an accountant; he also took night classes toward his bachelor's degree at a local community college and worked part-time at a private tennis club on the weekends. He hated this job because he thought the club members looked down on him. I suspect he was right. Even at nine, ten, eleven years of age, I was aware of how luckless our car looked in the club's parking lot, which was otherwise packed with sleek, metallic Jaguars, BMWs, and Mercedes-Benzes. And it's true that some of the club members were rude. For example, I remember a tall man with silky gray hair pounding on the bell at the front desk to get my father's attention one day. My father was in the back room—his boss's office—just off the reception area. Tracy and I were watching *Planet of the Apes* on one of the televisions suspended above the leatherette couches in the lounge area, but I'd propped myself up on an elbow to watch this exchange. My father looked tired when he emerged from the office. I remember thinking that he might have been napping. The man with the gray hair demanded that something be taken off his bill.

"I'm not authorized to issue refunds. But I'll be sure the manager sees this on Monday."

"Oh, right. You're just a clerk," said the man, before turning on his top-of-the-line tennis shoe and striding away, leaving my father hunched over the front desk, his cheeks bright red.

Tracy and I occasionally spent whole Saturdays at the club, flopped on those couches or doing our homework in the back room, where our father spent as much time as he could studying. All three of us would spread out our books and papers on the smoked glass coffee table. Sometimes he gave us change for the vending machines, and we'd bring back orange sodas and malt balls and peanut butter crackers and potato chips. In the lounge there was a long bank of plate glass windows overlooking the tennis courts, and sometimes Tracy and I would sclathe back and forth across these windows, trailing our hands over the glass, peering down at the activities of the little white-clad figures on the courts, figures whose actions seemed oddly disconnected from the sounds that floated up to our ears—pings and pongs and squeaks and occasional expletives. Sometimes we played Mad Libs, and sometimes we played hide-and-seek, putting the virtual jungle of ficus and rubber tree plants scattered all over the club to good use. Sometimes, if the courts weren't full, our father's friend Richie, who was an instructor, would set up the ball server for us so that we could whack away for twenty minutes or so. Neither Tracy nor I showed any aptitude for the game, and I remember the ball server as being a terrible bully. But Richie was handsome and nice and did an excellent imitation of Daffy Duck, so when he was around, we tried at least to look sporting.

Highway (1)

She was in one car, my father, Tracy, and I in the other. Sixty, maybe sixty-five, miles an hour. She kept making contact with the back bumper of our crappy old Chevy using the front bumper of our newly purchased Thunderbird. Each time, the Chevy would rock and sway, skittering dangerously into the neighboring lane.

"See? See that? See how much she loves you?" he said, wiping the sweat off his forehead.

Highway (2)

"Do you girls have your feet in those holes?"
"No!"
"I told you not to put your feet in those holes."
"They're not in the holes!"
"They'll get ripped right off! You'll have stubs for feet!"
"They're not in!"

I have always been a bad liar. Unconvincing. Red-faced, mumbling, eye averting. Even now, as a middle-aged woman, if I sense that someone suspects me of lying, if I sense they half-suspect me of lying, quarter-suspect me, suspect me even one atom of lying, I do these things, like a child. Yet I lied easily, without the least hesitation, to Grandma Ellen about the holes in the floor of the back seat in her car because lying to her was a cinch. There was such an airy quality to the woman. Although she spoke with great drama, it seemed like she was never really there. Lying to my mother was a different story, and she often caught me at it even when I was telling the truth. The thing is, as soon as she caught me, I got confused. It all seemed so fungible around her: reality, fantasy, truth, untruth. But to lie to my grandmother only meant risking our feet, and many times Tracy and I spent the entire ride to Dunkin Donuts—ten miles, maybe, each way—perched over the rusted-out holes in the floor of her decrepit Malibu, our feet flexed inches above the gray speckled blur of the highway. And which was more exhilarating—the act of lying or the sense that we were flying as we held hands and crouched below our grandmother's sightline, snorting with stifled laughter—I couldn't possibly say.

Hole

Y——, New Jersey, 1977

There are very few pictures of my father from my childhood because my mother destroyed most of them years ago. The ones that remain often show her to good advantage or him to poor, with just a couple of exceptions. Here is a photo out of which his image has been carefully torn. Where he would have been sitting at the head of the table is just a rough-edged rectangle of nothing. My mother must have deemed this one worth saving (for the most part) because it's a nice one of me. This was at a holiday dinner, although which holiday is unclear. The table is beautifully set with Waterford goblets handed down from the Aunts, a silver water pitcher, and the good, cream-colored china. I'm passing a basket of rolls wrapped in a white napkin. I am eleven years old, an age at which I usually look, in photographs, like the shy, awkward girl I was, but here, for some reason—the angle, the lighting—I look very dignified and pretty in an almost doll-like way. When I was a kid, people often thought I was Asian, and in this photo I can see why: my hair, nearly black, falls straight, like a plank, down my back; my eyes are long and dark. They seem to tilt up, even though I'm looking down and to the side, away from that void where my father once sat. I imagine he might have been raising his glass in a toast or carving a roast, but now there's just this hole.

Things are different now, between my father and me. Now he sends me chocolates on my birthday and spoils my kids and buys me books he thinks I might like: volumes of poetry, genealogies of myths, the complete works of Beckett . . . He hasn't had a drink in decades and is careful to say, "I love you," at the end of every phone call, every email. But as a child, I was well aware of the violence he inflicted on others; I saw it up close. And when I look at this photograph of me sitting to the left of that empty space where he used to be, I see, behind my perfect posture and the almost somber composition of my features, a girl afraid to move.

Holiday

It's Christmas Eve, and my mother calls to tell me a story. Because my father is visiting for the holiday and because my parents haven't spoken for over two decades and because my father is pretty much afraid of my mother, afraid that she will cause him some sort of career- or relationship-based misfortune (as, in fact, she has so carefully contrived to do in the past), I step outside, onto our porch, to talk on the phone with her, even though it is very cold and I'm not wearing a coat despite the fact that every surface—the picnic table, the porch planks, my bicycle—is covered with a glittering layer of hoarfrost. I've come outside mostly because I don't want my mother to be able hear, in the background, my father's voice among the many voices that fill our apartment tonight and also because I don't want her to feel isolated by the sound of all those voices in general since she is alone and uninvited and it is Christmas Eve.

My mother prefaces what she was about to tell me by saying that I need to listen very carefully because what she is about to say is going prove that I have to *believe* her stories, that I *should* believe her stories, and that I will now *understand*, with the telling of this story coming up, that she is not actually *paranoid*, only *unlucky* and *observant*. I walk over to the edge of our porch as I listen, so that I can see the strand of Christmas lights David hung up a couple of weeks ago—large, colorful, old-fashioned bulbs. These are the same type of Christmas lights my grandfather used to string on the enormously tall pine tree in his front yard when Tracy and I lived with him and our grandmother, back when we were very young. David's hung just a single long strand of lights—green and yellow and blue and red—along the edge of our roof, then loosely spiraled it through the limbs of the small fir tree under our bedroom window. But somehow it seems all the more magical for the minimal touch.

My mother's story goes like this: she went to Kinko's a couple of nights ago and stayed there for a few hours because she can no longer use the computer in her own apartment, as her every mouse click is being tracked. So, for twenty dollars an hour, she went to Kinko's and rented time on one of their machines. It was three o'clock in the morning, she said, when she arrived, and the people working the night shift were being really vicious to her. For example, at one point one of the clerks asked her to come over to the counter.

"Look up," he said. So my mother (who can at times be disturbingly compliant) looked up. "Not there," said the man, "there." He pointed.

She said she looked to the spot he'd indicated, and his coworker, a woman about his own age—midtwenties—said *real sweet only not really*: "Smile! You're on *Candid Camera!*" Then the woman behind the counter took a picture of my mother with one of those goosenecked cameras, the kind with a large, single eye, attached, via cable, to a computer.

"Now, Kimberli," says my mother, "*you* tell me, *why* would she do that? What *possible* reason?" And for once she is quiet, her voice pointedly held in check as she pauses, presumably to let this question sink in.

I know what she wants me to say. She wants me to say that, yes, with the telling of this story, I am now able to see, finally and with perfect clarity, what she's been talking about all these years—yes, this anecdote about a couple of completely assy dorks at Kinko's has finally made it clear to me that everybody is in on this thing, this plan, this scheme—that those two Kinko's employees are obviously in cahoots with DMH, which clearly proves that DMH is in cahoots with AT&T, and the whole lot of them are in cahoots with her various doctors, dentists, and shrinks. *Yes!*—she wants me to say, *Yes! I see it all of a sudden, clear as day! I see that every single one of these people—from the customer service representatives at AT&T to the clerks at Kinko's to your shrink to the highest-up mucky-mucks at McLean Hospital to every one of your last five or six landlords to the entire administration of your locally owned bank to some mysterious sector of Medicaid—I see that every single one of these people-slash-entities share but one single agenda, which is to put you back in the nuthouse.* She wants me to say: *I get it now. I finally, really, get it! And not only that—I understand the necessity of helping you with this problem, and I will put my own life on hold in order to see to it that you win these battles because deep down I am your Sancho Panza, Mom, I am!*

I know that this is what she wants me to say because it is what she always wants me to say, but I do not say these things. I do not say anything for a while because my mother is talking again, repeating the whole story more or less verbatim, only emphasizing different elements, probably in hopes of giving me a fuller picture.

It's bitter out here. The tips of my fingers are turning white. I've pulled the neck of my sweater up to my face to keep my mouth warm, but it doesn't work because my breath is getting caught in it, forming tiny drops of moisture that feel even colder than the surrounding air once they cool. In my chest or my brain, I can't tell, I feel heartbreak vying with guilt and guilt vying with impatience. Not surprisingly, impatience wins. I cut her off and say: "Maybe those kids know that you have problems, you know? Maybe they're just a couple of bored and nasty losers working the graveyard shift at Kinko's, and they know you have issues, and maybe they were just trying to get your goat. Maybe they thought the best way to do that would be to push one of your buttons, so they scared you, because they've figured out you've got this thing, this paranoia—"

"Oh, no-ho-ho-ho, Kimmy," my mother interrupts. "No. No. No. No! You *really* don't get it, do you? One day it'll be too late, and *then* you'll get it. You are just so *stubborn*."

The Kinko's story goes on for a while after this. Actually, it gets more complicated because it turns out there was also another customer, someone who made a big to-do over my mother's paperwork because he thought she was taking up too much space, but she thought he was just trying to look at her stuff, so there was a scuffle of sorts, which prompted the man to make a comment about her mental health, and this, to her mind, only proved his complicity.

When David pokes his head outside to tell me dinner is almost ready, a wave of laughter spills onto the porch. The warm air from indoors smells of saffron-laced fish stew and just-baked almond cake—our dinner ahead of us. I tell my mother I have to get off the phone. She says okay but doesn't stop talking, so I tell her I really have to go because dinner is almost ready and I should help set the table, and she says, okay, okay, but keeps talking. I say I am going to hang up now, and she says okay again, but she still doesn't stop talking, so I say, "Now is when I'm hanging up." But first I say, "Merry Christmas, Mom." And then I say, "I love you." And then I hang up.

Hollow

On a typical weekday Tracy and I would come home from school, grab some food, bring it into the TV room, and watch a string of old reruns—*Get Smart, Bewitched, The Brady Bunch, M.A.S.H.* These were followed by the Blockbuster Movie. After a break for dinner and a bit of homework, we'd return to our usual spots (me on the couch, Tracy sprawled on the shag rug) to watch sitcoms and family dramas. If it was a weekend, we'd stay up late watching movies, then *The Tonight Show, Saturday Night Live*, and *Second City TV*. Often we fell asleep in front of the set, waking only at the piercing noise of the broadcast signal, though Tracy sometimes slept even through that.

Not long ago, wandering randomly around YouTube, I found a video of two sisters watching television together, and they reminded me of us then. The girl who made the video, the one who'd set the recorder on top of the television—the older one—was using a curling iron on her hair and making occasional editorial comments about the show that was on, some kind of cartoon. But the other one just watched the screen. The girl curling her hair was probably about thirteen years old, her sister maybe eleven. The younger one sat in the corner of the couch with her arms crossed in front of her chest, and every once in a while she told the older one to shut up, but not impatiently, not meanly, in fact, in an almost affectionate way, if that makes sense. They sat in a room that looked eerily similar to the one Tracy and I spent so much of our childhoods in: small, plain, dimly lit. The video was six and a half minutes long. I watched it five times.

Home

The first family vacation we ever went on took place over Memorial Day weekend. The company my father worked for (not the tennis club but the computer manufacturer) owned a handful of small cabins near a beach on Cape Cod, and these they parceled out to their employees on a rotating basis as a reward for good performance. That weekend it was my father's turn to take a cabin.

It was a four-hour drive up from New Jersey. The minute we put our bags inside, Tracy and I took off to explore the beach. As we walked over the damp gray sand, studded with stones and shells, I remember thinking that our family had finally arrived. I wasn't sure where, just that we were in a better, different place. For example: I was wearing a new pair of exceptionally cute clogs, as was Tracy (they matched, like so many of our things: hers were red, mine blue, both with white polka dots). Also, we were on vacation in a famous place. Cape Cod! We were, in fact, on a "family vacation." I think the charm of that phrase was more exciting to me than the actual experience of being there and walking on that beach, which was actually a little cold.

Unfortunately, when we got back to the cabin, it became clear that our family had not arrived anywhere new at all because even on Cape Cod things were exactly the same as they were at home, only more inconvenient, because in the cabin our mother was having a hard time finding her NR tablets.

NR, or "Nature's Remedy," tablets were earthy-smelling pills that cured constipation, a condition that has plagued my mother since early childhood. At the time they were as necessary to her well-being as food or water, and even though she was sure she'd packed them, now they were missing.

Tracy said something—it was supposed to be sympathetic, only our mother took her words for sarcasm and decided that she was to blame for the missing pills. She built the story incredibly quickly. Just slapped it together. And suddenly there it was: an irrefutable fact. Before leaving for the beach, Tracy had taken the tablets from her suitcase and thrown them out the window at the back of the cabin.

"Why are you *such* a brat? Such a despicable little brat? Such a complete and utter *ingrate*? Why do you want *so badly* to ruin my one and only vacation?"

"Linda," said our father, "be reasonable."

"Why should I be reasonable?" she screamed. "If she's going to put the kibosh on my vacation, I'm going to put the kibosh on her vacation!"

Then she ordered us to look for the NR tablets outside, in a damp, leafy bank of earth that was piled up near the window. Tracy and I went outside and dug our fingers into the leaf mold for about thirty minutes or so. It was just for show, of course. I tried to lift my sister's spirits, but she kept sniffling. After what seemed like enough time—pointlessness goes so slowly—we came back inside to report that we hadn't found the tablets, and our mother told

Tracy that she had to sit on the bottom bunk of the bed we were sharing, in the corner of the cabin, until she changed her mind and decided to return the tablets.

"You can just stay right there until you come clean."

I tried to advocate for Tracy, as did my father, who at the same time continued looking for the tablets in the most inane places (the medicine cabinet, the trash can, the cracks between the itchy plaid pillows of the couch). I pointed out the obvious problem of timing—the fact that Tracy hadn't spent two minutes in the cabin before we'd left to walk on the beach, but my mother waved me off.

My father tried for a more practical approach. "I'll go into town tomorrow and buy some more," he said.

"They're not going to have NR tablets in that honky-tonk town!"

"Well, I'll buy you something else. Milk of magnesia."

She grunted and told him not to be an idiot.

Tracy lay in the bottom bunk crying quietly, and I lay next to her. There were still a couple hours of sunlight left, but the day was effectively over.

Eventually, my father found the pills. They'd slipped behind the silky lining in a corner pocket of my mother's suitcase.

"Oh," she said. "So *that's* where she put them."

Hope

The "only way of knowing a person," said Walter Benjamin, is to love them without it.

House

Y——, New Jersey, 1979

We've just finished making the gingerbread house—there's icing stuck to our clothes and splattered on the wall behind us. Tracy and I—eleven and thirteen years old, respectively—sit on our father's lap, one kid per leg, each holding a curious, tentative forefinger to his mustache. We stroke the black bristles as we might touch some small furry animal, a mole perhaps, and we are—all three of us—laughing. The flash makes a double flare in the lenses of his glasses, but behind them you can see that his eyes are closed. His arms are wrapped around our waists—both Tracy's and mine—but the thing is, we're really too big for this, and he has to clasp his hands tightly to keep us from slipping off. His fingers are knotted together, turning pink.

≈≈≈

Making a gingerbread house from scratch is a long, involved process. The first thing you have to do is to bake several large flat slabs of gingerbread. These will be the walls and the roof. Next you have to let the slabs dry in the oven on the lowest setting. Then you have to glue them together using royal icing. It's only after the house has been assembled and the royal icing has dried that can you even begin to think about decorating.

My father was assigned the job of building the house itself, sticking all the slabs together with the "mortar," but there were problems. For one thing the royal icing we'd made was too wet. It was thin and slick. Also, there were so many pieces—two roof slabs, four wall slabs, and a bunch of fussy chimney bits. In short, no matter how ingenious he was about propping things up with cookbooks and cans of soup, the whole thing kept falling apart—first this side, then that side, first the roof, then the walls. After a while, my mother started in with some hurtful accusations regarding his ineptitude, and these comments, of course, threatened not only the success of the entire gingerbread project but the general mood as well, which until that point had been fairly festive. Yes, for a while things were looking pretty bad, but somehow my father kept his chin up, and when it became clear that the propping idea was never going to work, he just sat down and held the whole thing together with his hands until it dried. This took at least an hour, maybe more. And all the while his glasses kept slipping down the bridge of his nose in the steamy air of the kitchen, and Tracy and I kept pushing them back up for him and scratching his cheek when he said it itched, and my mother kept snapping pictures, and there was a lot of laughing because there was icing everywhere, in his hair, on his cheeks, in streaks and globs on the front his sweater, even in the shiny black bristles of his mustache.

Hubris

I am not what happened to me, I am what I choose to become.
—*C. G. Jung*

Human Being

Personally, I am a slow forgiver. Maybe reluctant is a better word. In my efforts to become a more forgiving person, I have discovered a trick that provides a fair bit of traction in any forgiveness project. In my embarrassingly large collection of self-help books, this trick is frequently referred to as the cultivation of gratitude. What's most curious about this process, in my experience, is that even tiny amounts of gratitude can expand to perfectly useful proportions with surprisingly little effort. The biggest challenge can be finding something to be grateful about in the first place, no matter how small, although there's a trick for this as well, which is to "accentuate the positive," as the saying goes. True, there are situations in which it might take a bit of effort to figure out what "positive" there is to accentuate, but I've found it's generally worth the search.

For example, I have come, in recent years, to consider myself very fortunate to have in my possession a certain fork that once belonged to my mother's father. This piece of cutlery, which looks like something out of a fairy tale—out of some woodland cottage, with its four long iron tines and its dark wooden handle decorated with a small pewter cross—is what I use every time I make a pie crust or a batch of cookies, as it is ideal for cutting butter into flour. I suspect my maternal grandfather came to own this fork as part of his personal mess kit when he joined the Portuguese merchant marines, with which he sailed for several years despite the fact that he was, by birth, Swedish. This is just a guess, however. I know nothing, really, about this fork except that it once belonged to my mother's father. In any event I like this fork. It is my favorite fork, both because of its Germanic woodland cottage vibe and because pie crusts come out just right when I use it. I am therefore grateful for this fork and take some time to remind myself of this fact every time I use it, and every time I remind myself of this fact, I also think about my maternal grandfather, whom I never met but who was, after all, a human being—one who had to run away from home at the age of thirteen because he was afraid of his own father, whose beatings (at least according to the stories he told my mother and that she later told me) were daily events. I don't go far in these imaginings. Usually I just catch a glimpse of him—my grandfather as a boy standing alone on the deck of a great ship, his blue eyes looking up at the sky or out to the sea. It doesn't matter. What matters is that since I have been appreciating the fork he once owned, something in me has started to soften. Just a little, because it's a big thing. Maybe the biggest thing in me. But a little and a little and a little adds up. And I do bake a lot of pies.

Humiliation

Terror comes in two sizes. There's the big kind: gas attacks, earthquakes, a stranger with a gun. And the small kind, personal and rich with shame. It was the small kind of terror I felt whenever my mother threatened to "get out the scissors."

Tracy and I would beg her not to do it—"No, no! Please. Not the scissors!" It sounds comical now, but at the time to watch her cut up one of our father's business suits was like watching someone kill a small animal, some helpless thing. Snip, snip. It doesn't take much to do a great deal of damage with a sharp pair of scissors, and as the scraps of charcoal gray, navy blue, or pinstriped black fell to the floor, a terrible humiliation filled the room. My father's symbolic castration was clear enough to us even if we didn't know that word. Screaming, spitting, his cheeks bright, almost cherry red, he would pull at his own face as he stood over her while she kept working the scissors, cool as an insane cucumber.

Afterward the sense of impotence that settled over the whole house was horrible. Entire chunks of my childhood passed under the spell of that emotion. What I remember about it now is looking at things *through* it, like a lens that turned everything pointless, even the most innocuous details: the moist sugary shimmer of my mother's wax begonias, for example, or the nylon quilting thread of my flower print bedspread or the pale, nearly iridescent part in my sister's hair or the ionic blue glow that washed over us as we lay sprawled on the brown shag rug in the TV room, watching hour after hour of it didn't matter what.

Hunger

Y———, New Jersey, 1979

The flashbulb's light bounces off my forehead, my cheeks, my chin, the tip of my nose. It glows on the inside curves of the white serving bowl in the foreground and throws my shadow against the wood paneling behind me. My arms, sticking out of the puffy pink sleeves of my baby doll pajamas, look disproportionately thin. My hair is damp, my face chubby-cheeked and flushed; it seems as if I've just taken a shower, which makes me wonder if I'd recently come home from ballet class. There's a glass of milk next to my plate and a balled-up paper napkin in one hand. I'm smiling in the special way I'd contrived to hide the fullness of my lips: a constricted grimace. But despite this put-on, I really do look happy, which isn't surprising since it was dinnertime, and dinner, especially during those years we lived in the stucco house, was often a source of good feelings, good times.

My all-time favorite meal was meat fondue: bits of chicken and beef skewered on long forks, submerged in bubbling oil to fry until lightly caramelized at the edges, then doused with creamy sauces made with horseradish or curry or tomatoes and chives. Chocolate fondue ran a close second: a bittersweet pot in which we smothered apple slices, orange sections, strawberries, bananas, and broken halves of coconut cookies. Two fondues for my birthday was a tradition for many years, and they were wonderful meals, even if my father did once burn his tongue on the fondue fork twice in one sitting because he'd had too much to drink and kept forgetting you can't eat off the same fork you've just plunged in roiling oil. I can still see the pale double *Y* scorched on his tongue. But why bring this up? The thing that mattered was the conviviality. Fondue is a slow meal. Each morsel a miniature event. You have to take turns. Forks get mixed up. Negotiations are made. The discussions can take a long time.

Which do you like best?
The beef with the curry sauce!
The chicken with the horseradish!
The bread with the tomato sauce!

Fondue was my favorite, but many of our meals were great, and we were often happy eating them: chicken sautéed with rosemary and cream, sausages and fried potatoes, chili con carne, beef stew, ravioli with red sauce, TV dinners on occasion, yes, and frozen pot pies—but even those were eaten with gusto and a sense of communion. I know it doesn't compute, but it's true. Despite the addiction, the violence, the generalized group depression, despite my father's double shifts, my parents' night school classes, my mother's not-so-slow unraveling, we somehow managed to eat a tremendous number of excellent meals together, and we were often happy eating them.

Hush

Y——, New Jersey, Christmas Morning 1979

In a way the best pictures catch people off guard. Lampposts coming out of heads. Bad shadows. Cold sores. Regular spastic life. Me with some food not *quite* all the way in my mouth. My father wrestling—literally wrestling—a roast goose on its platter. My aunt Becky, clearly a little drunk (but in a wonderfully regal sort of way), unaware that she's flashing some boob . . . But the very best of these impromptu portraits, the photo that makes me absolutely giddy with love for my sister, shows Tracy and me on Christmas morning, so early that the sky through the dining room window is still black. We've been posed in front of the gingerbread house we'd made a few days earlier. I wear flannel pajamas with a repeating pattern of a little Dutch girl in a flower garden. I have that serious, spaced-out look I so often do in photos as a kid. But Tracy . . .

I remember those pajamas. Made out of some thick, fuzzy yellow material that's probably illegal now, they are school bus yellow and sport the iron-on image of a sappy-faced clown. They had plastic-bottomed feet that smelled horrible. Her shiny brown hair is lank, shoulder length, and parted right down the middle. She's looking sidelong at the camera, not so much smiling as propping up one side of her mouth. She's slumped—clearly, she could use about five more hours of sleep—but at the same time, she looks as if she's got big plans. These no doubt involve unwrapping the dozens of presents piled beneath the Christmas tree, glittering in the corner. Under her nose is one of those tissue burns you get when you have a bad cold.

I

Ice-Skating

She was making hot chocolate to put in a thermos to bring with
us. I was leaning against the kitchen doorway, watching her stir
the pot, and I remember for some reason feeling unusually tall
as I listened to her describe, in one breathless rush, how everything would unfold once we got to a popular ice-skating spot one
town over.

*All your friends will be there—it's always such a great social scene.
Today's the kind of day you'll remember forever, sweetie! Maybe there will
even be a boy—wouldn't that be nice? A boy who has a little crush on you,
nothing too serious—just an innocent childhood crush, he might even ask
you to skate—don't be shy, don't be bashful, you should accept. Maybe you'll
hold hands—just go 'round and 'round and 'round the pond with him.
There's nothing wrong with that, and when you stop skating, he can escort
you back to me, like a gentleman should—I'll be waiting for you, right
next to that steel drum they sometimes make a fire in. If they don't have
a fire going already, I'll make one! I can build a mean fire. It's so nice to
stand next to that big barrel when it's really cold out, like it is today—it
just makes you feel so alive. I'll be there with a big thermos of hot chocolate, pouring it out for anybody who wants some—all your friends. You
should always introduce your friends to your parents, you know that, don't
you? And make sure you introduce the younger person to the older one
first, if they're the same age, introduce the man to the woman, and when
someone introduces you to somebody else, if it's a man, you should always
hold your hand out first. The Aunts taught me that. I'll give all of your
friends a cup of my famous hot chocolate. Won't that be nice? Won't it be*

extra delicious right then! After you've skated so long and are so tired your legs are just numb with the cold and the skating. I just love that kind of tired, when my cheeks are all rosy and the air is so fresh!

Why did I feel so tall? And why did she look so slight, with her back to me, her elbow jutting out to the side as she stirred the hot chocolate with a plastic ladle? Looking back on that moment now, at the two of us in that kitchen—me leaning against the doorjamb, my mother at the stove, the black branches of a bare tree outside lightly tapping the windowpane with each intermittent breeze—I recognize in my own emotions something parallel to what I felt as a much younger child when I spied on my mother and Aunt Inga from the top of the stairs on my fifth birthday. Only this time the source of the exhilaration I felt was clearer to me. I was separate from her. She was different than me. Her weaknesses were not mine. My strengths weren't hers. With the arrogance of a teenager, I even pitied her as she spoke, now elaborating even further about the boy I would meet that day.

He might be a year or two older than you. That often happens. It's no big deal. He might be a little clumsy. That's okay. He could even have acne—it's not all about looks, you know. As long as he's a nice boy, that's all that matters. Your friend Donna will probably be jealous. She's a little homely. She can't help it. But she can't expect to skate with boys just like that. If she gets a bee in her bonnet, just ignore her.

And yet my inklings of autonomy weren't entirely pure. Something else was happening as I listened to her speak. Some part of me was shrinking, as it always did when my mother talked like this—about me but not me. Perhaps it was in order to reclaim this part of myself that I refused, later that day, to put on my skates at all but instead trudged in loops around the crowded pond, staring at the tips of my worn-out tennis shoes, which were the same color as the dingy slush I kicked with every step.

Infestation

"I am so *infested* with something. Some kind of fucking *parasite*. I think they're in my blood." She tells me she's spent the bulk of her day in the bathtub, expressing the glands all over her body. Many, many *thin, undulating, hairlike organisms* came out.

"There were a ton," she says, "I mean a *ton* from the Bartholin's glands." Then she explains the anatomy of the Bartholin's glands, which are located on either side of the vagina. I make an effort to speak calmly as I suggest that the things she's describing bear a creepy resemblance to sperm. "I know!" she says. "It's *so* gross!" I then suggest that it seems possible, even likely, that there is something psychological going on.

"You know, something about your father . . ."

She assures me that the exact same thought occurred to her and that this is precisely why she was so careful to perform the many experiments she performed on the squiggly little things that kept swimming so maddeningly out of her reach in the tub.

"I needed to be sure they weren't some kind of tricky lint!"

Inheritance

I inherited Grandma Ellen's hands, more or less, and a milder version of her dramatic jawline. I often take my tea with honey, lightened with cream or condensed milk, like she did. I am, as she was, a voracious reader, a good gardener, a lax housekeeper. Also, my grandmother wrote, although according to my aunt Becky, what she put down on the page was straight-up pornography. Nobody in the family knew anything about my grandmother's writing until after her death, when my aunt discovered two book-length manuscripts under her mother's bed. These consisted of two three-ring notebooks, the pages written out longhand—Aunt Becky told my mother (and my mother later told me)—in blue ballpoint pen.

In retrospect it shouldn't have surprised any of us that my grandmother had written so much since she was such a bottomless pit of a reader. In fact, my most abiding memory of Grandma Ellen is of her sitting near her kitchen window in an old red wicker chair with a book open on her lap, a balled-up tissue curled under the last three fingers of her left hand, and a cup of milky tea nearby. But what did she write in those notebooks? Unfortunately, I'll never know because just leafing through their pages, Aunt Becky said, made her "want to puke." So she threw them away.

Intermingled

I think they were pink, when I was growing up, not green, as they seem to be now, at least according to a recent Google search. Pink and heart shaped is how I remember Valium: a regular decoration of my childhood, like the wax begonias my mother was so fond of or the bobbled peds my sister and I favored or the corks in the kitchen drawer. Pretty, tiny pills one came across every so often, scattered on the floor of the car, at the bottom of her purse, or hidden deep in the cracks between couch cushions.

Instead

Because cutting up suits is an expensive habit and because my mother can be, when she feels like it, an extremely practical person, she eventually evolved her tactics so that instead of ruining my father's suits, she simply ripped them along the seams, a task almost instantly accomplished by running a pair of scissors through the stitches. The beauty of the seam-ripping approach, she once explained to me (laughingly and long after the fact), lay not in the destruction of the suits themselves but in the humiliation my father was forced to endure whenever he brought the deconstructed garments in to the tailor for repair.

Invisible

"*Kimberli*, if you don't get down here right now, I'll break *every bone in your body*."

"*Kimberli*, if you don't wipe that smirk off your face immediately, I'll break *every bone in your body*."

"*Kimberli*, if you don't clean up that mess pronto, and I mean *pronto*, I'll break *every bone in your body*."

It's not that I ever believed she would—I didn't—but a threat like this does something to you. Teaches you something. How to scuttle. How to get out of the way. How to hide before anyone starts looking.

Itty-Bitty

Tracy and I are running away. Our parents are chasing us, and we're afraid, but at a certain point we just get brave and say fuck it (only not in so many words because we're only kids), then jump into a car. It's always the same car, for some reason, a navy-blue vw Bug. Tracy usually gets to drive, but I don't care because no sooner does she start the engine than the car lifts off. Like smoke. Suddenly we're floating way up high. We can hear our parents behind us, but their voices are faint and getting fainter. We are already far beyond them. When I look down, they are tiny. We are so high up in the sky. So incredibly high in the sky, my sister and I. Laughing our heads off.

J

Jamboree

Isaac crawls up the ladder to our sleeping loft and squiggles into bed between David and me—warm soft little boy feet, chubby little boy toes, pokey elbows, bumpy knees . . . It's Saturday morning, eight, maybe eight-thirty. From downstairs Isabella asks if we're having pancakes for breakfast, and we shush each other. "Guys?" She climbs halfway up the ladder and, when she discovers us cuddling with her brother, says "That's not fair." She climbs the rest of the way up, then curls at the foot of our bed like some delicate, angular animal. David says, "Jamboree!" and the kids say, "Jamboree!" It's an old joke. Then everyone's talking at the same time—about breakfast, about sharing the blankets, about the movie we watched last night. I try to be in the moment because I understand the importance of staying with the instant that is but never remains, but I can't quite swing it because I keep thinking I have to remember this, everything about it, because this is it—the thing I've always wanted. The thing I want never to end.

Jane Birkin

I keep a photograph of my mother in our living room. People often comment on it. The other day a friend asked why I have a framed photo of Sophia Loren on the shelf. I said, "That's not Sophia Loren."

"Catherine Deneuve?"

"What are you talking about? Catherine Deneuve looks nothing like Sophia Loren!"

"Well, whoever. Jane Birkin?"

It's a self-portrait, but you can't really tell that just by looking at it. I only know because my mother has always taken pictures of herself, and also I recognize the hazy blur of light-blue wall-to-wall carpeting under her head. You can just barely catch a glimpse of her mask—studied, defensive—moving into place across her face. But it hasn't quite arrived. Instead, she wears an expression I've rarely seen her wear in real life. You could almost call it gentle.

Jell-O

From the bottom of a box of family photographs, I gather up all the old negatives. They are orange-brown, brittle with age, and seem slightly heavier than I expect them to be. I put them in an envelope and take them in to have them developed on contact sheets. When they're ready, I bring the sheets home and strain to see, through the little spyglass of a plastic loupe, long-lost details of the past trapped in the bars of intricate color hovering in fields of deep, glossy black. In one tiny square Tracy sleeps on the living room floor in the house with the pink shutters, her arms flung overhead. Her face is turned to one side, so you can see the straight line of her jaw, her small, pointed chin, the feathery layers of her hair. It strikes me, maybe for the first time, that something about the composition of her features, in particular the relationship between the nose and jaw, reminds me of Isaac. In another miniature image my aunt Elsa, maybe sixteen years old and slightly overweight, casts an imperious, blue-eye-shadowed glance over her shoulder. Another shows nothing but our dining room table decorated for my seventh birthday: crepe paper streamers crisscrossed overhead and eight paper plates.

I squint and shine my desk light directly on these miniscule photographs, which have a weirdly gelatin quality, a soft-edged, supersaturated intensity, as if they've been set in blocks of Jell-O. The stillness of these images is somehow more impressive than it is in normal photographs. There is, for instance, not the faintest suggestion of wind on the cloudy mountaintop where my mother stands in ski goggles and snow pants, and the clowning of my uncle Thor as he reaches up from the soft brown waters of Big Pond, pretending to drown, seems the art of the world's most silent mime, while in those overexposed squares in which Tracy and I eat green spaghetti from yellow dinner plates, our laughter is so fixed as to seem merely theoretical.

Jolly

My mother calls to inform me she's just been to a new dentist, and she actually sounds happy about it. Almost jolly. She says this dentist is young and caring and that maybe—who knows—maybe she'll be able to help her with her teeth.

"That's great. It's good to have a dentist you like."

"I made her cry, though," she says, and still, there's something bright in her voice.

"How?"

"I don't know! I just opened my mouth and she started crying."

Jug

Y——, New Jersey, 1979

In a sharply black-and-white photograph Tracy stands in the kitchen, holding the phone to her ear. The tightly coiled cord, wrapped behind her back, emerges from under one arm. She's eleven and either quite perturbed by whatever's getting said on the other end of the line or else eating something kind of tangy. She stands with a tomboyish swivel to her hips, and there's something mischievous in her—something impish and unpredictable. This was a strong physical characteristic of my sister when she was young—this upwardness, this springiness, or sprightliness. People carry their energy in different parts of their bodies, and in those years Tracy carried hers in her chin, in a playful thrust there. With the hand not holding the phone, she picks at the cork in a jug of wine on the kitchen table.

Juxtaposition

I was shy. Plus, we moved a lot, which meant that as soon as I started to open up, to make a connection, we were gone. But during the time we lived in the stucco house, I managed to make a small handful of friends. Four, to be exact. The closest of these was a girl named Lily Lundberg. I was friends with her twin too, Lila, but Lily was my blood sister, meaning that one day we licked our thumbs, then pricked them with a Swiss Army Knife, then smashed them together and said it was forever. We invented secret code names for one another and climbed pine trees and rescued half-dead mice from her cat and had Pop Rocks eating contests.

Temperamentally, I was much closer to Lila—quiet, observant— but that's exactly why I loved Lily, who was all angles and muscles and nerves. Lily reminded me of Kate Jackson, on *Charlie's Angels*, and Kate Jackson, the actress, reminded me of my mother, so obviously there was some complicated psychology going on. But Lily also reminded me of not-my-mother because she was fierce and happy and she never felt sorry for herself; even when she fell down and gashed her shin, she just got right back up.

K

Kale

It's Sunday morning. David is stirring melted butter into pancake batter. I'm making tea in our old pot, caramel colored and cracked with age. The kids are still sleeping, or else they're reading. In any case they're quiet. Outside the bank of windows near the dining room table, the snow in our yard is melting almost visibly. Three house finches dip their heads into a mud puddle and shimmy the water down their backs.

"You must have had a weird dream last night. You kept saying, 'Oh god.'"

"Oh my god, that's right!" says David. "It was sort of a bad dream and sort of a funny dream. About your mother."

I groan and say, "Oh no," as if I don't need or want to hear about it, but because I am and always have been and likely always will be obsessed with my mother—obsessed with finding clues that might offer the slimmest insight into the mystery that is my mother, I am in fact impatient for him to tell me his dream, but he's chuckling and shaking his head, so it's taking a while.

"Spit it out!"

"Actually, it was kind of gross."

"What?"

"My dream. She'd thrown up some kind of mess—it was horrible. Scary looking. All red and black. And she was all like, 'See, I told you! I told you!' as if she was dying, the way she always says she's going to. It looked so bad we got really worried and started getting ready to take her to the hospital. You were freaking out because you thought she was about to die. And Tracy was flipping out too. And all of that went on for a while, but then I realized—I just looked really closely, and I saw—she'd just mashed up a bunch of kale and mixed it with pomegranate juice. She'd just mixed them together, and I was like, 'Linda, that's just kale and pomegranate juice,' and she was like, 'Oh, *damn*! Well, I *almost* had you!'"

Karma

At heart, my mother says, she's a Buddhist. I say the same thing about myself, and curiously, so does my father, about himself, only I think we're all sort of Buddhist in different ways. My father is sort of Buddhist because he occasionally meditates and tries for a big-picture view and because I think he attempts, every day, to bring to mind—to the forefront of his mind—the quote from Plato with which he signs off every email:

Be kind, for everyone you meet is fighting a hard battle.

I am sort of Buddhist because I associate things like simplicity and humility and equanimity with Buddhism and strive to embody these qualities despite the fact that striving is pretty much antithetical to them.

My mother is sort of Buddhist because she believes in karma—past lives. Of her own past lives she once said: "I must have been one hell of a bastard! I mean I must've been some kind of *serious* bastard. Because how else do you explain all *this*?"

Katadin

Baxter State Park, Maine, 1979

Speckled in the lower-right-hand corner by a spray of red spots (photo developer? spaghetti sauce?), this photo is from our second and last vacation taken as a family—ten days in Maine. In the picture my father and I hold hands and jump as high as we can on top of Mount Katadin. I'd danced ballet for so many years at that point, it's not surprising that I've got some pretty impressive air under me. My legs are turned out, my knees sharply angled, my heels, in their hiking boots, neatly touch. My father leaps too, one leg outstretched to the side, the other bent beneath him. He's lacking what my ballet teachers used to call "extension." Still, you can't say he isn't trying.

Key

This winter has been a tough one, and there are predictions for a huge late-season blizzard to hit tonight, so David and I decide to bring my mother some groceries. She comes outside as soon as we pull into the parking lot in front of her small apartment complex but stays there only long enough to slip a bungee cord over the doorknob and attach it to a metal trellis that runs along one side of the front stoop.

"Now it will stay open when you bring them in," she says, meaning the door and the groceries. Then she points to the bottom of one of her flip-flops, which briefly touched the concrete surface of the stoop during the bungee cord operation, and says, "I've got to go spray this down."

We bring in six or seven bags of groceries, and I start packing away the frozen foods in my mother's worrisomely empty freezer and the more perishable items in her equally empty fridge, and as I do so, she comes out of the bathroom with her clean flip-flops to stand next to me, warning me that she has something important to tell me and that it's going to take a while but that it's *crucial* I listen carefully because it's for my own good and also I have to understand the background *fully* before I can understand the really *important point*, so I am just going to have to be *patient*. Already I am tuning her out. She starts talking about DMH and her hometown police force and also, for some reason, my kids. I don't like talking about my kids with my mother, so I get peckish pretty quickly.

"Just say what you need to say, Mom. We don't have much time."

The thing is, peckishness doesn't work at all with my mother. She takes it as a kind of bait or challenge, so in response she purposely slows her speech to a menacing drawl interjected with long hisses. This is something she has always had a talent for—hissing.

Her technique involves barely moving her jaw at all while at the same time setting her teeth slightly on edge and widening her already enormous green eyes. She can stare you down for ages like this, never blinking.

"Thisss—isss—important—Kimberliii. I'm trying to tell you. It hassss to do with the *kidsss*. Now you're *jussst* going to have to sssslooooowwww down and lissstennn."

"Oh Jesus Christ, Mom." I try to sidle past her and make my way to the door. "We really have to go now."

But she keeps talking, and I don't go as fast as I could because part of me is worried that maybe she really does have something important to tell me about my kids, even though I am at the same time beginning to understand the general shape of what she's say-ing and so on another level I know perfectly well that what she's talking about has nothing whatever to do with my kids in any real way because she's talking about some ancient lawsuit—one that may or may not have taken place (I've never been sure)—and the gist of things is that David and I need to find a way to purge our children's records because *everything is genetic.*

"Don't worry about it, Mom, okay? It's fine. Everything is fine."

"Don't be so *blasé*, Kimberli! It's your *kids* we're talking about. This is important stuff."

I tell her I'll worry about my own kids. She can take that off her list. And then I say we have to go.

"Don't you understand? They're tracing Isabella and Isaac's every move!"

I say we'll look into it, and I give her a kiss, which lands on her jaw, which is hard as a rock. Then David and I leave, but she follows us outside, still talking, this time apparently not at all concerned about the soles of her flip-flops.

"Don't you see? School records, dental records, medical records? Their chances of getting into a decent college are going to be *nil* if you don't take action *now!*"

Even as we get into our car, she keeps talking—still hissing, still bug-eyed and threatening. When I try to shut the passenger side door, she puts herself in front of it, so that I have to shove her out of the way in order to shut it, but that doesn't matter because as soon as I do, she opens it again, and we do that a few times, always with her talking and staring and setting her jaw on edge, until finally I succeed in not only pushing her out of the way and shutting the door but locking it as well, at which point David starts backing out of the parking space, while my mother looks all hangdog and rejected, standing there with her arms at her sides as wet, irregular clumps of snow get stuck in her hair. David is making a K-turn in the cramped lot when she starts trudging toward the front door, which is no longer bungee-corded open. When she reaches her stoop, I watch how she tries but fails to open the door and how she, at this point, turns back toward us, looking seventy-two times more hangdog than before. She nods or maybe shrugs—makes some kind of gesture, in any case, that seems indicative of her fate, which she considers cursed—and it is this gesture that gets me.

"Stop the car."

"Oh forget it. She's faking!"

"David, she's locked out of her apartment. It's freezing out. They're predicting a major storm. She's an old woman. I can't leave her standing there like that. I'd never forgive myself."

"Fine," he says, but he's shaking his head.

I get out of the car and start walking toward my mother where she is standing on the stoop, and as I approach, I ask impatiently if she's actually managed to lock herself out of her own building.

"I didn't do it!" she says. "*He* must have shut it—*he* must have moved the rope!" She flings her hand in David's direction. This doesn't make a lot of sense, but I just say, "Oh Jesus," and ring one of the six little brass buttons lined up on a plaque beside the door.

"What did you just do?"

"I rang a doorbell."

"And exactly *how* did you know to ring number *3*? Do you have any idea how *evil* that woman is?"

"I just picked a doorbell, Mom. Any doorbell. And anyway, I pressed number 2."

"Oh great!" she says, rolling her eyes in a huge circle. "She's even *worse!* Do you know what that woman did the last time Tracy visited?"

I say I don't care. I don't care who any of the people in the building are, I am just going to stand there and press every single one of the buttons until somebody buzzes her in, at which point my mother does this thing she does every so often that's sort of a relief and sort of just flabbergasting, sort of just mind-blowing, which maybe could be described as letting down her mask. What I mean is, all of a sudden she doesn't look quite so old or pathetic or crazy anymore but almost childlike as a smirk pops up at one corner of her mouth and she says, not hissy at all, just resigned, "Oh, *fine.*" Then she digs deep into the pocket of her sweatpants and pulls out a key at the end of a long black ribbon. And with this key she opens the door.

As she steps inside, I start walking back to the car. There's a familiar jellylike sensation in my legs that's getting worse with every step, but I manage to make it across the parking lot and wobble myself into the passenger seat.

"I told you," says David.

"Really?"

"I'm sorry. Are you okay?" He puts on the wipers and the blinker and waits for me to answer, but I don't. Not for a while. Finally, I shrug, and he gives my hand a squeeze, then we pull out of the lot.

Knife

Most everything I know about that night comes from my mother and from a police report I once read, years after the event, when I was helping her organize her enormous reserves of paperwork. There'd been a New Year's Eve party at the tennis club, and my father, who'd had too much to drink, had gotten mad when Richie danced for too many songs in a row with my mother.

He just sat there, she told me years later, *like a stone*, getting drunker and drunker, watching her and Richie having a *good, innocent time.* When he finally got up, he insisted on leaving and dragged her off the dance floor. Richie followed them downstairs, watched them get into their car, and decided my father was being too rough. So he got into his own car and followed them home. According to the police report, he wanted to make sure my mother got there safely. Twenty minutes later he watched again as my father pulled into our driveway and my parents went into the house. Apparently, Richie still didn't like what he saw, so he got out of his car too.

"He was just playing the gentleman," she told me. "He was so *very* young."

Tracy and I were upstairs, sleeping. I was thirteen, Tracy eleven. It's likely we'd stayed up late that night watching sitcoms and talk shows, eating peanut butter cookies. Even when Richie rang the doorbell, we didn't wake up.

The three of them stood in what we rather grandly called "the foyer"—a cold, square, windowless space with walls covered in cheap wood paneling. At first the disagreement was strictly verbal. I can, of course, only imagine the exchange, but it seems likely that my father would have demanded to know who Richie thought he was and that Richie might have said he just wanted to make sure things were okay. Then my father went upstairs. And this is the part I wonder about—the part that isn't in the police report. The part my mother never described because she stayed downstairs the whole time, talking to Richie, maybe about my father, maybe joking about him and his anger, his drinking, his jealousy. But upstairs in the kitchen, my father was looking for something. I imagine him rummaging in the dark, and I wonder: was he searching for it? Did he know what he was after? Or did the knife somehow present itself?

A beak-nosed paring knife is shaped, in profile, exactly as the name suggests: like a beak, or, to be a little more specific, like the curved beak of a hawk. Or the claw of a cat. Or its eyetooth. A doctor once explained to me as he stitched up my wrist (which I'd stupidly put between two fighting dogs) how lucky it was that I hadn't been bitten by a cat. "Dog teeth," he said, "are straight:

they go in and out, making simple punctures. But cat teeth are curved. They go in and tear a path out, ripping through everything in their way."

When my father went back downstairs, he'd hidden the knife in his hand so that at first neither Richie nor my mother understood what he was doing when he took a swing. Richie laughed, my mother told me, and said, "Jake, what kind of punch is that?" But even as he spoke, his shirt, which was white (again, according to my mother), filled quickly with blood.

It's easy enough to imagine the reactions of Richie and my mother at that point—though that's all I have, imaginings. I imagine Richie stopped laughing. And I imagine she started screaming, then ran for the phone. But my father? What did he do? When I imagine him, I come up blank. A man on pause. Mindless.

Tracy and I slept through it all—the fight and its aftermath, which included the arrival of the ambulance, the police, the paramedics, and their respective departures. We slept straight through until morning and even then didn't notice anything odd, since our father (who was being held at the police station) was often gone by the time we woke up. Our mother told us nothing, maybe because she thought she was protecting us. Or maybe because she wanted our new year to seem bright. Or maybe she was just tired.

L

Landlord Problems

Being authorities of a certain stripe, landlords are among my mother's favorite people to get embroiled with in complicated, usually vicious, often violent, sometimes litigious arguments that inevitably conclude to her disadvantage. For example, her last landlord, who happened to be an ex-cop, threatened her with a gun when she attempted to kick in the front door of his two-family house in M——. I might have assumed this story to be just another one of her many verbal inventions, but Tracy was there because it was Christmas Eve and she'd just driven out from Chicago. This was a few years ago. Tracy and my mother had come over for dinner at our place that night—roast chicken and apple pie—and afterward they drove to my mother's apartment, only my mother couldn't find her *key, and that's when the door kicking started.

Tracy saw the whole thing—how our mother rang her landlord's doorbell and how, because it was close to midnight, he didn't answer at first and also how, because there was no answer even after she'd pressed the bell several times, she said something in a very loud voice about the man's unbelievable laziness and vindictive nature. Then she leaned on the doorbell for a while.

"When he still didn't answer, she started kicking the door," Tracy told me a couple of days after the fact, when she came over for dinner by herself. "She was wearing those boots with the heels, and the heel started cracking the wood, making holes. I told her not to do it, but she was already gone." She illustrated the word *gone* with a facial expression I can only describe as "mental." "Needless to say, she ignored me."

We were making meatballs together—Grandma Bella's recipe—
when she told me this story. We were getting tipsy because that's
a thing we like to do—talk about our mother while cooking and
drinking red wine.

"After a few minutes of her kicking the door, the landlord finally
stuck his head out the window and told her to shut up. I tried to
shrug to show I wasn't part of it, but it was dark. I don't think he
could see. Mom told him to open up the fucking door or else
she'd kick it in. She said, 'It's Christmas Eve, you bastard! Have
you no heart?' Then she kicked the door again, and he said, 'Get
a locksmith.' And she said, 'Fuck you and merry Christmas!' And
that's when he got his gun. Actually, I think it might have been a
rifle. It seemed kind of long."

Late

I go to pick up Isaac from an after-school movie presented by the
PTO because it's a half-day, and when I come into the auditorium,
I find he's one of the last students left. The principal and vice principal are running around frantically trying to connect the remain-
ing students with their guardians. One boy is clearly struggling not
to cry. But Isaac, already in his jacket, backpack on his shoulder,
is calm. When he sees me, he hops up from his seat and takes my
hand, and as we walk out of the auditorium, he starts describing
the plot of the film, which concerns a lot of different kinds of food
that come alive and have adventures together. This explanation
takes a long time, and I find it hard to follow because I'm distracted.
Once we're back home, I put out a plate of chocolate shortbread
cookies and hand him a glass of milk. Then I apologize for being
so late to pick him up. He thinks about this for a second and says,
"Actually, it's more like the other parents were really early."

Laughter

My mother rode in the ambulance with Richie. In the story she tells
about that night, the paramedics were having a hard time staunch-
ing the flow of blood from his abdomen, and he was delirious. But

still he kept joking around, doing his Daffy Duck imitation. "Do you remember his Daffy Duck? It was so good! I'm telling you, he had everyone in that ambulance in stitches. Absolute stitches!"

The wound was complicated because of the shape of the knife, which had sliced through his intestines in several places. At the hospital he was rushed into surgery, and afterwards my mother waited with his parents all night for Richie to regain consciousness. Once he was awake, the police came by with a bunch of paperwork. They wanted him to press charges, and so did his parents. But he refused. He said he didn't want Tracy and me to grow up with a convict for a father.

My mother first told me all of this years ago. But much more recently I may have heard another take on the events from that night. I don't know for sure. It's impossible to say. But coincidences do happen. This was about three years ago. I was listening to an NPR special about the curative effects of laughter. The doctor on the show was a pioneering specialist in this field, and when asked how he got his start, he explained that he'd become interested in the power of laughter decades earlier, when he was fresh out of medical school, working in a hospital in New Jersey, and a young guy came into the emergency room with a terrible knife wound.

"His chances were slim," he said. "Extremely slim. I thought for sure we were going to lose him, he'd already lost so much blood. But he kept joking around as we got him prepped for surgery. He just wouldn't stop. He did this incredible Daffy Duck imitation. He was making everybody crack up, and the laughter was amazing. It buoyed us all."

Library

It's a beautiful spring evening—warm, and the magnolias are out. We're walking to the library, and Isabella is full of stories. These are mostly about her friends—the shy one who's good at math, the sweet but competitive one who cheated on a test, the insecure one who constantly checks her cell phone . . . I make a comment about cell phones, say something about how much I loathe them, and Isabella asks why I'm so bad with mine, meaning, why do I so often lose it or let it run out of juice for days at a stretch or simply don't bother to pick it up when it rings.

I used to speak in extremely tight circles about my mother to my daughter, but Isabella recently turned fourteen years old, and she is curious about her grandmother. Also, I think, she is curious about me. So, I tell her about the stretch of time, a few years ago, back before my mother was convinced that all her phones were being tapped, when she used to call me much more frequently—two or sometimes three times a day.

"It was just too much. I guess I started associating my phone with her. And you know what she's like."

"But you have that special ringtone for her—that duck. You could have just avoided the duck."

"Well, true. But she also texted, and texts just pop up on your screen. You can't really avoid them. They're just—boom—right there."

"What was so bad about her texts?"

"Oh, you know, crazy stuff. All her paranoid stuff. Plus, sometimes she can be mean. Demeaning. It hurts my feelings."

We walk for a while without speaking, and as we do, I rack my brains, trying to remember what it *was* about my mother's texts that had, during the years they'd been so frequent, made me so phobic of my cell phone. Then I remember. She used to send pictures.

"Of what?"

"Herself, mostly."

Normally, I would stop there, but my daughter is almost as tall as I am. We wear the same shoe size. And when I look at her, I see that her gaze is, for lack of a better word, searching. So I describe some of the photos my mother used to send, photos that were, more often than not, of her own face. I don't talk about the really disturbing ones: the pictures of her teeth or of her eye inflamed and red or those of her mouth "reacting" to something, in short, sad and gross photos offered as documentation of her many ailments. Instead, I tell her about my mother's more conventional self-portraits, some of which were just ghostlike hoverings in a mirror or a window or a computer screen and some of which were tight close-ups. And here I start hamming things up, framing portions of my own face to indicate the dramatic croppings my mother used: her mouth, her jawline, her cheekbones, her eyes.

"Looking right," I say, imitating my mother's expressions. "Looking left . . . Looking up. Looking down. Both eyes! One eye!"

At this point Isabella has stopped walking. We've made it to the library and are standing on the sidewalk at the base of the stairs leading up to the entrance. She is bent over, laughing, trying to catch her breath. Finally, she makes a funny little gasp, puts her hand on my shoulder, and says, "I had *no* idea!" as if the story I've just told her contained some astonishing piece of information.

"What do you mean?"

"I had no *idea* you were dealing with that!"

License

My mother loves driving, but she's very bad at it. Actually, that's not precisely the case. She is, in fact, a highly skilled but completely reckless driver. For instance, once she drove backward several hundred feet on the highway in the middle of the night at sixty miles an hour because she'd run over something and wanted to make sure it wasn't a body. It was Christmas, and David, Tracy, and I were in the car because her present to us that year (we were all in our early twenties) was a weekend stay at a cross-country ski resort. I don't remember much about that trip except that it rained both days and Tracy slept practically the whole time. But I do remember driving backward on the highway as we all screamed at her to stop. Needless to say, she ignored us, just kept zipping backward, jaw clenched, eyes squinting through the rear window. After she verified that the thing she'd hit was in fact a duffel bag (as we'd already assured her), she started driving in the right direction again, saying, "Gee, for a bunch of kids, you guys sure are wimps."

It's telling, perhaps, how much more vividly I remember those words than I do the ridiculous antic that preceded it. But that's how it is for me around my mother. I get lost so quickly. Especially if she scares me. I stuff the experience somewhere dark and airless. After we arrived at the cabin, before we went to bed, David, Tracy, and I took a walk on the deserted mountaintop road. The moonlight turned everything different shades of the same eerie indigo color. The gravel crunched under our boots with an icy sound. We walked into the white clouds of our breath, which grew bigger as we began talking about the stunt on the highway. David said, "She's crazy!" then imitated how my mother had looked peering through the back window. He and Tracy laughed and it sounded so good—so easy. I wanted to laugh too, and I did, eventually, but it took a while because I'd already buried the incident somewhere deep, where words don't reach and feelings don't register. It probably would still be there if David hadn't told that joke.

Lilacs

I ring the doorbell, then stand in the stuffy entry hall for several minutes—five, maybe six—while she slowly shoves the butcher-block counter out of the way because the door to her apartment opens directly into her kitchen, and in order to keep DMH and their various associates from sneaking in when she's asleep or watching TV, she keeps the butcher-block counter in front of it. This counter, which is set on wheels, is piled high with ancient boxes of paperwork as well as pots and pans, vases, and a wide assortment of cleaning supplies, all of which, of course, make the counter even heavier than it would be otherwise.

"Oh," she says, once she's managed to open the door maybe half a foot and can peek out of the crack. I'm standing there holding a bouquet of flowers. I offer them to her. "You remembered."

It's Mother's Day and close to dinnertime. Earlier, in the morning, David and the kids made popovers and eggs and fruit salad for breakfast, and we ate outside on the porch. The kids gave me hand-drawn cards, and David gave me a bottle of my favorite perfume. Isabella took a yoga class with me in the afternoon, and later Isaac curled up with me in the hammock to read Grimms'

Fairy Tales. Finally, I picked a few flowers from our yard—a couple of lilacs, the first pale pink roses (which smell ever so slightly of peppercorns), a single white daffodil, and some Scotch broom. "Are you sure you want to do this?" David asked as I wrapped the stems in damp paper towels, then stuck the damp paper towels in a plastic bag, then twisted a rubber band around the bag to secure everything together. "You don't have to," Isabella chimed in. But I assured them both I'd be quick, and I promised I wouldn't get depressed.

"Of course I remembered," I say. "Happy Mother's Day!" Then I hand her the flowers through the crack.

She mumbles the word *beautiful* and takes a careful sniff. She says something about my birthday, which was just a couple of days ago, and starts to explain why she'd forgotten to call, but since this explanation begins with DMH, I cut her off and tell her not to worry about it, and then, mostly in order to change the subject, I say, "Maybe you should rethink the butcher-block thing, Mom. In case of a fire it doesn't seem like such a safe thing to have it right in front of your door."

Considering the angle she has to work with—the six-inch slot between the door and the doorjamb—she has pretty good aim. The flowers hit me right in the face. Something snaps in my eye.

"Happy fucking Mother's Day yourself!" she shouts. "You think I need your fucking flowers? I don't need your fucking flowers! I just need you to *believe* me!" Then she slams the door and bolts it, and as I grope around for the exploded bouquet, tears swelling in my eyes, I can hear her struggling to shove the butcher block back in its place.

Limburger Effect

I don't actually, in real life, my everyday life, tell that many stories about my mother or my childhood or my mother's childhood because of a certain effect I've noticed my family history has on people whenever I discuss its details: something crosses their faces—a strained, politely muted, but unmistakable expression of dismay and some vague relative of panic. David knows what I'm talking about. He's seen it. He laughs when I joke that my stories smell like Limburger cheese—the Limburger part no doubt suggesting itself because it was one of the items my mother always listed as being on her father's special shelf when she told the Refrigerator Story. But to be honest, the Limburger effect makes me angry. Why shouldn't I tell these stories? Just because no one wants to hear them? Listen!

Liminal

I know from being married to an architect that a porch is a liminal space: neither inside nor outside. Connected to the home but not strictly part of it. Additionally, there is a door that leads to the porch from the house, and this door can be shut. If need be, you can lock it.

Local Paper

My parents gave me a beautiful winter parka for Christmas that year. It was pure white, down filled, with a fur-lined hood. I considered it the height of elegance and was certain it would change my image at school for the better. So, the first day after winter break (which is to say, two days after my father stabbed Richie, two days after he was arrested and then released, two days after Richie nearly died but didn't—only I didn't know any of this because nobody had told me) I put on this coat and wore it proudly to school.

I hung my new parka carefully in my locker and later in the day wore it onto the playground at recess even though it wasn't very cold. It made me feel like a movie star, and I was hopeful that wearing it would reveal to my classmates, and everyone else in the bleak and massive middle school I attended, my true nature, which is why, as I stood in line on the asphalt-covered playground, waiting to walk, single file, back into the school, I put my gorgeous fur-trimmed hood over my head and slipped my hands into my silky pockets and gently swayed in a manner I considered subtly movie star–ish.

"What are you so happy about?" asked the boy standing next to me. Not the boy I had a crush on. His best friend. "If I were you," he said, "I wouldn't be happy."

I found this less rude than scary. Was I so transparent? Were my faults—the ones my mother pointed out every day—so clear to the casual observer? I started to cry, and the boy apologized, but at that point the conversation took an even more confusing turn because he began talking about my father and his father and the police and some kind of a fight. A knife. A stabbing. New Year's Eve. Someone was drunk. It took me a while to figure out what he was saying, but eventually I understood that the boy's father had read an article in the local paper about my father, then told his son about what he'd read, and now his son was telling me, and what the boy's father had read was that two days earlier my father, my own dad, the man who'd bought me my beautiful winter coat and took a picture of me wearing it in front of the Christmas tree, holding up a stocking full of pistachio nuts, had stabbed another man in the abdomen with a kitchen knife.

"There was a whole article!" said the boy.

Locked Ward

There is some logic at work, no matter how private. For example, everything my mother does in service of her ever-growing paranoia is done to ensure that she will not spend the rest of her life in a locked ward in some hellish, state-run psychiatric hospital because, according to her private and deeply convoluted reasoning, it is only by being ever vigilant, by being wily and smart and constantly onto *them*, that she stands even the slimmest hope of avoiding such a fate.

Loft

I don't know what made me do it. Or rather, I know exactly what made me do it, but I know this only now. At the time I simply felt the urge come over me, and I acted on it. For some reason we were eating off paper plates that night: mashed potatoes, meatloaf, salad, bread and butter. Once the thought occurred to me, I didn't stop to reconsider, just picked up my plate, my satisfyingly hot and hefty plate, and sent it flying across the table. The simplicity of the action—a soft overhand toss straight at his face—seemed like magic, and for just an instant I felt powerful. But as I watched my father wipe the steaming mess away from his glasses, dread set in, and time did then what it does in nightmares—slowed down and speeded up simultaneously. I ran to my bedroom and fumbled at the lock. It took forever. The hollow core door jumped in its frame when he pounded against it, screaming at me from the other side. I don't remember what he said, but it didn't last long. My mother called him off, and the house grew quiet again.

I lay on my bed for a long time then, staring at my nylon bed-spread, dotted with colorful flowers, waiting for the electric discomfort of excess adrenaline to drain away from my limbs, listening to the muffled noises of my family: the clatter of dishes, the drone of the television, the toilet flushing. I felt so lonely.

Logic

I would have liked more of it when I was a kid. A lot more. For example, where is the logic in a commonplace statement such as "If you don't stop crying, I'll give you something to cry about"? It was like being trapped in an idiot world. I could have ripped out my hair with the frustration of it. But I didn't. Instead, I sucked back everything hot—tears, snot, anger.

Loony

I'm sitting outside at a pressed metal table at a Frenchy café eating French-type food, speaking French. Well, technically, "speaking" is stretching things because although my friend Emily is fluent, I can only crank out sentences in that language very slowly. Still, we're having a nice time, sitting in the sun, talking at two differ-ent speeds, praising our fresh pea soup and debating whether our waiter is handsome or simply young. But then we start talking about my mother. This is a topic I generally try to avoid in real life, but for some reason I'm just *in* it, describing the time my mother came to a birthday party at our place a few years ago. David and I have the same birthday, and two of his sisters were there too. And our kids, of course. I can tell as soon as I start this story that I ought to stop. Emily doesn't get my mother. She's never met her, and I often have the sense that she suspects me of exaggerating when I talk about her. This hurts my feelings, and I don't want to ruin the whole Frenchy, sunshiny, pea soupy vibe by getting my feelings hurt. On the other hand, I don't want to *not* tell the story just because of the Limburger factor because that makes me angry. So, I forge ahead and tell her—more in English than French— that on the night in question my mother brought over a paper bag full of photographs to give me as a present and that at some point during dinner she pulled a few pictures out of this bag and passed them around the table.

"Look—just look—at that body," she told my sister-in-law Judy, who was sitting next to her. I could tell from the expression that came over Judy's face that something wasn't right.

"Um," she said, holding the photos toward me, "I think you might want to keep these."

I grabbed the pictures and saw that in one I was standing on a beach in Spain, topless in a red bikini bottom, throwing a stick for our dog Oscar (whom we'd brought along on our honeymoon because we loved him like that, like a child, practically). Another picture showed me naked and heavily pregnant, flopped on our bed in *San Francisco*, my belly sagging sideways, my eyes half-closed. In the third I sat laughing with a friend on a granite boulder in front of a waterfall where we'd just gone skinny-dipping.

"Where did you get these?" I asked, my voice trembling.

"I don't know! How should I remember? I guess you gave them to me."

I tell Emily (whose expression I can't quite read behind her dark sunglasses) that after dinner, once everybody had left, I searched through the rest of pictures my mother had brought and found several more that didn't make any sense. These were photos she should never have had in her possession: pictures, for example, of my father with a girlfriend and some of a very young Isabella on vacation with David's parents.

"So, what are you saying?" asks Emily, in French, a little clipped. "You think your mother stole the pictures?"

"Yes! Or maybe. She just manages weird stuff. I don't know how she does it."

She tilts her mouth in a funny way and says, "You think your mother broke into your apartment and took the pictures when you weren't there?"

"I don't know! I don't know how she does it. But she's always done stuff like that. It's weird."

Something has closed off in my friend. Her lips look stiff, her brow stern. I want to prove that my mother really does sneak into my life and steal little bits of it. So, instead of shutting up, I tell her about the time my mother called me in order to read some printed-out pages she'd "found" in her apartment. She said that she had no idea where these pages came from or *who* could have written them but that the writing was so *elegant,* and for some reason it reminded her of *herself,* almost as if she was reading inside *her own head.* I listened, then, to the introductory paragraphs of an essay I'd been working on for months.

"The thing is," I explain, "I'm always really careful to throw away any print-outs of my writing because I don't want my mother digging through our recycling bin and finding them. I rip up my writing, if I've printed it out, into tiny, tiny pieces and put the pieces out with our trash. In our kitchen garbage. Underneath things."

"But that's kooky," says Emily, "that's loony." And I am dismayed to realize that it is entirely unclear exactly what the word *that* refers to in this sentence. "It just doesn't make any sense," she adds, before reverting to French and praising the pea soup once more, just as if we haven't already done so half a dozen times.

Lundbergs

After my father stabbed Richie, things got awkward, socially speaking, for my parents, so they decided to move. We'd always rented, but this time they bought a house a couple of towns away. Because it was the middle of the school year, they asked the parents of friends of ours—the Lundbergs—if they'd take Tracy and me to live with them until June, when school let out. I had been close for a long time with the two oldest children, Lily and Lila, and Tracy was friends with their younger sister, a beautiful black-haired girl whose name I now forget, though I know it started with an *L* because all the Lundbergs' children's names started with *L*. The five of us slept upstairs in a cozy refurbished attic outfitted with many beanbag chairs and green wall-to-wall carpeting that smelled, curiously, of mashed peas, Tracy and I in sleeping bags on the floor.

We ate dinner with the Lundbergs Monday through Thursday, then got picked up by our parents for the weekend on Friday afternoon. Although their food was less delicious than ours and much of it came out of cans, nobody seemed to mind. After dinner the father sat in an armchair to work on his duck decoys. The mother knit. Nobody mentioned what our father had done except once—an offhand comment by the brother that was quickly hushed. Still, I never breathed easy in the Lundbergs' house, and I know why: deep down, I resented both their charity and their happiness. And over the months I grew colder and colder toward my friends, even the lanky, good-hearted Lily.

Luxury Bath Products

Blah blah blah blah blah blah blah. Blah blah blah. Something about DMH. Something about the cops. Her landlord. A neighbor and their cats. I try to be patient. I fail. I say I have to get off the phone. She says I have to stay on. No, I really have to go, I have some things to do. Then, suddenly, she's furious. "You are so *unbelievably* jealous, Kimberli! Just like you've always been!"

"Jealous of what?" I ask, although I'm not sure she hears me because my voice sounds small, even to me.

"Jealous of *me*. Of every *fucking* thing about me! Every fucking *thing*!"

It's complicated, like origami, the folds in our relationship. My mother is talking about me, but really she is talking about herself, yet her wounds are my wounds; at least something in me hurts.

"I can't do this anymore," I say. Then I hang up.

Later, after the kids are in bed, I climb into a steaming hot bath. Luxury bath products are good for days like this, which is why I buy so many of them. My current stock includes: a lemon-scented bath bomb (fizzes on contact with water); a large jug of jasmine- and honey-scented all-natural shower gel; a vial of hops and valerian-based organic German bath oil; a slim white brick of camellia oil soap from Japan; a heart-shaped "bath melt" composed of cocoa butter and infused with aromatic oils; a creamy white soap molded to resemble a scallop shell and scented with Nag Champa incense; a bottle of traditional fir-scented bath oil from Switzerland (disgusting, actually, but novel); and a tub of mustard-based muscle tonic powder from India. It's this last that I throw into the bath in double the suggested dose. As I lean back, the gritty powder bubbles beneath my legs, making tiny, scorching explosions.

M

Maddening

The thing I worry about with my mother's eye isn't worms, it's shingles. Because it's true—her left eye does not look healthy. It is often red, and the skin around it is very chapped, and both of these are symptoms of shingles when that disease affects the eye. Shingles of the eye is a highly contagious disease, which if left untreated for too long can cause blindness. But when I explain these things to my mother, she yells: "Don't be stupid! Shingles don't give you worms!"

Mashed Rutabaga

For most of my life, I'm not sure why, I had miles of fuse with my mother. Miles and miles and miles and miles of fuse. In fact, for many years my reserves of patience for her seemed virtually endless. But that changed all of a sudden one Thanksgiving about four years ago. David and I were hosting, and after some debate we decided to invite my mother. When I asked if she could come, she said: "Oh, Kimmy. Thank you so much! I'm so excited! It's going to be so wonderful!" She even asked if she could arrive early in order to help prepare the meal, which she said was half the fun. So, for the week leading up, she called daily in order to pin down our plans, checking to see what she could bring and when she should come and also to ask what sort of gifts I thought the kids might like because she'd forgotten both of their birthdays that summer. She said she'd like to make a spinach dish that had been her specialty years ago, a dark silky mess of chopped spinach in cream sauce topped with slivers of hard-boiled egg. She also said she'd give me tips on the gravy because she makes a "mean" one, but when I said I already knew how to make good gravy, she said that really she'd just be my sous-chef.

"There's just so much to do on Thanksgiving. You can tell me, 'Chop this, chop that.' I'll do whatever you say. Dishes. Table setting. Watching the kids. Whatever!"

The truth is, I was getting kind of excited about having her over. She seemed so happy about it, so unusually centered and even considerate. We'd invited only three other people, friends of ours named Jess and Peter and their daughter, Sophie. Although we'd known Jess and Peter for many years and they are among our closest friends, they had never met my mother. So I warned them ahead of time that she might be a little hard to deal with— hyper and extremely talkative, maybe about inappropriate things.

"Don't worry," said Jess. "I'm sure it'll be fine."

We said we'd eat at four o'clock, and my mother told me she'd come over at one thirty to help get things ready. Because she is notoriously late, I asked her to call before she left so that I'd know when to actually expect her. At two o'clock she phoned to say she was getting into her car. She lives fifteen minutes away, so at three o'clock, when she still hadn't arrived, I called to see if she was okay. She said she'd forgotten something, but she was leaving that *very moment,* in fact she was getting into her car as we spoke, then she slammed her car door to prove it. At four o'clock Jess, Peter, and Sophie arrived with a salad, two bottles of wine, and a loaf of homemade bread. The turkey was behind schedule, but we had plenty to eat with the appetizers, which included a mushroom salad Grandma Bella used to make: quartered button mushrooms, chunks of Pecorino, olive oil, salt, pepper, chopped parsley, lemon juice.

"This is amazing!" said Peter, about the salad. "Jess, we must remember this recipe. It's so simple and good."

At five thirty I texted my mother to tell her we were starting the meal without her. She texted back:

Soooooo sorry. Unexpected delays. Just down the street b 5 mins.

I don't like turkey, but everyone else said it was good. I'd prepared it with a stuffing that included garlic, basil, and parmesan cheese, which is how I remembered one of my great aunts on my father's side making it once.

"So, I guess your mother's not coming?" Jess asked halfway through dinner. I shrugged and said it was probably for the best. Isabella told Sophie (who is exactly her age), "My grandma is a little funny." We cleared the plates, and Jess and Peter asked to look at the pies I'd made so they could at least ogle them since they'd promised to have dessert at Jess's cousin's house.

After they left, David, the kids, and I decided to take a walk before starting dessert. I texted my mother once more to say we'd be out for a while but that if she wanted pie, she could come by around eight. She texted back:

Apple?

It was cold outside, but we walked for a long time anyway. The streets were virtually empty, and the air felt as if it were full of tiny, invisible needles of ice. At one point we wandered into the main commercial district of B——, and for some reason I remember this part of our excursion with tremendous tenderness. I remember, for instance, that as we crossed a deserted Beacon Street against the light, David took my hand and said, "You can't really expect her to do what she says she's going to." I said that it had been a beautiful meal anyway. I asked if he'd liked the turkey.

"Honestly, I wasn't crazy about the garlic stuffing," he said. I told him Grandma Bella would never have done it that way, even though her sister had. She'd always done her turkeys with just the most basic sage and sausage stuffing. He said that was his favorite kind of stuffing too, and I resolved to do it that way from then on.

When we got home, I put on the kettle for tea and checked my cell phone, but there were no messages. The pies, if I do say so myself, were excellent. One apple, one squash. We ate thin slivers with whipped cream while watching *Pink Panther II*. It was about nine thirty—we were halfway through the movie—when I heard a faint knocking at the door. I said, "She's here," and David said he didn't hear anything, but then she knocked again and he asked if I wanted to let her in and I said not really but I guess we should, so he went to open the door, and she came in talking a mile a minute about the bottle of fancy wine she'd brought.

"It'll go *great* with the turkey!"

David asked if she'd like some pie, and she said: "Well, what I was really hoping for was some turkey and mashed rutabaga—I've been dreaming about mashed rutabaga all week long! Is there any left? I'm just *dying* for mashed rutabaga."

"We ate hours ago, Linda. Everything's been put away."

"Just a little plate?"

From across the room I said, "No!" Then I marched into the kitchen, cut her two slices of pie, dolloped them with whipped cream, and put the plate in front of her. She picked at these while telling Isaac about all the presents she was going to get him for Christmas. As I listened to her speak, my stomach started lurching around. This is often the case when I'm near my mother. You can actually see it move. That night it was so bad that I couldn't stand up straight. I just wanted her to leave so we could get back to our movie, but I didn't say so because I could feel the anger bubbling inside of me and I knew that if I opened my mouth, what came out if it would be ugly, and I didn't want to be like that in front of my kids, so instead I hobbled over to the ladder that leads to David's and my sleeping loft, climbed upstairs, and crawled under the covers of our bed to wait for her to leave. After about half an hour David started shepherding her toward the door.

"The kids are tired. It's late. It's been a long day." It took him ten minutes to get her out. Right before she left, she shouted, "Good-bye, Kimberli!" But this was barbed because she only uses my full name to indicate displeasure.

Once she was gone, I hobbled back downstairs and told Isaac that he shouldn't get his hopes up about the presents.

"I know," he said.

David asked if I was okay. I said, "Let's just watch the movie." He turned it back on, then leaned over to give me a kiss, but I pulled away. I said, "I'm done. I'm done with her. For real." He said, "That's probably good. There's really no point. It doesn't help her, and it only hurts you." Once again he leaned over to give me a kiss, and again I pulled away, but then I leaned back.

Massachusetts

A state full of *sadists*. A bona fide *hellhole*. A *living nightmare*, where everyone is *in cahoots* with everyone else and nobody ever gets off her back.

Material

Once, many years ago, I helped my mother run an especially exhausting and fruitless errand. I was in my midthirties when I put Isabella in her car seat and drove an hour and a half south of Boston to visit a tiny jewelry store, where I was supposed to act as a kind of character witness for my mother while she laid out a handful of blurry Polaroid photographs and unpacked a shoebox full of expensive rings and pins on the glass counter in front of the store owner, all the while spewing a nonstop verbal explosion of deeply paranoid logic. Needless to say, things ended badly, but it took a really long time—almost two hours—because the jewelry store owner was an exceedingly polite man.

At the conclusion of this mortifying exercise in futility, I was not only humiliated but exhausted and hungry, and Isabella had long ago passed cranky. Luckily, we found an old-fashioned diner just a few doors down from the jewelry store, and there we ordered three grilled cheese sandwiches, two iced teas, and a glass of chocolate milk. Once we'd finished eating, the waitress brought us our check, which—I just so happen to remember—was for the very modest sum of twelve dollars and eighty-six cents. After glancing at this figure, my mother pushed the bill toward me. I was annoyed, but of course it wasn't that much money, so I tried to let it go.

Unfortunately, as evidenced by the fact that I still recall the precise amount, I have not as yet managed to succeed on that score.

After lunch we took a walk across the street, where there was an old graveyard on a hill. This graveyard was of the type New England is known for, with slate headstones tilting at odd angles and inscriptions so old they're often worn away and, when still legible, tend to describe tragically short life spans. It was a beautiful place—peaceful and cool and quiet, shaded by tall maples whose crowns merged to create a canopy of leaves that rustled every so often in the breeze. Overhead, pigeons flew in deep arcs. As we walked, I bumped my sleeping daughter's stroller gently over the buckled brick path, and I remember thinking, *This isn't so bad . . . walking with my mother . . . talking . . . it's actually kind of nice.* Then, for a little while, it got un-nice. Then it got nice again. And then—I forget how it came up, but at a certain point my mother turned to me for some reason and said: "You know, you can write about me if you want, Kimmy. I don't mind. I know I'm your material."

Memory Lane

The memory was gone—for years, decades. But then, suddenly, it's here. We're at the table eating macaroni and cheese, the kind that comes out of a box, when Isabella complains about not being able to enjoy things like corn on the cob and candied apples because of her braces. Beyond the windows, behind my children, I can see our yard, and beyond our yard I can see the grounds of their grade school, with its track and its baseball diamonds, its basketball court, its picnic tables and swings. I know better, which is why I try (briefly) to reason with myself, but it doesn't work. I dive in anyway.

"When I had braces, do you know what Mormor used to do if she didn't like what I was saying or how I was acting? Can you guess?"

I ask as if we were playing a fun game. My children look a little worried, and a voice in my head tells me to shut up, but I don't listen. "She used to take my face in her hands and squeeze my cheeks. Really hard. Rub them back and forth, back and forth, squishing them into my braces." I imitate my mother crushing my cheeks between her hands, but it's weird because I'm trying to be both me, as a kid with braces, and my mother, with the hands. Then I laugh. Ha ha.

"That's not funny," says Isaac.

"That's awful," says Isabella.

"Well, you know Mormor," I say, trying for an airy tone.

Mental Illness

In my embarrassingly large collection of self-help books, I have found very little that's truly illuminating on the subject of mental illness. Thich Nhat Hanh, for instance, often speaks of "difficult" people, though not of mentally ill people, and there is of course an enormous distinction to be made. Generally speaking, most authors of the sorts of books that fill my collection, no matter how lucid they may be on the broadest spiritual truths, are content to say things that are plainly half-assed when it comes to mental illness. For instance, one idea frequently articulated is that difficult people ought to be seen in a special light, one that reveals them as valuable teachers who can reveal important truths about things like patience and empathy and also about our own neediness and other shortcomings.

Once I heard Eckhart Tolle say something completely ridiculous on this subject in a YouTube video. Generally speaking, I like Eckhart Tolle. I have learned a lot from his YouTube channel. But I remember thinking that his rambling answer to this particular question ("What is the purpose of mental illness? How can something that is consciousness depriving have its necessary place and function?"), asked by a nervous and pained-looking young woman, was absurd in the extreme. I remember growing increasingly irate as I listened to him go on and on about the supposed "purpose" of mental illness. And yet afterward something curious happened. His answer stuck in my head, and over time I began to understand what he was really saying. He was saying that mental illness, as it manifests in the individual, is actually a reflection of a wider, vaster, deeper illness in the human species as a whole and, for this reason, should be understood as an indication of humanity's lack of compassion or insight or maturity because we are all connected, and ultimately, if one of us is mentally ill, all of us must to some extent, on some deep, psychic level, share that fate. At least this is what I thought he said. But when I finally re-watched the video some time later, I realized that I'd gotten it all wrong—he actually was talking in circles. Still, I like the answer I *thought* he gave. In any case it remains the only explanation that makes any sense to me at all.

Mess

There's a predictable narrative arc to the dreams I used to have about my grandmother's house. It always opened the same way, for instance, with great news: I inherited the property. What a boon!

In this dream I used to drive straight down to New Jersey and roll up my sleeves. Not surprisingly, the house was always a mess: dirty, even disgusting. There were smells and sights to make me gag, but I had vision; I could see past the surface grime. And the thing of it was, now that the house was mine, I realized how badly I needed it! It was the answer—or would be, if only it weren't so dirty—to all of my problems. Free housing: who could possibly say no to that? Plus, we were having another baby, or David had just been transferred to New Jersey, or we really, really, really needed a kitchen garden, so badly it was a matter of life or death . . .

In these dreams, as in real life, the land all around Grandma Ellen's house was green and gentle. But in my dreams it was always summer and always sunlit, and sometimes there were woods covering a hill that wasn't actually there, and sometimes there was a lake or a mountain range. But the house was always the focal point because it offered such unheard-of potential. Maybe that's why I loved this dream so much. Or maybe I loved it because it allowed me to revisit my grandmother's house. In either case I looked forward to this recurring dream in much the same way I look forward to the first big snow of winter—as a magical occurrence. And I missed it when it evaded me for too long, as it has for the past several years.

But back when the dream recurred more reliably, it always unfolded the same way. In it I really threw myself into the cleaning. I would clean nonstop. But no matter how hard I cleaned, nothing ever changed. The dirt was just so deep. The dirt was just so dirty. So dirty I might work for hours scrubbing a single corner of one room, and yet the minute I turned around, it was only to discover exactly how enormous the task at hand really was, how much bigger than I. Slowly, I'd come to realize that I'd never finish. Of course, it didn't help that things kept changing. For example, as soon as I turned my back to my one little scrubbed square foot of floor or wall or what have you, it would instantly become dirty again. It would become *filthy.

But then, just as I was about to give up, something very good would always happen: I'd find the secret room. Or else sometimes it was a garden, and in the garden there'd be a secret shed, which would become the secret room. Sometimes the room was in the basement, and sometimes it was in the attic, and sometimes it was off the porch. Sometimes it was simply a matter of cutting a hole for a door and the room would be right there, where it always was. The point is, no matter how many times I dreamed this dream, it was always exhilarating when I discovered the secret room because this room was always very special. Sometimes it reminded me of Café Pamplona in Harvard Square, and sometimes it reminded me of England. Once it was on the seashore and Seamus Heaney lived next door. And for some reason this room—and only this room—I could actually clean, even if the rest of the house remained forever dirty. This room I could really spiff up. There were even times when I found more than a single room, when I stumbled across an entire suite of rooms, a suite so large that the original house could be used for nothing but dead storage.

Every time I dreamed this dream it was a little different but not much, at least until the last time, when things ended badly. This was five or six years ago—right around the time Isaac was born. I remember this: an ominous feeling pervaded the whole thing.

And during the long, exhausting process of cleaning, before I got to the secret room, I unplugged some kind of weird storage compartment. It was like a boarded-up closet, only high above my head, and as soon as I did this, something loud and toxic and airborne came streaming out of it, spraying out of it as if out of a gigantic aerosol can. I ducked, of course, but the sense I had in the dream was that I'd been badly damaged by this stuff, whatever it was, permanently damaged somewhere inside.

Metaphor

Little puzzles, little toys, things to play around with in your brain, things that stand for other things that with the right mental shift can turn into still other things or even back into the original things. A glossary, for example, can be seen as a messy and confused attempt at storytelling as well as the exact opposite—an insistence on orderliness and organization indicating an enormous level of control freakishness borne of a profound sense of impotence stemming from an exceptionally heavy pair of *boots.

Me Too

I was laid up in bed, sick with the flu. My mother was away on a business trip, so my father stepped in to take care of me. He did so with surprising tenderness. For example, at one point he brought me a bowl of homemade chicken soup, at another a plate of saltines and a glass of room-temperature ginger ale. At still another he put his hand—unfamiliar, soft, dry—on my forehead to check for a fever. Perhaps it was after this brief, slightly embarrassing contact that I asked him to shut the door. He paused in gathering up my used tissues to make a joke. It was a very good joke, perfectly timed and low-key, because my father's humor, when it does surface, is like that. In addition, the joke was in French, which is a language I was (and remain) deeply enamored of and one I assumed he didn't know the first thing about, but apparently he did, because his accent was pretty good.

"Je t'adore aussi," he said.

Mildew

My mother's apartment is about a quarter-mile away from the Charles River, which is why, from the bay window in her living room, you can just catch a gray glimpse of it, where it runs parallel to the Mass Turnpike for a while. It is near this window in her living room that something strange is happening to one of the walls: it's begun to belly out, and the paint, where the wall is bulging, has begun to sag so that it looks like wrinkled skin, and in the creases of these wrinkles there are fine black lines that appear to be mildew. My mother has a special term for what's happening to the wall, but I forget what it is. It's a technical term that she looked up on the internet, and she says that this technical thing that's happening to the wall in her living room is an indication of internal rot on account of excess moisture because of the proximity of the river and that her landlord knows perfectly well what's going on—he knows all about this technical thing—but he doesn't want to do anything to fix the situation because he wants her out because she complains about the neighbor's cats too much and also because she knows he's spying on her and because she refuses to turn a blind eye to numerous safety violations in the building overall. Eventually, she says, the wall will simply fall down, probably on top of her, and at that point her landlord will be under no legal obligation to house her. "He has it all planned out."

She's been complaining about this situation for more than a year, and although I have always doubted the veracity of her account, it's not until I come by to drop off a large, heavy box from Williams Sonoma that she had, for some reason, shipped to our address instead of her own, that I suspect she might really have a mildew problem because it's only then that I notice two small machines in her living room set directly under the bulge. These look like humidifiers with upturned spouts, aimed right at the wall, which is why I say: "Why do you have humidifiers under that bulge in the wall? Won't they just make it worse?" She says, "Those are de-humidifiers." And I say: "Oh. They look just like humidifiers. That's funny." And she says, "Well, I have things to do," and practically pushes me out the door.

Mindmap of My Mother's Childhood

Over the years all the stories my mother's told me about her childhood have come to take up a lot of room in my brain. By now they've all fused together to make an extended landscape, a kind of mental diorama. There are many people scattered throughout this map. My maternal grandfather is there, for instance, as is Grandma Ellen, and so, of course, is my mother when she was just a child, and all of her siblings are there too. There are several neighbors, some dogs, a few horses, a hermit, a handful of crickets, a bus full of kids, an unkind teacher, a cheerleading squad, and, of course, there's my father standing on line at a movie theater when he was still just a boy and he saw my mother for the first time . . . There are countless details glittering all over the place: tiny bottles of nail polish, larger ones of vodka, a wooden headboard, some raw potatoes, a slice of damp bread, an old yellow dress, a pair of red canvas sneakers, a white woven blanket, a box full of thin mints, a pot roast, an ironing board, a blue chair, a plate of raw beef, a fistful of candy . . . All of it's packed in my brain, serving, as far as I can tell, no purpose. I mean, what am I supposed to do with something like the story she once told me about the time Grandma Ellen showed her, when she was no more than eight or nine years old, one of her miscarriages floating in the toilet bowl?

"Come and see," she said (my mother told me—so long after the fact, sitting in one of her rooms in one of the psych wards in one of the hospitals in which I have visited her over the years). Grandma Ellen wept as she took her daughter by the hand and led her into the bathroom, where she pointed out the wasted miracle floating in the pink water: ten nearly microscopic toes, ten impossibly small fingers, the almost invisible slub of a nose—all bright red. She was crying, and my mother, kneeling by her side, was crying too, though I suspect for different reasons. My grandmother showed the miniature corpse to my mother, and decades later my mother showed the miniature corpse to me. I can see it that clearly.

Mired

M——, New Jersey, 1981

We're at Grandma Ellen's house, and the meal appears to be more or less over: a couple of empty plates, a few bottles of beer, an ashtray, some crusts of bread, are all that's left on the table. My mother's talking to Aunt Inga, leaning over her in a domineering way (although it occurs to me that maybe it only looks like this— maybe she's just getting up from the table). Aunt Elsa, chewing something and glancing sidelong at her sisters, is apparently riding some great, barely controlled wave of annoyance. Emily, Uncle Lucas's girlfriend, a woman I adored, is dancing into the room with a cup of coffee in her hand. (Why is it that Emily dancing into the room with a cup of coffee in her hand is so real to me? Even the precise shade of milk in that coffee seems absolute.) Mrs. Anders, my grandmother's neighbor, in brown pants, a blonde wig, and bright shaggy pink slippers, is bouncing somebody's baby on her knee. And I'm there too, sitting in a blue-and-white lawn chair, reaching a hand across the table. My head is tilted in the direction of Emily as I watch her dance into my memory.

All of these people are oriented toward the table, even if not seated at it. Only my father, in the unfocused foreground, sits alone and angled away from the rest of us. He's staring off, out of the frame of the photograph, through the semi-opaque plastic covering of the window in my grandmother's kitchen. He's heavy here, though not as heavy as he will eventually become. In one hand he holds a glass. It's almost empty.

Mishap

The reason I think my mother hasn't given up her license voluntarily, as she has always maintained, but has had it revoked is because I know something she doesn't know I know: she had an accident right before she decided to *opt out*. I know about this accident because David saw it, only she doesn't know he saw it. This was maybe a year and a half ago. David called me from the street sounding breathless and furtive. Nothing at all like he usually sounds.

"God, I hope she can't see me."

"Who?"

"Your mother!"

"Where are you?"

"I'm walking. I don't think she sees me. I feel so guilty. The cops are there."

I told him to slow down and start from the beginning, so he took a deep breath and explained that he'd been outside getting lunch in the neighborhood where he works, and had been waiting to cross the street at the corner of a large intersection where five roads converge when he heard someone lean hard on their horn.

"There was this huge BANG! At first I thought, what kind of idiot would do that? because there was a car that had tried to cut across two lanes of traffic. They wanted to make a right-hand turn, so they just cut across as soon as the light was green. But then I looked closer and I thought, Oh my god, that's Linda."

"It was my mother?"

"Yes! For a second I thought I was seeing things, but it's definitely her. It's her car, the old gray Honda, and I could see her in the driver's seat. She looked all nervous and worried. God, I have this sick feeling in my stomach. Probably I should have stayed and helped. The other driver was totally pissed off, of course. There was all this smoke. Oh my god, I feel so guilty. She's probably still there."

"Are you a hundred percent sure it's her?"

"Positive."

"What did you do?"

"I just turned around. Now I'm walking in the other direction."

This, I knew, was probably smart. Probably sensible. Because to get embroiled in my mother's problems is to waste many, many hours, and there's never any payoff, even for her. It's also very likely what I would have done had I been in my husband's shoes, standing on that corner. But to tell the truth, I'm not at all sure I've ever forgiven him for it.

Modest Split Ranch

It was obvious from the start that we couldn't afford it—a modest split ranch ten minutes away from the yellow stucco house. But it was a nice place, in a nice neighborhood, and my mother really threw herself into it. First, she had the whole thing painted pale gray. Then she had a pine fence erected around the yard. Then she had the front hall floor covered with dark slate and the kitchen counters covered with delicate blue tiles. She sewed curtains and chair cushions, and every day after work, weather permitting, she took a gin and tonic outside to tend her flower garden in the front yard. There, over the course of the three years we lived in that house, she planted phlox and aster and lily of the valley, Japanese iris, French iris, tulips, daffodils, lilacs, rose of Sharon, allium, hydrangea, bleeding hearts, and a stand of bright pink peonies.

Morale

On the first day of my freshman year of high school, I invited a classmate over after school. My mother was home for some reason that day, and in an unusual display of domestic busyness, she decided to bake us some chocolate chip cookies. Liz, who was also new to the town that year and also a freshman, wore small pearls in her ears and had a fancy way of pronouncing certain words. For instance, she said "litrah-lee" rather than "literally." This seemed to put my mother on guard because I noticed that pretty soon, she, too, started talking funny.

Liz and I sat at the kitchen table discussing our first day of high school. Our conversation was a bit stilted because my mother was just a few feet away, making the cookies. We could have gone down the hall to my room, but I didn't want Liz to see it. I considered it an embarrassment, with its garish metallic wallpaper and bent-up Venetian blinds and bizarrely textured wall-to-wall carpeting with a rust-colored stain over half of it.

"It's just an ordinary room," I told her. "But it doesn't feel like me yet. I'd rather stay here."

"Please?" said Liz. "I just want a peek."

"Let's just sit in the kitchen."

"Really, it's no big deal," she said. And then she jumped up to trot down the hallway in her designer jeans and cashmere sweater. "I'll be right back!"

In the kitchen, waiting for her return, my mother and I said nothing to each other, although she did crank out a fairly good imitation of Liz, silently wiggling her shoulders and flipping her hair.

When she returned, Liz said: "It's not so bad. You shouldn't feel ashamed." And my mother, still working on the cookies, said, "She's not ashamed!" Then she tossed an eggshell over her shoulder. It landed on the floor with a surreal little splat. "She's not ashamed of anything!"

Mormor

A Swedish compound noun usually defined as "mother's mother" (although I think a stricter translation might be closer to "mom-mom"), *Mormor* is what my mother asked we teach Isabella to call her after she was born. I liked the idea on account of my own fixation with all things Swedish, but for my kids I suspect Mormor is closer to an abstract concept than a real name indicating an actual person (much like the name Pop was to me when I was young), since they so rarely see my mother at this point. Isaac in particular understands her, I think, almost as a kind of living ghost, a fast and jumbled voice at the other end of the telephone, a fixture of confusion and loss in his mother's mind perhaps best identified as a facial expression—an etched-in disappointment that I often catch, myself, in the bathroom mirror, one that I try to erase with the assiduous application of expensive creams and to accept with a devoted, some might even say obsessive, yoga practice.

Morose

He could shut out the world and just sit there, turned inward, a miser of regret tallying his grievances. Although he never said so, it seemed obvious that my father's biggest regret must have been getting my mother pregnant when he was just nineteen years old, and so, by extension (according to my calculations), his biggest regret was *me*.

I remember a period of weeks—I was fourteen, fifteen—when his silence and stillness were at their most extreme. It was a dark time: we were going bankrupt. During these weeks my father took to sitting in a velvet-covered armchair in his study for hours on end, whole days even, on the weekends, staring into the vague middle distance, refusing to speak. I fought with my mother almost every day at that point, but I never confronted my father (the occasional throwing of things notwithstanding). In fact, we barely spoke. But his habit of slumping in that chair and exuding all that funky black energy really bothered me, and one day as I walked past him I hissed, under my breath, "I don't know why he has to be so goddamned morose!" I said it like that, in the third person, but he didn't bat an eyelash. It was only my mother, who happened to be around the corner, in the kitchen, who reacted.

"That's it!" she said, grabbing my arm. "That's it! That's *exactly* the right word! I've been trying to think of it for *years*!"

Muck

R——, New Jersey, 1982

She looks a little like Michael Jackson's wacky white sister in this picture. She's got gloves on, for one thing—long white rubber gloves that reach all the way to her elbows. Also, a white oxford shirt buttoned up to the neck. Her nose is dwarfed by a pair of enormous sunglasses, while her hair, which is apparently in the awkward stages of an out-growing perm, lies flat at the crown of her head but gets fluffier and fluffier as it descends past her shoulders. She's in the backyard, picking a path through some kind of muck, arms raised for balance. So, yes, she looks wacky, but she also looks happy because my mother truly loves cleaning, and whatever it is she's fumigating or sterilizing or scouring or scraping out there in our yard seems to be an especially rewarding challenge.

Munchausen Syndrome

To roughly paraphrase the Mayo Clinic website, Munchausen syndrome is a serious mental disorder in which a deep need for attention results in the pretense (or even in the artificial manufacturing) of illness. A person with Munchausen syndrome may invent symptoms, push for high-risk operations, or try to rig laboratory test results in order to win sympathy and concern. It is notoriously difficult to treat people afflicted by the syndrome as they go to such great lengths in order to avoid discovery of their deception. It should be noted that Munchausen syndrome is not the same as inventing medical problems for practical benefit (such as getting out of work or winning a lawsuit), nor is it related to hypochondria. Symptoms may include (but are not limited to): dramatic stories about numerous medical problems; frequent hospitalizations; vague or inconsistent symptoms; conditions that get worse for no apparent reason; eagerness to undergo testing or surgery; extensive knowledge of medical terminology and diseases; seeking treatment from many different doctors or hospitals; having few visitors when hospitalized; reluctance to allow health professionals to talk to family or friends; arguing with hospital staff; and recurrent requests for pain relievers or other medications. People with Munchausen syndrome have been known to falsify their medical histories, manipulate medical instruments in order to skew results, tamper with laboratory tests, fake symptoms, injure or sicken themselves in inventive ways, take medications with effects that mimic diseases, and repeatedly interfere with the natural healing process.

Mute

Like clockwork, I used to get a painful ear infection right around Christmas. When this happened, my mother would fill the afflicted ear (usually the left) with hydrogen peroxide, then dig around in the bubbling liquid with a bobby pin, searching for pieces of wax. These treatments lasted about half an hour and did nothing to relieve my pain or resolve the infection, which meant that eventually my parents would take me to the doctor, who would prescribe antibiotics, and, god, how I loved those antibiotics. The sweet, spreading relief of them.

Sophomore year of high school I had an especially bad earache, but because we were so tight on money, I didn't go to the doctor for a long time. Instead, I received many bobby pin treatments, one after another, several days in a row. At a certain point the pain took me somewhere else—inside myself but far away—and I stopped talking.

When we finally did go to the doctor, I saw someone new—a man who must have been covering for my regular pediatrician. In the examination room the doctor told me that my eardrum had been perforated but not completely torn. It would heal eventually. He explained that sometimes these things happened when an infection goes on for too long—the pressure builds, and the eardrum bursts. He said I'd have some trouble hearing for a while, but he could give me pills that would at least stop the pain. Then he asked why it had taken us so long to come in. My mother explained, in the half-joking tone she often used when complaining about me to other adults, that I was a bit of a whiner and that this made it hard for her to know when I was really in pain or when I was just being a baby. She also mentioned that she had been working on the situation with her hydrogen peroxide–bobby pin method. And as she spoke, I noticed that she faltered. I also noticed something on the doctor's face and on his assistant's face too, which made me wonder if my mother hadn't been wrong about the bobby pins and about the pain and about my whining. I tried to see her then as the two of them seemed to be seeing her, and for the first time in my life, I caught a glimpse of a nervous, somewhat strange woman.

Muzak

Once I threw an apple at my father. We were all getting into the car—Tracy, my father, and I—on a Sunday morning, about to drive to the bakery. It was midwinter and very cold outside, ice everywhere. I was eating an apple—a green one. My father didn't do anything to prompt my action, just got into the car. But he was slow and fat, and I think that might have been what upset me. I don't know why, it just made me so mad. I threw the apple—hard—and it got stuck in the puffy folds of his down coat. Without saying a word, he examined the fruit where it had landed in the soft ridges of his sleeve, plucked it out, and dropped it onto the icy driveway before shutting the door, starting the engine, and pulling away. We drove to the bakery then, as we always did—with the radio on low. And once we got there, we bought the usual things: a pecan ring, a loaf of rye bread, a loaf of sourdough, a half-dozen cupcakes.

My Room

Spurred by the awkward encounter with my classmate Liz, my mother spent more money redecorating my bedroom than she did on any other part of the house. Whenever she showed someone my room, she was careful to point out the various design features, such as the two subtly different wallpapers and how they tied in with the carpet or the frilly lace pillowcases she'd sewn herself and the exorbitantly expensive drapes she'd had made. A symphony of blues and greens and creams, crowded with faux antique furniture and two twin beds topped by two handmade lace coverlets and masses of pillows that had to be carefully "carelessly" arranged every morning, my room was devoid of anything even tenuously connected to my own ideas of beauty or comfort. Even my telephone was a faux antique, impossible to hold.

Just down the hall, Tracy's room seemed to exist on another plane entirely. "That's Tracy's room," my mother would say when giving family and friends the grand tour. Often she didn't even open the door.

The wallpaper in Tracy's room was the same stuff that had come with the house: a beige plasticky corduroy. There were posters taped to her walls, and she had a sprawling stereo system, which I wasn't allowed to have in my own room because black, bulky machinery would have clashed with everything else. Tracy's room smelled like Cheetos and spilled chocolate milkshakes and broken pens' leaking ink and my sister's sleepy body. It felt private, and I liked it a thousand times better than my own room, which is why, whenever she stayed over at a friend's house, my sister let me sleep in her room. That's where I was the night my mother accused me of being with a boy. She banged open the door to Tracy's room and stood there, wearing a long white night gown and making crazy eyes. Her hair was a wreck around her face and for the first time in my life, I thought, "She's insane."

"All right!" she shouted. "Where is he?"

"Where's who?"

"I heard you in here, the bedsprings, where is he?" She stomped over to the closet and looked inside it.

"I don't know what you're talking about," I said. "You're crazy."

We fought then, about whether or not she was crazy. Finally, I said, "Why don't you check under the bed?"

She cocked her head. "You think you're so smart, don't you?" Then she marched over to the bed, dropped to her knees, and lifted the dust ruffle. When she didn't find anyone there, she said: "I don't know how you did it, Kimberli, but you'd better be careful. I'll catch you next time."

As she was leaving, I said, "You're nuts," but so softly she didn't catch it.

"What was that?"

"Nothing."

"It had better be."

After she was gone, I waited for my heart to stop hammering. Then, one centimeter at a time, I rearranged my limbs on my sister's soft, lumpy mattress. It took forever, but finally, with my arms crossed over my chest and my legs stretched out straight, I willed myself back to sleep.

Mystery

R——, New Jersey, 1983

The street is shiny with snowmelt, the power line hanging over my father's head encrusted with ice. Where it hasn't been shoveled or plowed, the snow stands about three feet deep and is dingy near the road.

Although he's in his midthirties, overweight, and bundled in a puffy blue parka, there's a boyish jauntiness to the way he negotiates the slush on our front walk as he makes his way from the front door to the car in the driveway. This sense of jauntiness is probably on account of his neck, which is exposed and seems thin and therefore vulnerable and therefore young. Or maybe it's on account of the way he's high-stepping it, holding both arms slightly out to his sides, grasping one glove in each hand, carefully picking a path through the icy gray mousse in his big black boots.

≈≈≈

If I were a playwright, I'd write plays with interesting special effects. For instance, if I were to write a play about a household in which generalized group depression constituted, as it did in my home when I was growing up, the usual atmosphere, I would have the characters slug around on their knees, not walking upright. And I would have them speak through some kind of kazoo-like device so that their voices were distorted and difficult to understand but also sadly comical. I would include directions for clouds to float across the stage while the characters spoke in more or less unintelligible tones to one another, and these clouds of strange colors—colors indicating some kind of disease or pollution: brown, acid pink, greenish yellow—would float above and between them. Sometimes the characters would flop down, no matter where they were—on the kitchen counter perhaps or under a table, on the front stoop of the house, or at a schoolroom desk, maybe even over the shoulder of a disinterested boss—they would just flop down (as I so often flopped down on my bed) and lie there with their eyes open, staring, clearly at something, but exactly what would be unknown, even to them. Every character in this depressed household, if I were to write such a play, would also own an exceptionally heavy pair of boots—large, black, extremely bulky, and difficult to lace up. And every morning each one of these characters would spend a long time getting themselves into these boots as well as some additional time inserting the kazoo-like distortion devices into their own mouths. Yes, if I were a playwright, I would include stage directions like these. But I am not a playwright. I am a glossator.

N

Nada

Negative adjectives are popular vehicles for some of the most common forms of verbal abuse. For example, "You are *miserable*" or "You are *pathetic*" or "What are you—*retarded?*" Such adjectives are frequently followed by derogatory nouns, resulting in constructions like: "You spoiled little brat" or "You disgusting little slut." For some reason diminutives are employed with great relish by verbal abusers, probably because the point, when all is said and done, is belittlement, reduction, even a form of erasure.

However popular they may be, it should be kept in mind that adjectives and derogatory nouns are but two of the most basic tools at the disposal of a truly inspired verbal abuser. Indeed, there are times when the most elemental declarative statements (e.g., "You look fine") strike deepest—though the effect of such statements, of course, depends directly on irony, sarcasm, and/or the slick dynamics of faint praise. For an example of this last tricky maneuver, consider the compliment my mother once paid me when I was sixteen years old: "There is at least," she said, "one positive thing I can say about you—you always have a nice toothbrush."

Naive

Thirty years ago she went to a famous endodontist to get treatment for an abscess. As this man was operating on her molar, he discovered several strange objects stuck deep under the gumline. These included the broken tip of a pink plastic toothpick, a tightly curled metal shaving, and two or three extremely small balls of what appeared to be some type of super-absorbent fiber. I know because my mother saved all these things in a tiny green caper bottle. This bottle, a fixture of my childhood, is still hanging around—the last time I saw it, it was sitting on a little glass shelf in her bathroom, next to some potpourri.

You might wonder how this odd, not to say eerie, assortment of miniature objects could have possibly wound up deep under the gumline of one of my mother's molars. But if you were to address this question directly to her, as the famous endodontist did some thirty years ago, she would tell you (as she told him, as she has since told me) that another dentist put them there. If you were at that point to express even the gentlest hint of doubt regarding this explanation, she would likely respond with a look of withering pity because dentists, in my mother's book, are all, to a man, *patently* evil, and anyone who doesn't understand this is hopelessly naive. Case in point: it was that very endodontist—the world-famous one—who pierced her maxillary sinus during that very treatment. And this was not a mistake but *an act of pure aggression.* On top of this, that operation, with its malicious piercing, is the *root cause* of the infection that has over these past three decades spread to the *deepest fibers* of her body, evolving into a *deadly systemic bacterial infection* that will ultimately, she often assures me, kill her. It's only a matter of time.

Names

The only presence I've ever experienced in a ghostlike capacity is that of my mother's mother. I might have preferred a visit from my father's mother, but I've never received one of those. Grandma Ellen's visit occurred in a dream, which I know makes it sound like it was just a dream, but there was something about the encounter that was more saturated, more substantial than that. How can I explain? I heard her voice, for one thing—I mean her actual voice, an embodied thing, full of vibration and feeling, a real physical presence. When she was alive, my grandmother's voice was remarkable for being simultaneously hoarse and musical. I'd

forgotten that odd combination, a sort of wheezy lilting punctu-
ated by violent spells of coughing, but it all came back to me in
this dream as I was talking—listening mostly—to my grandmother
over a very large, old-fashioned telephone set.

I'm not prone to mystical thoughts, so of course I've pondered
how a woman who's been dead for decades could possibly possess
a voice. After all, a voice is the product of a specific physical body,
shaped by real tissues—the tongue, the throat, the teeth, the lips,
and many of the facial muscles. It is fed by the lungs, which were,
in my grandmother's case, deeply scarred, supported by the dia-
phragm, and amplified by the hollows in the skull. All of which
suggests that no matter how convincing my dream may have been,
it was not really my grandmother's voice I heard during it but my
own vivid imagining of that voice. And yet in all honesty, when I
think of that dream and the things my grandmother said, I feel
certain that it really was her, some version of her, talking to me.
Yes, deep down, I can't help but believe that something—let's call it
my grandmother's spirit—actually managed to organize itself and
move through some kind of time or space hole in order to visit me.

The dream, her visit, took place at the yoga studio I go to every
morning. I was sitting in the small reception area, wearing my
old peacoat (the one I wore when I was pregnant with Isabella),
holding my yoga mat. It was much busier than it is in reality at the
hour I normally arrive (before dawn), and for some reason I felt
it necessary to avoid eye contact with all the other people in the
room, which left me with little to do but study the many rubber
tree plants arranged randomly throughout the space. Despite all
the people milling about, things were more or less quiet until, at
a certain point, the phone jumped to life—a strident trill. The
woman sitting behind the reception desk picked up the heavy,
old-fashioned receiver but was clearly reluctant to speak into it,
as if she thought it might be coated with germs. Nevertheless, she
somehow deduced that the call was for me and held the bulbous,
shiny thing, attached to a long and intricately tangled cord, in
my direction.

"Hi, honey. It's Grandma," said the voice at the other end of the line—a voice that, as I've already described, was rich with life. It was also, I noticed right away, nervous. Almost shyly, my grandmother told me that she wanted to read me something she'd written. I have always been deeply curious about the novels she composed in secret during the last years of her life, and so I encouraged her to go on, thinking that maybe I'd gain some insight into whatever those lost manuscripts might have contained.

She started reciting a predictably creepy narrative (I have not yet perhaps mentioned this, but my grandmother loved scary stories and told them with gusto). It began in the third person but quickly transitioned to the first and concerned a young woman who had traveled to Portugal, where somebody slit her throat, as a result of which, went the gist of things, she was drained of all promise. I could, of course, piece this puzzle together: my grandmother was the girl, and the man who slit her throat was her husband—his identity made clear by the country of Portugal, since my grandfather sailed for many years with the merchant marines of that country. I was silent for a while as I absorbed the import of this story.

"Are you still there?" asked my grandmother. I assured her I was, and she continued reading, only now she spoke of her garden and all the flowers that she'd grown in it when she was still alive, when she had been, in fact, an inspired although somewhat haphazard gardener. Her words at this point began to feel like a set of instructions gravely delivered, as if she had sought me out all these years after her death simply in order to impart some gardening advice, which struck me as a bit frivolous considering the many pressing mysteries that surround my mother's early life and my grandmother's early life and before that, even, the early lives of the Aunts . . . I was trying to come up with a polite way of interrupting her so that I might bring the conversation around to these much more important topics when I realized she was speaking of individual roses and lilac blooms that she'd grown in her garden, single flowers recalled with great affection.

"If they were special, if they were beautiful," she explained in her strangely tremulous voice, "it's because I named each and every one of them: Thor, Inga, Linda, Becky, Nils, Elsa, Lucas—" In this way she listed out the names of all seven of her children. She was, of course, speaking in code by this point, but I understood it, and I knew that what she was really telling me wasn't that I should name all the flowers in my own garden (although the thought did, fleetingly, cross my mind) but that she had tried her best as a mother and had loved her children in ways I could never hope to fathom.

It's astonishing really how dreams sometimes manage to unlock such long chains of emotional logic in us, miles of it, but that's exactly what happened when my grandmother listed out each tulip and lily and, at one point, for some reason, even a potato by its individual name. As she did so, I understood that all the strange and unhealthy behaviors she'd exhibited during her lifetime— which I have always considered, ever since I was old enough to make such judgments, selfish and essentially perverse—weren't, in the final analysis, so much a series of choices as a set of limitations.

"Do you understand what I'm saying?" she asked me finally, her voice more unsteady than ever, and I thought very carefully in my dream about how to answer her. On the one hand, I felt I should give my grandmother no quarter because for most of my life I have blamed her for not protecting my mother from my grandfather and in this way I have considered her guilty of aiding in the destruction of whatever essential thing my mother has always, for as long as I've known her, been missing. I could almost feel my grandmother's anxiety pulsing on the other end of the line as I considered how much of an effort she must have gone through to arrange a call like this. I thought about all the wounded things that seemed to live in her voice and about how old I was now and about how, when I was much younger, she had been so much more than just a voice, so much more than just part of a story. Strange, messy, spiteful, intelligent, masochistic, and probably mentally ill— somebody who made good pot roast and drank gallons of tea and wrote novels in secret and had a special understanding of flowering perennials. And for some reason, in my sleep, I suddenly felt incredibly light. It was a tremendous relief—as if something in me had let go. And finally I was able to answer her. "Yes, Grandma," I said, "I think I know what you're saying."

Narcissistic Personality Disorder

Of all the labels that doctors have given to what's wrong with my mother, the only one that ever struck a chord for me is Narcissistic personality disorder. This is the only one, in any case, that begins to explain the extreme hermeticism that defined my childhood, that explains, even now, my state of mind when I find myself in the same room or even just on the phone with her. Wars might start or end, children might be, have been, conceived and born, people tortured, buildings razed, presidents elected, but speaking to my mother, you'd never know any of it. 9/11 came and went, and her only comment, when the phone lines finally cleared, was: "Oh, Kimmy, I've had such a terrible day."

Nasty

I'm digging around in my baking cupboard, trying to remember what's the best way to set a blackberry pie—with cornstarch or flour? tapioca? gelatin?—when my mother taps on our screen door. Bad timing. It's August, and I'm packing up kitchen supplies to go on vacation for two weeks on a small island in Maine, where we try to go every summer. This time of year there are blackberries everywhere up there.

"You're not going to believe this," she says as I step out onto the porch. "But he did it. The nasty son of a bitch finally did what they wanted him to do all along."

"Which son of a bitch?"

"He's totally hooked into DMH. You realize that, right? It was obvious from *day one*. Honey, I don't want to nag you, but I think you should have that looked at." She touches a mole on my cheek. "It's getting bigger."

"Mom, what are you talking about?"

"Ha!"

My mother has a special way of making this noise in times of great crisis. Sort of barky. Her neck strains in a way that makes it looks extra skinny. I think she's going for tough, but she just looks scared. "Jerry kicked me out. As if I didn't know *that* was coming!"

"You got evicted?"

She nods in a super huge way, like the absurdity of it all is just too much, then describes the entire humiliating scene to me. It's all extremely déjà vu since she's been evicted three times before, and yet you wouldn't know it, judging from the tones of shock and outrage woven though her description of the moving truck, the police escort, the curious neighbors, the taciturn landlord, and the three social workers who kept asking her (*"as if* they really cared, *as if* they actually gave a flying fuck"*) what she planned to do next. She is particularly annoyed by the social workers and finds significance in the fact that there were three of them, all pushing cards and telephone numbers and addresses at her, because she considers their concern, their insistence that she stay at a shelter, nothing but a poorly veiled attempt to get her one step closer to a locked ward.

"But where are you going to go?" I ask, trying not to let my eyes dart toward our bags and suitcases, which are already lined up on the porch for our departure tomorrow morning and which are overflowing with beach towels, board games, swimming noodles, knitting projects, stuffed animals, sun hats, fishing rods, and a waffle iron, all ready to be loaded into our car.

"I don't *know*," says my mother, letting her own eyes land quite pointedly on our bags. "I really don't know. I guess I'll just have to stay at a B&B."

I say I guess so, and she asks if she can leave a few things on our porch while she gathers her thoughts and comes up with a plan—just a few things she doesn't want to put into storage but that are too bulky to carry around.

"Everything's still in the cab," she says. "The cabbie is probably totally pissed at me by now. He already thinks I'm trouble. Says I'm giving him *agita* and he should charge me double. He definitely won't help me bring down my bags." This clearly is a hint, but I just raise my eyebrows. Actually, I am seething. But I tell myself I'm just raising my eyebrows. I watch as my mother scurries back up the path to the street, looking small and hunted, and then I go inside to finish packing.

It takes a while for her to lug everything down. Then she hangs around on our porch, arranging and rearranging the two enormous duffel bags, a suitcase, and three cardboard boxes stuffed with a mixture of paperwork and cleaning supplies, but I don't talk to her again, just stay inside doing the dishes, folding towels, and packing up a bunch of dried goods to take to Maine. When the kids come home, I can hear them talking with her. She laughs, and they politely but quietly laugh with her. When they come inside, Isabella asks me what's going on with *Mormor*. I explain that she's been evicted, then I explain to Isaac what the word *evicted* means. I tell them not to worry because there's nothing we can do about it. I say this kind of trouble, this kind of discombobulation, is just part of my mother's sickness, which is why she gets into situations like this so often. Isabella gives me a lopsided smile and a hug.

"I'm sorry, Mama," she says. I hug her briefly back and say, "Thanks, sweetie," but it sounds clipped. It's only when David comes home from work and I tell him about what's happened, tell him why all my mother's junk is out on our porch, that a bunch of wet, crappy little tears fall out of my eyes. And it's only when my husband gives me a hug that I allow myself to say something about how she might pull herself together, maybe, this time, and David says, "Shh."

Standing limply in his arms, I'm quiet for a minute before I say something even more hopeful, even more hypothetical, even more imaginative, about how my mother might really surprise us this time, might actually, finally, maybe, do something really interesting, something that would shock us all, like, who knows, you never know, it's impossible to say, become a *florist* or get a boyfriend or go back to school.

Nearly Adult

Our family was changing quickly, falling apart. I'd just turned seventeen when we lost the split ranch. I'd recently gotten kicked out of the boarding school my parents had sent me to for my junior year of high school, during which time I'd become completely unmoored—gouging my own skin, throwing up half my meals, smoking unfiltered cigarettes, skipping classes, and sneaking off campus several times a week. Not surprisingly, I got expelled, or, as the administration politely put it, "uninvited" for my senior year. When I came back home, there was no home—at least not the one I'd left.

After the bank repossessed our house, my mother moved into a two-bedroom duplex three towns closer to New York City. She and my father had already started divorce proceedings. Officially, he lived mostly in South Jersey, where he worked, but on the weekends he often stayed with us in the new apartment, sleeping on the foldout couch in the living room, which only added to the confusion. By this point my mother was taking all kinds of pills—pills for the pain in her teeth, pills for the pain in her neck, pills for the pain in her head, pills for the pain in her jaw—and my father's drinking, although still invisible to me, was, as we would soon discover, worse than it had ever been.

College, adulthood, freedom—these things were so close I could taste them, but they weren't quite mine, not yet. I knew all I had to do was be patient. Tracy wanted out too, of course, but she had longer to wait, and her philosophy seemed to be to just hunker down. For example, she stopped talking except when strictly necessary and slept in her clothes. She slept, in fact, in her boots.

Nice and Lean and Lanky

Because she was always late picking me up, by the time I was a senior in high school, I'd adopted the habit of adding a half-hour to whatever plan my mother and I had made, and still I often had to wait five, ten, fifteen minutes before she showed up. Only once that I can remember was I late to meet her using this method. It was a Friday afternoon, and we'd planned to meet in the small parking lot at the back of the high school I attended that year. When I came out of the heavy double doors, I found her parked about thirty feet away. I waved at her and noticed her face soften as an expression of relief came over her features. I thought this might have been because she'd been worried about my being late, but when I climbed into the passenger seat, she said: "Oh, my god, thank *god* it's you. I was so confused. I mean I was completely *mystified*! A little while ago a girl came out of those same doors, and I thought: 'Wow, I didn't realize Kimberli was so *dumpy*! I thought she had *style*!' But then the girl kept on walking, and I realized it wasn't you. Then *another* girl came out of those doors, and I thought: 'My god, I didn't know Kimberli was so *chunky* and *ungraceful*! I thought she was nice and lean and lanky!' But then that girl kept on walking, and I realized it wasn't you either! Then finally *you* came out of those doors, and I was like: 'There she is! That's my Kimmy—*long like a cool drink of water*.' And I was so relieved!"

Nicknacks

E——, New Jersey, 1984

Someone's lying on the couch in the new apartment. This could be any one of us—it's impossible to say because whoever it is has thrown an afghan over their head and upper body. Only the legs are partially visible, clad in jeans, and the feet in black socks. The whole scene is drenched with silent hysteria. At least this is how I see it now. The couch is hideous—a big, tufted, suburbo-colonial thing with huge sprays of mint- and salmon-colored peonies on the upholstery. There's an empty vase on the floor propping up a framed charcoal drawing of my mother. On the end table is a school portrait of Tracy at about thirteen. Her hair is flipped back in intricate layers, her teeth gray and complicated-looking with braces. There's a chessboard on the coffee table and a few nicknacks: a tiny malachite turtle, a hotel ashtray, and the candle chimes we took out at Christmastime. The idea for these was that the heat from four small candles would send a tiny brass angel spinning over a set of bells. With the tip of his trumpet, the angel would strike each of the bells one at a time and make a steady tinkling sound until the candles burned down.

Niche

Before we leave for Maine, I spend some time thinking about where to hide our spare key. Normally, we put it in with the clothespins, in a small wooden box that we keep on the steps of our porch. I've always considered this a fairly clever hiding spot, but suddenly it seems completely stupid. Any idiot who really wanted to find our key would discover it in about five minutes. No, this time I want to find a really, really good hiding place.

"What are you so worried about?" David asks when he finds me hunting around the yard. "We have to get going, or we'll hit a ton of traffic and miss our ferry. You don't actually think she'll try to get into our place when we're gone, do you?" But then, before I have a chance to answer, he makes a *hmm* sound and starts helping me look.

"It has to be a really, really good place!" I tell him as we hike the perimeter of our yard.

It takes a while, but eventually David spots a small chink in the mortar of the foundation of the house: a tiny crack between two gray fieldstones. I stuff the key into the crack, then stuff the crack with some pebbles so that it's practically invisible. Then I lean an old folding chair against the wall, and then, just to be on the safe side, I stack some tomato cages in front of the chair. Finally, in the interest of thoroughness, I drag a potted impatiens over to the tomato cages and wedge it casually between their tines.

Night Party

E——, New Jersey, 1984

Extraordinary pallor. Layered "shag" haircuts. Tracy and I sit at the kitchen table, slouched to the point of seeming only semisolid. We're staring at a small birthday cake—my birthday cake.

I'm turning eighteen. It seems I've just blown out the candles, and for some reason my sister and I both appear to find this very amusing—but not too amusing. We're laughing yet at the same time we look as if we might just fall face-first onto the tabletop and start snoring. We wear pajama-y clothes—Tracy an old T-shirt and the Brooks Brothers robe the two of us fought over for years, me a loose white button-down shirt and an inside-out sweater haphazardly thrown over my shoulders. Our faces are sleepy, our eyes half-closed behind the drooping plastic frames of our glasses. It looks as if we both are either very sick or someone has woken us up at three in the morning for birthday cake. I feel certain that five years ago I would have been able to tell you the story behind this photo. The memory's no longer there, but I know (what do you call the memory of a memory?) that it once was.

Nimble

I didn't even know we owned a baseball bat, but suddenly there it was, slicing through the air at the back of my neck. Certain elements from that instant remain in focus with bizarre clarity, as if the room had suddenly opened up in a 360-degree visual sweep so that even to this day I remember the dictionary on its intricately carved wooden stand, the paneled closet door with its dull brass knob imprinted with an art deco design, the forest-green wall-to-wall carpeting, and the brightly colored flowers and interlacing vines on the wallpaper.

I ran in a circuit through the living room, with its tufted couch, its glass-topped coffee table, its parquet floor and foldout daybed, into the dining room, which was cool and dark and which contained, I believe, my father, who seemed to be reading a newspaper by the dim light of the north-facing windows, then I swept back into the front hall and scrambled upstairs, taking the steps two at a time.

As I ran, I could hear the bat behind me banging against things—banisters, doorjambs, it was hard to tell. In the bedroom I shared with Tracy, I hopped on top of my mattress, and then I hopped on top of Tracy's, and then, as my mother filled the doorway, I slipped under her raised arms and ran back downstairs. And the whole time I was running, I was thinking about logistics. For instance, I considered the weather: it was a hot summer day. I also thought about the fact that I had no money. I thought about the fact that I was wearing an old pair of jeans with just a couple dollars in one pocket, and I knew that a couple of dollars wasn't going to get me anywhere. My father, however, almost certainly had money in his wallet, and his wallet was almost certainly in his jacket, and his jacket, I knew, was downstairs in the armoire near the front stairs. As soon I'd put these elements together in my adrenaline-drenched brain, I had something like a plan, so once I was back downstairs (my mother still after me, though lagging), I stopped briefly at the armoire, where I dug around in my father's wallet and extracted sixty-eight dollars. Then I raced out of the building and onto the street.

I felt nauseated but kept running, taking only quiet side streets because I was worried that my mother might jump in her car and follow me. Eventually, I made it to the bus stop, where I bought a one-way ticket to New York City.

I was about to make a string of very poor decisions, but at the time I had no idea of this. At the time I was only thinking about how I'd just succeeded in getting away from my mother, and that made me feel invincible. I felt nimble and young.

Once I got to the city, I called everyone I knew, which amounted to four people. None of them were home. My best friend at the time was a girl named Annie, whose parents were divorced and whose mother lived on West 74th Street. Annie often spent weekends with her mother, so I went to the Upper West Side, thinking I'd call every hour or so until one of them came home. But nobody picked up that night. Nobody picked up at the home of an ex-boyfriend either, and nobody picked up at the apartment of a boy with a cleft lip whom I'd met just a month earlier on Block Island. Even the shrink I'd seen for a while after I'd gotten kicked out of boarding school didn't pick up.

I bought two hot dogs and an orange juice at Gray's Papaya, then walked around. At some point I wandered into a trendy clothing shop. I was only looking to kill time, so I tried on things I couldn't possibly afford, but the owner didn't seem to mind. In fact, when I told him I was stranded in the city and didn't know what to do with myself and that I was only there because I had no place else to go, he said that I could try on as many things as I liked for as long as I wanted. I can't remember his name, only that he was passingly handsome and had an accent. He might have been from Morocco, but that's a fairly wild guess at this point. He wasn't tall, and he wasn't short; he wasn't thin or fat; he wasn't pale or dark. His hair, though, was pitch-black and so richly oiled that it gleamed under the track lights. He smoked unfiltered Gitanes and had very long eyelashes, and it was these, I believe, that contributed to the impression that he was smiling even when he wasn't.

I tried on many things that night, especially as it had started to rain, so I couldn't walk around outside anymore. The man with the long eyelashes let me use his telephone, but still no one picked up at Annie's or at my ex-boyfriend's or at the home of the boy with the cleft lip or at my old shrink's office. Once I came out of the dressing room wearing a very short black shift made of thin T-shirt material, and the shop owner let out a long whistle. The dress cost over ninety dollars, but he said he'd sell it to me for half that if he could take me out dancing later.

Of course, I was still young, though I don't see, now, why I'd decided to take such a narrow view of my own fate that night. But at least I had a place to sleep, and that seemed important. I suppose I was lucky in the grand scheme of things: I didn't have to camp out on a park bench, and there were no lasting physical ramifications of our time together. It wasn't a terrible night, but in another sense it wasn't anything at all. After the dancing we went back to the man's apartment, where he lit a dozen candles in his living room, with its leather sectional seating and huge windows that looked out over the Hudson. He poured me a glass of alcohol, something amber colored, of which I took micro sips. A bit later I had a moment of drama in the bathroom, as I stared into my own eyes in the mirror above the sink before joining him in his bedroom, which I remember as being cramped and smelling faintly of sour milk and garlic. The comforter was beige and pilled and lightly stained. Underneath it I felt nothing at all.

No Doubt

Stone fruit, which includes plums, peaches, and apricots, cannot propagate unless their hard pits (their stones) are cracked open. Only then can the life potential of the seed hidden inside be released. The same is true for us, wrote Khalil Gibran: just as the fruit's stone must break wide open to free the germ, so must we know pain in order to release the understanding hidden in our hearts.

Nutcracker

E——, New Jersey, 1984

By the time this picture was taken, I was already going to college in New York City. Freshman year. I'm only back for the holiday— just a quick visit. My father's back too, even though this is not his home. It seems we've just decorated the Christmas tree because my parents are standing in front of it like it's an event. At the top of the tree the little angel with the white candyfloss hair holds her hands together in prayer. The green satin pear and glittery gumdrop man dangle nearby. The tall wooden nutcracker, with his soft rabbit fur beard, stands sentry on the coffee table under a pitch-black window. My father has taken off his glasses, but you can still see the imprint of them on the bridge of his nose. My mother hugs him, nestling her head against his chest. She smiles as she looks into the camera, seems almost at ease. With exaggerated weariness he tilts his eyes up to the ceiling. We'd fallen so far as a family by this point. And yet we had no idea. There was so much further to go.

O

Obscure

"Word salad," also known as "expressive aphasia," is a speech disorder in which words are strung together in nongrammatical, non-
sensical combinations with the cadences of normal speech. On the
afternoon of January 1, 1985, my father suddenly produced long,
angry strings of this type of speech while brandishing a *knife at
my mother, Tracy, and Grandma Ellen, who was visiting for the day.
Somebody—I've never known which of the three women—got away
and called 911. The police arrived within a matter of minutes to
arrest my father and bring him down to the police station. There
they gave him a choice: jail or rehab. He chose rehab.

I know none of this firsthand. I was a freshman at Barnard College
and had opted to spend almost all of Christmas break in New York
City, in my abandoned dorm, mostly in order to avoid spending
time with my mother because by then we fought almost constantly.

My parents had already officially divorced, although they still tried
to "keep things friendly," which is why we'd spent Christmas together
and why, I assume, my father was in my mother's apartment on New
Year's Day. But why did he snap? That he was drunk seems likely, and
yet normally my father was taciturn, *morose, and withdrawn when he
drank, but that day he was quite talky, even if the words themselves
made no sense. I've asked Tracy about what happened many times,
but she's close-lipped when it comes to the past, especially the ugly
parts, and for years, whenever I pressed her for details about this
event, she would tell me only that it had been "no big deal" and that
it "sounds worse than it was." But last Christmas, when she came out

from Chicago for a visit and she and I went for a walk after dinner along the Muddy River, I asked her again about that day, so long ago now, and for some reason she opened up a little.

"Honestly, I think he just couldn't take it anymore. You know what she's like. *Di-di-di-di-di-di-di!*"

It was dusk, and there aren't many lights along the river, but I could still see the gesture she made with her gloved hand, touching her fingers and thumb together in imitation of a mouth talking very quickly.

"You know how it is. She just wouldn't shut up, and it was like his brain finally snapped and he just—" Here my sister made a bunch of squeaky high-pitched noises, then stopped to give me a look of impatience because she didn't like my expression. She thinks I take things too seriously.

"No, really," she said, walking more quickly all of a sudden so that she was a good three or four feet ahead of me. "You had to be there. It wasn't scary at all. It was just weird. Almost funny. Or pathetic. Or sad mostly. Really, it was just sad."

Obvious

David was at Columbia when I was at Barnard. We'd been dating for just a few weeks when, one Sunday afternoon, he decided to make a pot of black bean soup in his dorm kitchen. It didn't look like much—dark, lumpy. But it smelled like delicate woodsmoke, and we ladled it into chipped mugs, then brought the mugs, for some reason, outside. It was very foggy that day, and the streets—at least as I remember them now—were almost completely deserted as the mist swirled through them. Walking together, talking, eating that soup (inky, earthy, salty, sweet), I suddenly felt that at least one thing in my life was clear.

Ode

We've been lucky so far up here in Maine, on the island: the weather's been perfect—warm and sunny through the belly of the day, cool at night, foggy in the mornings. We've been feasting on blackberry pancakes, blackberry pies, blackberry jam, and blackberry anything else we can think of. I'm lying in bed, listening to my family. There's not much in here: just a bed, a dresser, a painting on the wall, a few rusty sliding screens. Our window is open, and through it I can smell the sea of ferns at the base of the hill, and beyond the ferns I can smell the glossy brown mud in the cove because the tide is out. The mud smells like life, and the ferns smell green and vaguely buttery and also a little like hay. It's a smell that reminds me of the one that comes off of newborns' heads, their fuzzy scalps.

When we're up here, we all tend to read a lot. We play mancala, Uno, Monopoly, chess. I knit and do yoga. David and Isaac go fishing. Isabella takes long, solitary walks from which she returns, each time, a little more wild, a little more grown-up. She and I tend to wake up late, David and Isaac quite early—sometimes hours before dawn to study the stars or to launch the rowboat for a predawn troll. We eat huge, sumptuous breakfasts and fill our days with hikes and berry-picking expeditions, walks on the beach, and quick forays into the freezing blue-gray waters. Sometimes we picnic on the flat rocks that border the cove; sometimes David and the kids dig for clams in the flats; sometimes we visit the lobster dock. In other words, all the clichés are in play up here—the jigsaw puzzles, the fog, the seashells on the windowsills, the homemade pies, the crickets in the grass, the star-encrusted skies, the deer in the woods, the sand in our beds—only they're not clichés, they're real, and right now I'm just listening to it. The plenitude. The bare feet on the cabin floors. The pots and pans. My husband's voice. My children, laughing.

Off Guard

For a while, after my father was pretty much entirely out of her life and she and Tracy were living together (yet more or less separately), my mother's drug of choice became Xanax, its frequent use justified by her teeth, neck, and jaw problems. She said it made her feel *relaxed*. It was supposed to be a joke. Like—her, relaxed! For some reason she openly admitted not only to using but to loving

Xanax. The idea was that she was such a prim type, such a teetotaler, such a staunch opponent of all things druggy or addictive, that having a favorite pharmaceutical high was just sort of cute.

On Xanax my mother spoke extremely slowly, with swollen vowels and extended, vaguely embarrassing plosives. It really let down her guard. For example, on Xanax she didn't care whether she was dressed or not. I know because I once came home to find her standing in the kitchen completely naked except for a pair of baggy old nylon underwear. She was eating a raw English muffin near the window, which was open.

"Mom!" I said when I saw her. "I'm home. I'm here!"

"Oh, hi, sweetie!"

"You're naked."

"I'm sorry," she said, looking down at herself, then back at me. Grinning crookedly, she took another bite of the muffin, then explained, "You caught me off guard!"

Oily

G——, New Jersey, 1973

This photograph was taken from a child's low perspective in front of the house with pink shutters. My mother sits on the front stoop, smoking a cigarette, wearing a pair of jeans she'd altered with a bottle of bleach (uneven splotches and dashes and dots of white are scattered all over them) and a scoop-necked T-shirt with tassels dangling from the collar and both sleeves. She smiles behind a pair of oval John Lennon–style gold-rimmed eyeglasses. I wore those glasses sometimes when I was in college. They were the entirely wrong prescription—much too strong. They made the world seem oily or underwatery. I couldn't judge distance in them at all. But I wore them anyway because I thought they made me look elegant.

Old Enough

New York, New York, 1987

Aunt Millie stands at the head of the dining room table, which is laid for three: the Aunts and me. White china plates, real silver, linen napkins. Wearing a sober black knit dress with short sleeves and a strand of fake pearls, she holds perfectly still for the camera, which I am holding. I'm in this picture too, reflected in the mirror above the sideboard. I wear a white T-shirt and a pair of ochre-colored parachute pants, and I'm smiling, encouraging my great-grandaunt to do the same, but I don't think she can hear me. Gazing straight into the camera, as if she were staring down death itself, she wears a completely neutral expression. She looks pretty fit considering she's pushing ninety. She is, in fact, very near the end of her life. They both are. If I'd realized that then—if I hadn't been such a dope—I might have spent more time with them. But as it was, I only paid them a couple visits when I was in college, despite the fact that it was just a quick subway ride downtown.

Aunt Millie served meatloaf and steamed spinach and mashed potatoes that day. Afterward, while she was doing the dishes, I sat in the living room with Aunt Gert and asked her about the old black-and-white photograph of a handsome man on her secretary desk. I'd always wondered about him but had never bothered to inquire before. The man in the picture was her brother, she said. His name was Edgar, and he'd died from a gas leak in 1951, when everybody else happened to be out of the house. They'd found him with his head resting on his neatly folded hands at the kitchen table.

"Maybe," I started to say, "Maybe he didn't—maybe it wasn't—"

But Aunt Gert quickly cut me off. "It was an accident," she said.

Since we were on the topic of family, I asked about "Pop." The old woman licked her lips, looked intently into my eyes, and said, "He was not a good man." Aunt Millie, who was extremely hard of hearing, was banging around pots and pans in the kitchen, making a huge racket. It smelled like the warm stewed fruit we'd soon eat for dessert.

"I'll tell you one story," said Aunt Gert. "Because you're old enough to know certain things." Then she went on to describe a trip she and Millie had taken to their niece's house many years earlier, decades earlier, not long after my oldest uncle—my grandmother's first child, Thor—had been born. She said my uncle was still crawling around in nothing but a diaper because it was hot that day.

"And above the diaper," said Aunt Gert, "there was a bruise. A huge dark bruise. It covered his back, and it was shaped exactly like a man's shoe. With a heel." Here she sketched the outline of the thing she was describing in the air between us. "And a toe."

Orangeade

When he went into rehab, my father lost his job. When he got out of rehab, he moved to New York City, and for a while he lived with the Aunts. Right around the same time, my mother lost her job. I think it was the drugs. She and Tracy had to move out of the duplex she'd started renting after we lost the house, and now they lived in a tiny one-bedroom apartment just a couple of blocks away from the on-ramp to the George Washington Bridge. This apartment had red-white-and-blue shag carpet in the living room and floors that sagged when you walked across them. The whole place smelled like rotting wood.

Tracy waitressed several nights a week at a large Greek diner and on the weekends, too, to help with the rent. Once David and I took the bus to Jersey to visit her at the restaurant. This was an enormous place with a menu at least a dozen pages long. Tracy wore a pink dress with a white apron, white sneakers, and sheer nylons, just like all the other waitresses, only she was ten years younger than the youngest of them. On her suggestion we ordered two western omelets and two orangeades, which were a specialty of the house. As we waited for our food, I watched Tracy run around from table to table to kitchen to counter. She seemed happy and spoke in full sentences instead of grunts and eye rolls, as she did at home. She even smiled and laughed. Everyone seemed to like her: the customers joked with her; the older waitresses helped with her table clearings and coffee refills; and the owner—a short, stocky man—flirted with her almost bashfully. She was so pretty.

"What's wrong?" David asked. But I couldn't explain. It didn't make any sense. She was right there, and yet suddenly I missed my sister so much.

Orientation

Things I've thrown at my father (in chronological order):

a plate of food;
a green apple;
a box of art supplies;
a heavy, old-fashioned pencil sharpener;
a sixteen-ounce jar of bitter orange marmalade.

The marmalade was part of a care package I'd assembled for him after he got out of rehab. Also in the care package were a bar of goat's milk bath soap, some black tea, and some pistachios. These things were meant to be a kind of "welcome back" or maybe something closer to a "let's start over" or a "no hard feelings" gesture. I was very nervous to see him. He'd been out of my life for six months. On top of that I realized that I now needed to get to know him in a different way, with the label "alcoholic" hanging over his head, so to speak. Growing up, I'd never thought of him like that, but after the incident with the word salad and the months in rehab, I finally understood that this was exactly what he was—what he had always been. Only knowing it made him seem like a stranger.

We met in the West Village, on the corner of Seventh Avenue and Tenth Street. He'd come with a friend named Sam.

"Sam's my AA sponsor," he explained as we stood awkwardly on the sidewalk. I'd come with David and introduced him as my boyfriend. The four of us shook hands, made forced pleasantries. It was sunny—summer was on its way—and this made me feel optimistic, but I was also tense, and when my father said the thing he shouldn't have said, the thing that pissed me off, I just picked up the nearest small heavy object and hurled it. Now, of course, I understand that my father said what he said because he, too, was nervous. I know this because I am a parent and so have firsthand knowledge of the fact that parents can at times feel quite nervous in front of their own children, and when parents are nervous, they, like anyone else, can act like idiots. But back then, I was just a nineteen-year-old kid holding a goofy little woven basket full of things like soap and marmalade, looking at the man who was my father and realizing I hardly knew him.

In actuality I'm pretty sure there were just one or two things he could have said that wouldn't have prompted me to throw something at him. Something like "I missed you, sweetheart" or "It's so good to see you, darling." But such statements fall far wide of my father's personality, even at his most affectionate moments. *Sweetheart* is simply not in his vocabulary, and when he says "I miss you," it is usually in code, and that code is almost invariably edible. In any case, instead of saying one of these impossible phrases, he held me at arm's length and asked in a jokey sort of way what all the "spots" were on my face, at which point the marmalade practically hefted itself.

Orlaya grandiflora

I notice as I walk down the path that leads to our apartment that the little patch of a garden by our gate looks spectacular. There's not a single weed, the pink tickseed is exploding, the roses are in full bloom, and the leaves of our potted oleander—normally a bit sickly—are a deep glossy green. This is weird because we've been in Maine for two weeks. Then I notice that our old plastic watering can—which I distinctly remember tossing in the garbage the day before we left on account of a hairline crack—is sitting at the base of our tomato plant, and my heart starts thumping way up in my head.

I push open the gate, and there, as I half-knew would be the case, is my mother. She's sitting on an old stump of wood that she's pulled onto our porch, staring at the screen of the brand-new iPhone Tracy recently bought her, wearing a pair of earbuds, lightly bopping her head and chewing on her bottom lip. She doesn't see or hear me, not even when I crunch across the gravel path and get very close.

"Mom!" I yell. "Mom!"

She stands up and turns toward me, squinting as if it were dark out. Stepping closer, holding out one hand as if she were blind or as if I were some kind of a ghost, she waves her arm back and forth until her fingers finally touch my chest, then she says: "Oh, Kimmy, I didn't recognize you. Can you believe this? It won't let me do *anything*. Brand-new iPhone. Blocked already. Ridiculous! Plus I can only get reception if I sit here. Right *exactly* here, precisely on this *exact* piece of wood. It's the only place in the *entire* neighborhood. A four-block radius. Rather curious, wouldn't you say? Simply amazing, the lengths they'll go to." She shakes her head.

"What are you doing here?"

I ask this question even though I know exactly what she's doing here. She's staying in our yard. All her bags are open on the picnic table—clothes and papers and cleaning supplies tumbling out of them. A huge gray sleeping bag and a pillow are stuffed into our hammock; a toothbrush is balanced on the base of an upturned clay pot.

"I know it looks bad. I know it doesn't look like it, but I'm actually staying at the B&B down the street. It's just they're giving me a special discount, and there are all these rules. One rule is I'm not allowed to stay in my room during the day. Also, I have to clear out all my stuff until 4:00 p.m."

I sigh. But it is not a simple sigh. It is a sigh with many things in it. Resignation, disappointment, guilt, anger. Other things, too, but I'm not sure what they are.

"So, I've been coming here. Just for the daylight hours. It's really been gorgeous. I've been so lucky. Did you notice the garden? Doesn't it look amazing? I've been working on it every day!"

"I'm tired."

I walk past my mother and start unlocking the door to our apartment and notice as I do that she's looped the handles of a plastic bag around the back of one of our lawn chairs. It is filled with water, and nearby is a damp washcloth. On our woodpile an *Elle* magazine is opened face down. Next to the hammock there is a long stick on the ground and a pair of flip-flops.

David comes down the path holding a bunch of suitcases and bags. He looks at me, then he looks at my mother, then he says, "Linda."

"Oh, he's so good. When he gets mad, he just gets polite. Such a good man you married."

"Mom, I can't believe you've been staying here."

"I *promise* I haven't been sleeping here. I know it looks bad, but really."

I ask what she's going to do now, but she doesn't answer because the kids are clomping down the path. Isabella is holding her backpack and an armload of board games, and Isaac is right behind her, and neither of them says anything to any of us; they just march straight into the house as if on a mission. Isaac's cheeks are red.

"Did you know you have a rare strawberry plant in the herb patch back here? Did you know that? Purely decorative. You'll never get a strawberry off of it, but it's *so* charming. Pink flowers. And be careful with the tarragon. It looks exactly like a weed. But it's *so* delicious, especially with chicken."

"I know," I say. It sounds very harsh. Too harsh, I think, so I add, "I love tarragon with chicken." Then I let her show me around my own garden, as if I'm on a tour. She shows me all the plants I put in the ground myself and tells me their names and how to care for them.

"Be careful with the mint! It can take over. It was *all over* this whole side of the herb patch. I had to trim it *way* back, but don't worry. It's tenacious. It'll grow back in no time."

She explains about the watering can at the top of the path—about how the crack in the base is perfect for watering the roots of the tomato plant very slowly, all day long, just the way they like it. "And this," she says, pointing to a small clump of white lace flowers I bought at a nursery a few weeks ago, "I haven't seen this since my mother was alive. She used to love this flower!" As I watch her talk, something in me deflates. After a minute Isabella comes out of the house with her sneakers on.

"I'm going for a run," she announces to nobody in particular, then jogs up the path. Watching her leave, my mother shakes her head and says, "Gorgeous."

Osteria

After he got sober, my father lived for two years in a seedy SRO in Lower Manhattan, across the street from a park frequented by homeless people and junkies. I saw the inside of his room in this place just once: it had a single window covered by a grid of thick iron bars and was so small it fit hardly anything beside his bed. The walls, if I remember correctly, were painted black.

It took a while after the orange marmalade incident, but eventually we met again, this time for dinner. And as that event unfolded in a more or less civilized manner, we decided to do it again. This quickly became a routine. In fact, we met for dinner every Tuesday for the next three years, until I graduated from college and moved to Boston.

Every so often, he would come uptown, to Morningside Heights, but usually I took the R or the N train down to 23rd Street, then walked to his SRO and asked the "concierge" (in his bulletproof cage) to ring my father. I'd wait for him on the front stoop, trying to avoid eye contact with the junkies in the park, and with what always struck me as incredible alacrity, he'd appear next to me, dressed in what was at that time his everyday uniform: jeans, sneakers, and a T-shirt. We would walk down Second Avenue to our favorite restaurant, a tiny hole-in-the-wall place called L'Osteria, where we ate cheap and simple but well-prepared food from Southern Italy—food that reminded both of us of Grandma Bella.

For the first several months of this weekly routine, our conversations were absurdly cramped since we strayed only reluctantly from a handful of topics that were clearly safe. Among these the one that gave us the most mileage—and the one we enjoyed the most—concerned the foods we were eating, which, at L'Osteria, were often things my grandmother used to make: golden *arancini*, silky eggplant parmesan (dark and bitter, without a trace of mozzarella), sautéed *rapini*, stewed escarole, *mozza en carozza*, Sicilian style macaroni . . . Sometimes we talked to the owner, who spent most of his time at the front counter ringing up orders and making *vasteddi* (sandwiches composed of thin slices of oil-basted sheep spleen and a handful of matchstick shavings made from salted, cured ricotta). These sandwiches sold for a dollar fifty, and in this way, I'm pretty sure, L'Osteria kept several people in that neighborhood alive.

I usually ordered iced tea, which came from a powder mix and which was almost unnaturally quenching, though sometimes I had a glass of wine. My father drank San Pellegrino. Gradually, the tiny circles of our conversations grew more expansive. I sometimes talked about David or my classes. Eventually, he told me about his AA meetings and his new job. He paid for our meals and always left a big tip. If it was nice outside, we often wandered around the Village for a while before heading to the subway station, where he would walk me up to the turnstile and give me two tokens—one for my ride home that night and one for my trip back the next week.

Overcoat

I was supposed to meet my mother to talk about "something." I was nervous, but being with David made everything easier, even my mother, and I was relieved to have him by my side as we took the bus out of the city, then walked through curtains of freezing rain, first to a grocery store, where I bought a box of Mozart chocolates as a preemptive peace offering, and then to the one-bedroom apartment my mother and Tracy shared.

When we arrived, my mother was nowhere to be seen, and Tracy was asleep. Because the apartment was so small and my mother's queen-size bed took up most of the bedroom, Tracy slept on a cot, the foot of which had been shoved into the closet. For privacy, at the head of the cot, she had hung an overcoat on a piece of twine using clothespins. We might not have noticed her there behind the coat, lying with her arms crossed over her chest, except that she was snoring. Just a little.

We decided to wait—either for my mother to show or for my sister to wake up. To pass the time, we washed and dried the dishes that had piled up in the kitchen sink: pots, pans, plates, and bowls, all with caked-on remnants of canned chili and minestrone and mac 'n' cheese. We emptied the ashtrays that Tracy had filled to the brim with her cigarette butts (Marlboro Lights). Then we sat on the couch in the living room and waited a little longer. Finally, we put on our coats. But before we left, I went into the bedroom and leaned over my sister to whisper that I loved her. She mumbled something in her sleep and, without opening her eyes, found my hand with hers. She brought my fingers to her mouth, gave them a dry little kiss, then rolled over onto her side.

P

Pair

New York, New York, 1988

What are we? Puppies? We're so cute, it's unreal. A light rain hangs
in the air; umbrellas are up. My graduation gown, pale blue with
small black crowns at the shoulders, is dotted with drops. My face,
sheltered under the tipped mortarboard of my graduation cap, is
aglow. I don't think there's another word for it. David isn't wearing a hat or using an umbrella, but he is so young, so fresh faced,
I suspect he's just naturally water-repellent. I hold my hand over
the single button of his blazer. My nails are painted a bright man-
darin red. His tie—a Liberty print of tiny blue flowers—matches
my gown. We are children. Our hair is curly. Our eyes enormous.
Our smiles just slightly uncertain.

Paltry

Last night I dreamed about grandfather in a different setting
than the usual bathroom labyrinth. This time we met in a small
windowless room. I understood this space to be the foyer of one
of my mother's old apartments. She and I were chatting, though
what about I can't remember, when somebody rapped at the door.
My mother explained that she'd asked her father to come over so
they could discuss a knotty problem of hers. It was obvious that she
was both nervous and excited to see him and also afraid—so afraid
that she refused to open the door. I very much wanted to meet
my grandfather at last, so as my mother receded into the shadows
of that strange little room, I swung open the door. He barged in,

charged past me, talking a mile a minute with a heavy Swedish accent. He was tiny, perhaps only five feet tall, and rail thin. His skin was a deep, burnished bronze color, his features tight against his skull. He had no facial hair, no hair on top of his head, and it strikes me now, as I write this, that he was essentially mummified. His accent swung up and down in a Swedish, singsongy way as he admonished my mother, telling her that she needed to grow up, needed to stop dwelling on problems of the past. But he couldn't fool me. I saw right through him. I knew this talkativeness, this aggression, was only his way of trying to camouflage himself so as to prevent our attention from settling on him too long.

I finally stepped right up to him and told him who I was. I insisted on shaking his hand, which I found, as soon as I took it, to be extremely small and fragile, almost friable, like something that's been baked too long. Though I can't say for sure, I think it was more out of curiosity than malice that I squeezed his hand harder and harder until the bones splintered and disintegrated in my palm. I had the sense, as the dream thinned out and I began to wake (the sky was gray this morning, smeared with bits of blue), that I could easily keep crushing my grandfather—different parts of him—if I wanted to: his arms, his neck, his head.

What's so unsettling to me now about this dream is the lack of satisfaction that final image provided. I spent so much energy as a child fantasizing about the various ways I might save my mother—fixing her teeth, taking her far away from my father, doing everything she asked of me . . . But there I was, face to face with the root of so many of her problems, crushing him like a bit of charcoal, like—how weird dreams are—the chicken wing I ate for dinner last night, and nothing changed. My mother, cowering in the shadows, stayed there.

Papaya

I was waiting for a bus that I was going to take, for some reason, downtown (normally I'd head north after one of our dinners), and my father was waiting with me. It was summertime—sunlight flashed off the shop windows and spiked off the ground glass in the sidewalk. The bus stop happened to be right next to a Korean grocery store, the kind with fruit and flowers arranged in opulent outdoor displays. One of these was an enormous pile of papaya, each fruit cut in half and individually wrapped in plastic so as to reveal the vivid orange interior, with its shining black seeds. These must have caught my father's eye because he said, "I'll be right back," then hurried into the store.

I'm not a huge papaya fan, and I remember thinking it was a little awkward, this gift of half a papaya that he gave me—awkward to carry, to hold, and eventually, to dispose of—but the gesture must have touched me in some way because when the M-103 pulled up to the curb, I said something to my father that I hadn't said in many years, tossed it over my shoulder. I pitched the volume of these words (there were just three of them) so that the driver wouldn't hear but my father would. Then I took a seat by the window, and holding the seeping piece of fruit in my lap, I looked outside to find him exactly where I'd left him, standing there on the street corner. Only now he was doing something funny, something that struck me as tremendously private, pinching the skin on either side of the bridge of his nose—pressing the inside corners of his eyes, which, although tightly shut, still glinted in the sun.

Paperwork

The day it finally hit me that she was actually gone—that I'd really lost her—she still had a home, a car, and a functional cell phone on which she called to say she was parked in front of our building.

"Can you come outside for second? I can't leave the car. I have something for Isabella."

It was hot outside. She was sitting in the driver's seat with the windows rolled up, the AC blasting. Staring pensively ahead, she played nervously with a strand of her hair. When she saw me, she opened a window and said, "Oh, good, you're here," then gave me a card full of tiny iridescent hair clips, every color of the rainbow. "I saw these at CVS, and they just screamed 'Isabella!'"

"Thanks, Mom. She'll love them."

"Hold on a minute," she said, then got out of her car. She motioned for me to stand closer to her and started picking her hair again.

"Now that I have you here, there's something you should know. Things are really heating up. I'm not sure when I'll be able to see you again. I may have to go into hiding."

"What do you mean?"

"What do you *think* I mean? Do I have to spell it out every time? You know perfectly well what I'm talking about." She looked up and down the street.

"Mom, nobody's there."

"I can't even leave my *house* anymore. They're so desperate to get me out of the way. I've started using Peapod because I can't leave my paperwork unattended for more than *two minutes*, max. That's all they need to get their hands on this." She gestured to the boxes in the back of her car, familiar boxes that I knew were full of ancient X-rays and MRI films, doctors' reports, dental records, medical reports, insurance vouchers, outdated leases, rumpled old Day-Timers, bills, decades-old mortgage receipts, bank statements, and, of course, her own illegibly scribbled notes on god knows what. These were boxes she'd been lugging around with her for half her life, maybe more. "Just two minutes, and years and years of work would be over. Kaput."

"Mom, I hate to say this, but I think you're being paranoid."

She repeated the word *paranoid* almost silently, with her eyes shut, as if miming great exhaustion. "This is so much more serious than you're willing to admit. When are you going to realize that?" She made a funny gesture then with her hand. Forefinger extended, thumb cocked above it. She seemed to be making the sign for a gun.

"Are you telling me they want to kill you?"

"Sh!" She looked around once more, then got back into her car and leaned out the window.

"One day you'll believe me, Kimberli. But by then it'll be too late, and boy oh boy, do I feel bad for you on that day because you are going to feel *so* guilty, only I won't be around to see it."

Paralyzed

After a couple of years of living in New York City as a sober man, my father—still youngish, newly single, and thin again—got a good job, a decent apartment, and a cute girlfriend. It was at this point that my mother decided she actually liked him after all, decided he actually was the one and only for her, and became increasingly obsessed with getting him back. Unfortunately, her tactics were decidedly scary. For example, she pulled the suicide card, and when that didn't work, she called his girlfriend to tell her that her new boyfriend had once stabbed a man, and when that didn't produce the expected results either, she called his boss and told him the same thing, then faxed the police report to prove it. He was fired the following week.

"I suffered all those years," she said when I asked her why she'd done it. "I lived with the crappy Jake. I trained the violent Jake. Why shouldn't I get the benefit of the nice Jake now that he's stopped drinking?"

But my father didn't see things the same way, and when he cut off all communication with her, she started getting creative. For a while this meant calling him and leaving messages to the effect that either Tracy or I had been in a terrible car crash and were paralyzed from the neck down. But after she did that a couple of times, he stopped calling her back, so she started calling a police precinct that happened to be just a block away from his new apartment in order to get a cop to personally deliver equally awful messages to him. I found out about this because a cop once called me from my father's apartment in the middle of the night to make sure I was alive.

"I'm just calling to see if you're all right," said the unfamiliar voice at the other end of the line. "You all right?"

"I'm fine. Why?"

"Well, I'm standing here with your father, and I'm here because your mother called the precinct and . . . Frankly, I don't know who to believe. Your mother. Your father. I mean, I don't trust either of them."

"What are you talking about?"

"Your mother said you were in a car crash. Actually, she said you were in a four-car pileup and 'burnt to a crisp.' Said you were 'incinerated,' and she was trying to get in touch with your father because it was an emergency and he wouldn't take her calls, but he needed to know because you were dead. So, I come here, and I knock on the door, and I say, 'Sir, your daughter's been in a serious accident,' and he rolls his eyes at me, and I say, 'Sir, there's been a terrible accident involving your daughter,' and he says, 'That's bullshit,' and I say, 'Something's wrong here,' and your father says, 'Yeah, my ex-wife is wrong.' But I guess I just don't trust him—I mean, no offense, but I don't trust the guy. So, he says I should call you, and that would prove that you're alive, and I guess you are, cuz we're talking. I guess he is the one to believe after all because I'm talking to you, so you must be alive."

"Well, I guess that's right," I said, gazing at the window box that David had hung outside our bedroom. We lived in a tiny apartment on Beacon Hill. The box was full of red and pink geraniums, but they looked black at night. Staring at them, I felt, as I so often did in those days, a curious shade of nothing. Not sad, not mad, just zilch.

"Geez!" said the cop. "I can't imagine how anyone could do that. Actually say those words about her own kids. I mean. I'm a parent, and I can't even . . . The bond is not like that. It's not natural. I mean, just thinking about putting those words in the same sentence as my kid's name makes me want to throw up. I feel sorry for you, miss. Your mother—she's a sick lady. If I were you, I honestly wouldn't know what to think."

Partially Cropped

J——, New Jersey, 1989

When Tracy left for Chicago to go to college, my mother started living alone for the first time in her life, and I think that was the problem. The solitude. It didn't take long before she got laid off from her job, which she'd held down for many years. Fortunately, she quickly found another gig at a smaller computer company, doing a job that paid less and was more demanding, but at least she could afford to move out of the cruddy one-bedroom where Tracy used to sleep in the closet. Her new apartment was the garden unit of a classic brownstone in a gentrifying neighborhood about thirty minutes from downtown Manhattan. The building was owned by two soft-spoken gay guys who made it a point to stay out of my mother's hair, and it was there, in that large but somewhat gloomy space, that she would go through the experience of losing many more things. For example, she lost her new job. And then, a short time later, she lost a third job because by then she was taking so many pills that she could no longer get up in time to get to the office before noon, and when she finally did get there, she slurred her words and got into fights with clients, bosses, and coworkers. She'd already lost her husband, of course, and both Tracy and I were gone. Even her boyfriend—married but at least he was company—didn't work out.

These photographs were taken in that apartment. There are three of them, all very similar. In the first (there's a clear chronology suggested) she stands about ten feet away from the mirrors that run the length of the living room. She leans gracefully against the couch, twisting slightly at the waist in order to face the mirror. A Christmas tree, decorated with ornaments I remember from childhood (the pink gumdrop man, the beaded satin pear), stands in one corner. The heavy black camera completely obscures her face.

In the next photo she has taken off her glasses and moved a few feet closer to the mirror. She holds the camera with one hand, now to the side of her face. Her features, in this picture, are composed but uneven—the two halves quite distinct. She looks unusually intense.

In the last picture she stands just a foot or two away from the mirror, which has the effect of placing her so far to the left that her shoulder is partially cropped. She has put her glasses back on and now holds the camera—a 35 mm Canon—with both hands, near her head. My sense is that she's not trying to present herself in any special way here—she's not striking a pose, only trying to capture something. She studies herself in the mirror the same way she might, I imagine, inspect the anatomy of some unusual insect. What I mean is, there's a strikingly neutral quality to her gaze. Every defect in her normally beautiful face is accentuated: her mouth and the tip of her nose veer to one side; shadowy rings extend under both eyes; the bones of her forehead look bumpy, her neck thick, her skin tired. The reflection of the camera's flash hovers in the dark plane of the mirror—a milky blue bar surrounded by a greenish aureole.

Passage

Ever since we came back from Maine three weeks ago, my mother's been spending a lot of time hanging around our place, sitting every day for an hour or two on the stairs of our porch, doing searches on her iPhone, and rummaging around in the bags and boxes she dropped off the day she got evicted. The rest of her things have been moved by her ex-landlord to a storage unit (which Tracy is paying for) about an hour away.

To be honest, I don't know where she goes the rest of the time. I've asked, but she's vague, and I haven't pushed. Some days, I've noticed, are better than others. Some days she's angry and her eyes are gone, and it's obvious she's taken too many of the pills that rattle around in her gigantic purse. But other days she seems almost centered, even sweet. For instance, today, when I come home from a grocery run with two armloads of bags to find her looking through the pages of her overstuffed Day-Timer, I can tell by her posture that she is in one of her better moods. She even looks cute, in a long dark-blue dress and a pair of sunglasses with purple plastic frames and a really huge, super-enormous black visor. When she sees me, she says, "Oh, hi, Kimmy," and all of a sudden those bits of her face that are visible behind and beneath the sunglasses and the visor crease into a lopsided smile.

"Look at you!" she says, taking two steps toward me and putting her hands on my shoulders. "Just look at you!" She shakes her head so that the shadow of the visor makes dark swoops across her chest. "You're perfect! Absolutely perfect! A little brainwashed, maybe, but basically *perfect.*"

What blooms up in me then? So ancient and hungry? It rises instantly: grudgeless, happy. I give her a hug and ask how she's doing, and she says, "Oh, you know." I ask if she has any clearer idea about what she's going to do next, and she says, "Well, I'd like to tell you my plans, sweetie, but if I do, you have to promise not to tell anyone. I mean *anyone.* If anyone calls you—any of my doctors or shrinks or DMH—just act stupid. I mean, you know *nothing.* Okay?"

"Okay."

"I'm going back to New Jersey. Now don't get upset. I actually have a plan. I know it doesn't seem like it, but this whole thing, this whole eviction thing, is really for the best. The universe is telling me something. It's time to get out of this hellhole. I'm finally going to get my life in order. This state has fucked with me for the last time."

"That's the plan? Do you even know anybody in New Jersey anymore? Everyone in our family has moved out of there. Do you have any kind of a network down there? Any kind of safety net?"

"My 'network,' as you put it, has practically killed me up here. Anyway, New Jersey's just a pit stop. I have bigger plans. I'm putting together a whole new life for myself. I just have to get organized."

"But you have no support system in New Jersey. Here at least you have doctors and social workers."

"That support system has done nothing but try to fuck with me ever since I stepped foot in this state. They all want one thing and one thing only, and that's to see me put away for life in some backwoods nuthouse mental institution where I won't be a threat anymore. Seriously, Kimberli, if you ever listened to me, you'd know that. You'd know the whole thing. But for now you'll just have to *trust* me. I need a fresh start. I know it doesn't seem like I'm on track, but believe it or not, everything's going according to plan. I just need to get a small efficiency apartment. Just someplace to land. Somewhere to sleep and study and plan the rest of my life. I only need a computer. I want to learn Spanish. You know Rosetta Stone? I'm going to learn Spanish using Rosetta Stone. And then I'll get a part-time job—something easy, no stress, a little cash. And then, when I've learned Spanish and saved enough money, I'm going to move to Costa Rica, and in Costa Rica I'll finally be able to relax. And if I lived in Costa Rica, you'd be excited to visit me, right?"

"Yeah. Sure."

"Anyway, I can't stay here. My whole life is in danger. A federal agent told me."

Pasta

One day, over the phone, she told me she wanted to kill herself, so David put two plane tickets on his credit card, and we took the first flight we could get on, Boston to New Jersey. When we arrived at her place, she answered the door wearing nothing but a silk bathrobe, untied, wide open. I pointed out the problem, and she looked down at herself, laughed, then fumbled with the sash.

When I remember that moment, it's complicated because I know so many things now that I didn't then. For instance, I know now that in the desk we walked past as she led us into her apartment, there was a drawer filled to the brim with empty prescription pill bottles. I also know what my mother's father did to her when she was a child because she would tell me about it for the first time a couple of days later. But at that moment, as she tried and failed to tie the sash of her robe, all I knew was that she'd recently been fired from a job she'd had for only three weeks and that before that she'd been fired from a job she'd had for only a couple of years and that before that she'd been fired from a job she'd had for more than a decade. I also knew she'd been talking with increasing fervor and determination about getting back together with my father but that he had no interest in such an arrangement, and this rejection was making her crazy—needy and desperate in a childlike way I'd never seen her act before.

That night David and I ordered takeout from a nearby Italian restaurant because my mother said they made her favorite dish in the whole world there on Friday nights, and even though it was expensive and we'd already spent a fortune on last-minute plane tickets, we wanted to do something nice for her. This dish was an elaborate creation made with two kinds of sauce poured over a gigantic mound of angel-hair pasta. We ate it at the coffee table in her living room, sitting cross-legged on the floor. The sauces came in two separate containers: one was white and creamy, the other red and flecked with bits of lobster. When mixed together, the two became a beautiful coral pink. My mother's eyes rolled weirdly in her head as she ate. She called the food "ashooludilish." David and I watched as she jabbed at the pasta on her plate, sometimes missing it, sometimes feeding herself forkful after forkful without chewing, so that the pasta kept falling out of her mouth and long swags of creamy pink angel-hair hung down past her chin, and the whole time she was talking, but we didn't understand a thing.

Patronize

When it became obvious that the situation was even worse than we'd feared, David called a friend of his family—a psychiatrist—to ask for advice. This man suggested we get my mother to a hospital, preferably one in *Massachusetts, so that she'd be near us. He stressed the importance of keeping her safe until then and told us we should do a thorough search of her apartment, looking for what he called "sharps." After David got off the phone, he and I dug into every drawer and cabinet and closet in the place, gathering up steak knives, razor blades, shish kebab skewers, even a pair of pruning shears and an electric carving knife. All of these things we put into a heavy-duty black trash bag, and we put the bag I forget where—someplace out of her reach. My mother agreed that this precaution made sense, though she didn't help, which seemed reasonable, considering. Besides, she had a migraine and was laid up in bed.

At one point during the search, I found, in the bottom of her desk, in a legal-sized file cabinet drawer, dozens upon dozens, maybe even hundreds, of empty emerald- and amber-colored pill bottles for things like Xanax, Soma, Valium, and Percodan.

"For insurance purposes," she told me when I brought a large handful of them into the bedroom. "I'm saving them to get reimbursed. Believe me, it looks like way more than it is." She was propped up on a huge pile of pillows, leafing through a fashion magazine.

"There are a ton of them, Mom!"

She gave me an exasperated look and said, "Don't patronize me, Kimberli."

Pekoe

David had gone out to buy groceries, and I was making a pot of tea when my mother wandered into the kitchen, still in her bathrobe (half-open again). There were patches of moisturizer on her chest and neck that she'd forgotten to rub in. Even though the water had come to a boil, and I was holding the tea bags in my hand, I left the kettle on the stove because I didn't want to miss what she was saying. It was hard because she was slurring—I couldn't understand all the words. But I understood enough. She spoke of her father and her sisters and of the things he did to them at night when they were young. Sometimes, she said, she pretended to be asleep when he touched her. And sometimes she liked it. When she said that, her whole face collapsed. Something about her went away. Just disappeared. It was as if the light had gone out inside her.

All the girls slept in a single large bed, she told me, and he would "favor" (that was the word she used) one of them for a while, before moving onto the next, but he did so in an irregular pattern, so they never knew whose turn it would be on a given night. It began when she was five years old and continued until she was thirteen. As I listened to her speak, I felt many things. Some of these were emotions you'd expect anyone in my position to feel: shock, sadness, anger. But I also felt relieved. I know that sounds strange, but I *was* relieved. Relieved the way you might be if you'd spent your whole life wading through an opaque fog and then one day the sky opened up to reveal the sun's position. What I mean is, it seemed to me that there was suddenly a north and a south. An east and a west. A reason for the way my mother was.

Pithy

You desire to know the art of living, my friend? It is contained in one phrase: make use of suffering.
—*Henri-Frédéric Amiel*

Pressure of Speech

A medical term indicating, essentially, the inability to shut up. A person afflicted by this condition—also called "pressurized speech"—may seem to possess an almost fantastic disdain for logic. Indeed, his or her thoughts often appear to be strung together by only the most tenuous threads even as the sentences unreel at a fantastic speed, slamming one right into another, without pause for breath or a whisper of concern regarding the auditor's patience, interest level, or response.

Probably (1)

Childhood decides.
—*Jean-Paul Sartre*

Probably (2)

"I'm all id and superego," my mother once told me. "No ego whatsoever."

Problem

We did most of the packing. She still had that headache. David and I drove the U-Haul with all her stuff in it. She followed behind in her Corolla, blasting Ry Cooder, John Prine. In the rearview mirror I sometimes watched her driving. She looked not unhappy. Picking her hair.

She stayed for a while at a b&b in Cambridge until a space opened up at McLean Hospital. It's a famous place. Sylvia Plath went there. *Girl Interrupted* was set there. Anne Sexton and Robert Lowell both spent time there. Located in a quiet Boston suburb, McLean looks more like the campus of a fancy New England college than a psychiatric hospital. Eloquently winding roads connect handsome old mansions that were once private residences but now serve as individual wards specializing in various psychological conditions. The slightly run-down grandeur of the place combined with the spotless confidence of its Harvard teaching staff made it seem, for a while (at least to me), like it was the answer to all my mother's problems. But she never liked the place.

"I'm nothing *like* these people," she said when David and I visited her there for the first time. She'd been placed in a ward that specialized in obsessive-compulsive disorders, addiction, eating disorders, and depression. She'd already picked up one new habit since arriving: holding and puffing on an unlit cigarette.

"It calms my nerves."

We'd brought her a bouquet of flowers in a swirled glass vase, which was now sitting on her bureau, next to her bed. Her room was sunny with tall ceilings. Even her roommate seemed all right— neat, not too talkative.

"Half the people here are *addicts*," she whispered, gesturing toward this woman, whose back was curled under the covers of her bed. "I'm not an addict. Not a *true addict.* Yes, okay, maybe the Percodan got a little out of hand, but given my dental issues, that's understandable. True addicts are different. My brothers and sisters are all *true* addicts. My father was a *true* addict. Your father is a *true* addict. But I couldn't be more *different* than those people. I've never been into drugs. You know me, Kimberli. I'm a Goody Two-Shoes."

At McLean the doctors stressed the importance of family therapy, so for several months my mother and I met with a social worker named Mary Ann Frederickson. Mary Ann's office was in the attic of my mother's ward, in a space that smelled strongly of creosote, for some reason, and also of tuna fish, which seemed to be Mary Ann's preferred lunch and which she sometimes ate during our meetings.

The time we spent in that office did nothing to improve my mother's and my relationship, but it wasn't entirely pointless because I found it informative to watch someone else watch us, to see how someone else reacted to the way my mother and I interacted. For example, Mary Ann often noted that I rushed to comfort my mother, while she rarely comforted me.

"You constantly try to placate her," she said. "It's as if you're the parent."

"That's not true!" said my mother. "I was an *extremely* nurturing mother. I always have been. I still am! You just don't like me."

"That's not true, Linda," said Mary Ann. But I actually think it was.

Our sessions, though stressful (I invariably had stomachaches for a day or two in advance and a day or two afterward), also provided many clues for my secret detective. For example, it was during one of these sessions that my mother first told me why she'd left for Florida the day after my fourth birthday.

"I knew I had to leave when I realized you were afraid of me," she said. "I just waited until you were four so I wouldn't ruin your birthday."

"How could you tell I was afraid?"

She said it was obvious. I asked how so, and she said, "Some things are better left unsaid," at which point Mary Ann leaned across her cluttered desk and said, "How so, Linda?"

"Oh. All right. It happened in that little apartment, the one we moved into after I got out of the hospital. One day I called you for lunch, but you didn't answer. I called and called, but you didn't make a peep." My mother was crying now, pressing a tissue against one eye, then the other. "Finally I got worried, and I went to look for you. I was afraid you'd gone outside. We lived on a busy street. But I found you just standing—perfectly still—in the middle of your room. You were just sort of braced there. It was like you were paralyzed. Your little shoulders up around your ears. I said, 'Kimmy, are you okay?' and you didn't say a thing. It was like you were frozen on the spot, and when I came toward you, you looked right at me—your eyes were *wide* open—and you peed. That's how scared of me you were."

My mother bit her lip and shook her head in a tight little semi-circle. I moved to put my hand on her knee but stopped myself, as this was precisely the dynamic that Mary Ann had so often warned us against—me rushing to comfort my mother when it might just as easily go the other way around.

"How does that make you feel, Kim?" Mary Ann asked, but I didn't answer because my mother was now openly weeping, and I didn't want to make things worse. We were both sitting in these huge, boxy modern chairs that had high, squared-off sides, and in these chairs you had to sit with your arms squished right next to your body.

"That's when I decided to leave for Florida," my mother continued. "I couldn't stand the idea that I scared you that much. I knew you'd be better off with your grandmother." Then she reached awkwardly toward me around the arm of her chair, opening and closing her fingers in a way I knew meant "Quick, quick, hold my hand," so I reached awkwardly around the arm of my chair to do just that. And Mary Ann Frederickson sighed.

Proclivity

During her first hospitalization at McLean, my mother still let me talk to her doctors, who asked me many questions about her personality in hopes of settling on an accurate diagnosis. They asked, for instance, whether or not she'd seemed depressed when I was growing up or whether she'd been addicted to prescription drugs for a long time. Mostly I didn't have any answers for them. I think this is because the constant, active denial in which I was engaged at the time was more or less indistinguishable from genuine ignorance. At one point, however, somebody asked me a question I could answer without the slightest hesitation. It had to do with whether my mother had ever displayed signs of mania. To help me out, the doctor listed several behaviors typifying this condition, such as "seems to lack impulse control," "goes on cleaning jags that last days at a time," "speaks extremely quickly, perhaps even foaming at the mouth," and "goes on huge shopping sprees, spending large amounts of money they may not be able to afford."

Yes! My mother went on huge shopping sprees. No! She could not afford them. This had been the case for as long as I could remember. In fact, from the time I was about eight or nine years old until I was a teenager, my mother would drag Tracy and me with her to the mall several times a year, and there she would drop six, seven, eight hundred dollars at a time, money that didn't exist except in plastic form. She spent the bulk of her time at the makeup counters, where she put on embarrassing airs, waving sales clerks away or summoning them with imperious gestures. Bored practically to the point of tears, of physically melting, yet sick to our stomachs with the knowledge that an argument between our parents was in the near future, Tracy and I would sit on the tall, spinning stools and wait for her to finish debating shades and textures, demanding samples, more information, other brands, other sizes, and racking up the terrifying bill.

Afterward she was always incredibly happy, almost childishly so, as she reviewed her purchases in the car, right in the parking lot, opening, sniffing, touching, and sampling again each and every cream, wrinkle treatment, lipstick, soap, and perfume.

Psychobitchcunt

A verbal invention of Tracy's. Something from the old days. Used in such sentences as, for instance, "I just got off the phone with *psychobitchcunt.*" Or "Have you heard from *psychobitchcunt?*" Or "*Pscyhobitchcunt* told me I need to lose weight."

For a while the term was a favorite of ours. But eventually it got old, as all such jokes do. Now neither one of us would refer to our mother in this way, except perhaps as a shorthand way of pointing to those years when we were both much younger and our anger seemed, on some convoluted, unspoken level, to function as a kind of *hope.

Puppy

M——, New Jersey, circa 1958

The photo is black-and-white, but there's no black or white in it, just dense and denser grays. My mother stands in front of some deciduous trees on a patchy lawn. This must have been in the backyard of the house where she spent the first part of her childhood—a house I never saw but one that for some reason I know was painted red.

She's about ten years old, maybe eleven, and she looks so much like Isabella. She has similar eyebrows. A similar forehead. She has the same smile! She's laughing the way Isabella often laughs, with her chin slightly tucked. And she's skinny, almost painfully so, like Isabella is, like I was.

In baggy trousers, a cap-sleeved sweater, and somebody's fedora, my mother stands alone in the middle of the weedy lawn. There's a bicycle upended in the background and a scrap of something pale—newspaper?—nearby. Her knees are slightly bent and she's holding one hand up at her side, as if she's about to snap her fingers. I can't look at this photo without imagining a radio playing somewhere and the voice of one of her favorite singers—Otis Redding or maybe Buddy Holly—floating through the still, gray atmosphere. Her knees knock, her shoulders hunch, but she's laughing. A round-bellied puppy near her feet looks up at her and raises a front paw as if to touch her leg. It wants to play.

Q

Quabalpa Porshitrosa Tanipnosnet!

In my twenties I started speaking a made-up language. It was a very intuitive thing. I never knew exactly what I was saying, and neither did David, but he still listened. Sometimes I whispered the words frantically, and sometimes I shouted them. This language had no grammar, but it possessed inflections and rhythms that suggested something like meaning, no matter how fuzzy. There were times, especially late at night, when I went on at surprising length in my language. The slightly harsh musicality of it made me happy; sonically, it seemed a mix of Swedish and Yiddish with a bit of Russian thrown in. And a dash of Chinese. Sometimes the words came out kind of squeaky, and that was fun. Squeaks, I discovered, can be wildly therapeutic if you really throw yourself into them. Occasionally, while speaking my private language, I would also cry—but just like the words coming out of my mouth, the tears coming out of my eyes were unattached to specific thoughts or images, so I was never really sure what they were about.

It was fun for a while, but eventually, even I had to admit that pretend words weren't cutting it. I needed to talk to someone for real, using real words. I found a psychologist—someone cheap because she was fresh out of school. Rachael had a serious face and dark eyes that never rolled and never glared and never pointedly shut. In fact, she never drifted even slightly when I was talking to her. If I forgot what I was saying, she remembered. Our conversations, of course, were ridiculously one-sided, and they were often boring—even I knew that. But she never seemed bored, only earnest and interested.

Over the years that I saw her (twenty altogether), Rachael helped me understand many things, such as how *boundaries* work and how guilt has two modes—fact and feeling—and that these are often unrelated. Meaning: there's a difference between being guilty and feeling guilty. In other words, you can experience guilt without actually being guilty, which is why it's so important to make distinctions. She also gave me excellent advice regarding marriage and children, and on occasion she even helped me write businessy-type emails because those make me nervous. But the thing she did most of all, the thing Rachael was really tireless about, was teaching me that it's okay to be happy. In this regard she was unbending and never once failed to remind me—when I needed reminding (which was often)—that willfully sacrificing one's own happiness doesn't help anybody, no matter how mentally ill that person may be.

Quacks

My mother is many things. Inventive is one of them. For example, once when I'd come to visit her at McLean, I noticed, as she shuffled toward me while I was signing in, that she was wearing two pairs of eyeglasses, one right on top of the other.

"Well now, Linda," said the nurse who was checking my bag for sharps, "why might you be wearing two pairs of eyeglasses?"

"I already told you," she mumbled.

After I was done signing in, she took my arm, and a guard led us to the art therapy room, where I gave her a shawl and a one-pound box of fudge. She fussed appreciatively over both of these things, then gave me a kiss, which was wet and which I surreptitiously wiped away. Dozens of pictures were taped to the walls. There was a rose with every petal a different color, a girl smoking a cigarette, several cloudscapes, a unicorn or two . . . There were also many coloring book pictures of puppies and kittens, all carefully crayoned and sometimes dedicated to the art teacher.

"Where's yours?" I asked.

"Oh. They don't let me in here."

"Why not?"

She sighed. "Ask them."

"So, Mom, why are you wearing two pairs of glasses?"

She explained. It was complicated, but basically they were part homemade bifocals and part protest since her real bifocals were in her car and they wouldn't let her go to the parking area to get them.

"Do you get it?" she asked. I said I did. And she said: "That's good. The people around here are too stupid."

It was on that visit that I started to worry about her in a different way. It suddenly occurred to me, actually for the first time in my life, that she might be seriously mentally ill. I know that sounds odd. After all, she was in a psych ward. But I'd allowed myself to believe that she was there simply in order to get weaned off the drugs she'd gotten hooked on in New Jersey and that once this was done, she'd go back to being "normal." But as we moved through the ward that day, I saw many things that surprised me. For instance, I saw a man I'd passed on my way into the building still leaving the building.

"He does that all day," said my mother. "In, out, in, out. I'm telling you, there are a bunch of quacks in here."

Another patient, a young woman who, according to my mother, was taking a break from Harvard, wandered the halls with a small plexiglass suitcase filled with water. In the water a goldfish swam narrowly back and forth, back and forth.

"That's actually bigger than the first one. They made her get a bigger case for it."

Later, in her room, my mother showed me her roommate's bed, which was still unmade. "They don't let her make it," she whispered, so the nurses wouldn't hear. "She has OCD, and if they let her make it, she takes all morning. So, instead, she 'unmakes it." Exactly the same way every day. It looks messy, but actually it took her *all morning* to get it like that. Of course, they haven't caught on. The dopes!"

And still later, as I was signing out, I watched another patient float past me down the hall. It was impossible to say how old this woman was, but I think she was probably younger than she looked, probably around my age, early to midtwenties. She moved extremely slowly, as if trapped in an invisible network of pain. It was obvious she was going to die because her skin was so pale it hinted at blue and she didn't blink and she didn't have a nose anymore because she was in the most advanced stage of anorexia nervosa, meaning her system had already devoured its own cartilage. At that point it was starting in on her organs.

"She'll be dead next week," said the nurse who was checking me out, after the woman had passed us. "The thing is, they have to want to be healthy."

Quadrillion

I won't lie, the guilt is fairly staggering at this point. Every day she comes by, and every day she seems a little more ragged, a little more deranged. Some days her eyes swim. Some days they don't. When they swim, I stay away. When they don't, I ask about her plans. She's got a train ticket for New Jersey and has put her paperwork in storage. She says she's found a place to land down there, a decent hotel that's not too expensive. Part of me can't wait until she's gone, maybe because I want to believe what she keeps saying—that a better life will begin as soon as she leaves this state. Or maybe I just want her to go away so I don't have to witness her falling apart anymore. Also, it's late September. Soon it will be cold at night, and I have no idea where she's sleeping.

Today, when she comes by, I am up in my study, finishing a website design that's due next week. This space is crowded with books and papers and art projects and yarn and wires and cables and photos and old mugs of dried-up tea and fancy pens and pretty stones I've found on various beaches. The window is open, and I can hear her muttering to herself on our porch. I notice that she speaks differently when she talks to herself. The whole pressure of speech thing drops away. Her words sound soft, worried. Eventually, I realize I haven't been working for several minutes because I'm too busy listening to her zipping and unzipping her bags, sorting through papers, and making noises that sound vaguely exclamatory or inquisitive, like "oh!" and "huh?" After a while David comes home from work, and I listen to the two of them exchange a few words. When he comes inside, he says, "You're mother's out there."

"I know."

"It's good you don't feel obligated to engage with her."

I know he means this to be encouraging, but it just makes me sad, so I hop out of my chair and go downstairs, and as I head for the door, he says, "Are you sure you want to do this?"

On the porch I see that my mother has her things spread out all over the place, piles of toiletries and clothes and papers.

"Oh, hi," she says.

I say hi and ask if she's looked at the packet I printed out for her a couple of days ago—pages I got off the internet that list out resources for homeless and mentally ill people, pages I left on our picnic table for her in a manila folder with her name written on it in huge block letters.

"Yes, I got them, and I know you meant well, but those are *exactly* the kinds of people I need to get away from."

She is actually using the back of one of the pages I printed out to make a to-do list.

"Any more news on what's next?"

"As a matter of fact, I'm all set to leave for New Jersey next week. But don't worry, sweetie. I'm going to be okay. I really am. It's going to be a *quadrillion* times better once I get there. And—this is important—I don't want you to help me."

"I can't help you."

"I know, you have enough on your plate."

"That's not what I meant."

"There's only one thing I need you to do," she says. "If you can just promise me this one thing, that's all I need, and then you don't need to feel guilty about anything else just so long as you do this one thing." That sounds like a pretty good deal, so I ask what it is, and she says: "Just take care of Tracy. Be there for her if she needs you. You're all she has. Can you promise me that?"

"Yes."

"Good. I'm so relieved."

"That's easy, Mom. But I'm not worried about Tracy. I'm worried about you."

The conversation gets a bit confusing at this point, but I don't mind for some reason. She's talking about her old landlord and the storage company and the owner of the B&B down the street. I just stand there and listen. I don't even feel that impatient. I just want to be near her, I guess. But at some point I get a great idea, and I go inside to get a bunch of clothes I think she might like—things I don't wear so much anymore or things I don't really need, like a rust-colored blouse with a yellow fleur-de-lis pattern on it and a pair of brown corduroys and a blue lace cardigan I knit for myself a while ago but never wear because it's too heavy and I think it makes me look frumpy. When I bring these things out onto the porch, my mother tries them all on. She likes the blouse but not the corduroys. She takes a gray thermal, and the sweater she loves.

"It's beautiful!" she says, pulling it on. "How does it look? It's a gorgeous color. Do you know the name of this color? This is a very *specific* blue. Prussian blue. *Extremely* hard to find a true Prussian blue."

I tell her it looks great on her because it does, because even though I'm a pretty good knitter, I am not a perfect knitter, so the sweater has a decidedly handmade look, and I've noticed that when people wear handmade sweaters, it's clear to anyone with half a brain that somebody, somewhere, loves them.

Quagmire

It was harder when I was a kid, but now I can tell. Now I know when my mother's lying because of how she holds her hands or where she looks—for instance, if she looks too penetratingly at me while asserting something, I can be pretty sure she's lying.

Likewise, if she blinks in a way that seems strangely timed or if she tilts her chin slightly upward when speaking or if she closes her eyes entirely. Also, when she speaks very, very slowly through clenched teeth, she is almost certainly lying. Ditto when she speaks extremely quickly while looking sideways. In fact, I'm pretty sure my mother lies most of the time, but it's confusing because she lies about things that make no sense, that serve no apparent purpose, which makes a conversation with her feel a bit like walking around a house with squishy floors and rotting walls because everything is constantly shifting, everything feels uncertain and potentially dangerous and most of all pointless.

The first time I caught her red-handed in a lie was when I discovered that she'd stolen my father's laptop. She'd recently been released from McLean and was living in a halfway house in Boston. Actually, the laptop in question didn't technically belong to my father but to the fancy New York City accounting firm she'd gotten him fired from by sending his boss the police report about the time he'd stabbed Richie. The company had been asking my father for over a year to give back their laptop, but he didn't know where it was. Or he did know where it was—only he didn't know how to get it back. So for a long time he just kept asking me to ask my mother if she by any chance happened to have it.

Back then, laptop computers were rare and very expensive. I knew that my mother likes rarities, especially expensive ones, and I knew, too, that she liked to hurt my father, but the idea that she would have actually stolen the computer just didn't make sense to me, even on a logistical level, because she would have had to have snuck into his apartment when he wasn't there, and then she would have had to have actually taken it—snuck it out—and then she would have had to have lied to me for over a year, because my father didn't have a thousand dollars to replace the machine, and so every month or so he'd ask me to ask her yet again, and I would.

"I wish he wouldn't do that," I once complained to David. "If she says she doesn't have it, she doesn't have it."

"Of course she has it," he said. "That's the sort of thing she does."

But every time I asked her, she said she didn't have my father's stupid laptop, and what would she do with his stupid laptop anyway, and why was I always taking his side, and when in her *entire* life had I ever known her to steal *anything* or lie about *anything*?

Still, the issue of the missing laptop just wouldn't die because my father was persistent. Or maybe he was desperate since he'd have to pay for a replacement if he couldn't return it. So I kept finding creative ways to ask. For instance: the move up from New Jersey had been rushed and confused. Maybe it got shuffled along in the rest of her things without anyone noticing?

"No, no, no, Kimberli! I don't have the man's laptop. Seriously— how would I even get his laptop in the first place? I mean, you're saying I *stole* it, for god's sake."

Then, one day when I was visiting her at the halfway house, she asked me to look in her closet for a blanket to put over her because she was lying in bed and felt cold. I went over to the closet she'd indicated and pulled a comforter from the top shelf, revealing in the process a dense black slab of plastic.

"What is this?" I said, marching over to her with the laptop in my hands.

"Oh, *please*, Kimberli. You poor fool. What's the big deal? He owes me *way* more than that."

"I can't believe you lied to me for so long!"

"You are so naive! Anyway, why shouldn't I? He's the lying cheating scum. He's the stabber. He's the drunk. He's the liar. Not me."

Quandary

It is very simple to be happy, but it is very difficult to be simple.
—*Rabindranath Tagore*

Queen

At the halfway house, she got the idea to dig out her jugular with a pair of cuticle clippers (pedicure variety), but the jugular is located deep within the tough and intricate anatomy of the neck, so she didn't get further than the first layer of muscle. Despite this, medical records state that she was officially dead for almost two minutes due to the effects of shock. This, in any case, is what my mother has always maintained.

Soon she'd be back at McLean, but first she was sent to a regular hospital to get patched up. When I went to visit her there, the nurse on duty asked me which patient I wanted to see. I said my mother's name, and she looked puzzled, so I gestured feebly toward my neck, and she said: "Oh, the drama queen. The queen of drama." Then she led me to a large double room that my mother had, for some reason, all to herself. The sun was setting outside the tinted window, but there were still several bright strands of lavender and fuchsia near the horizon.

"Kimberli," she said. She sounded disappointed. I figured her tone was probably a reference to her suicide note: a four-page letter addressed to Tracy and me listing our many filial faults. I threw this letter out long ago, but I remember the gist of it: we were selfish, dishonest, judgmental, untrustworthy, uncaring, disrespectful, and entirely lacking in perspective. But mostly, we just didn't love her enough.

"How are you?" I said, but I was speaking nothing. Canned blah. Pseudo words. My mother shrugged. I moved to kiss her, but this too was pure gesture; I merely hovered briefly over her shoulder, then pulled away. There was a massive chunk of gauze stuck to her neck with three strips of white, semitransparent tape. Under the tape her skin was purpled and puckered. That's mostly what I remember from that visit: the skin, the bandage, the clouds outside. Also: just wanting to get the fuck out of there before the sun went down.

Quiet Room

I've rarely known my mother to be quiet. Sometimes, yes, when she's really nervous, she'll hold her tongue. For instance, I've seen her quiet around David's family, when we occasionally used to have holidays together. Yes, around my husband's well-off, articulate, highly educated, suavely boastful relatives, I've seen her be very quiet. But there are only two subjects about which she is reliably reticent. One is her childhood poverty. The other is her father—or, rather, the things her father did to her. About these acts she has only spoken to me very briefly and in the broadest of terms. To fill the horrible blank spot in my mind, I have just a few details. A chair by a bed. A grown man's stubbled cheek. His dirty nails. The smells he left on her. Smells that rose up around her on the school bus in the mornings. Mostly what she has told me—what she has whispered—is: *I felt so ashamed.*

If my mother's paranoia is an ever-enlarging imaginary world taking over her mind (and I think it is), at the center of this world stands a locked ward, and in the center of the locked ward there is a quiet room. A quiet room is where troublesome patients are put in psych wards. Acting out? Screaming your head off? Losing your shit completely? You'll get put in a quiet room. My mother has spent significant chunks of time in several quiet rooms, in several hospitals, but it's my impression that all quiet rooms are more or less the same: small and bare, they contain nothing but a mattress, to which patients are often strapped with four-point restraints, then left alone until they "calm down." This might be for a few hours or it might be for much longer than that. A quiet room is a kind of inverted straitjacket: an environment in which, so goes the thinking (clearly wrongheaded), you cannot possibly hurt yourself.

R

Rae

"Hi, I'm Rae," said Rae, as she stuck out her hand. I liked her immediately because who does that? She pointed to her sweatshirt, across
which were stretched the letters MIT, and said, "I teach there."

"Oh? What do you teach?"

"Physics."

I believed her because she was clearly eccentric, and I figured
MIT physics professors are probably eccentric as a rule. Plus, she'd
been scribbling in a notebook, so everything kind of clicked. But
in reality Rae was not a physicist. She was a patient, like my mother,
and she'd come out of the ward to sit in the underheated waiting
room in order to spy on me as I waited to see my mother because
even though theirs was a locked ward with plexiglass windows and
stainless steel mirrors, Rae was such a long-term, good-natured,
reliably amenable patient that she was considered low risk and the
staff buzzed her out whenever she wanted.

Half an hour later, in my mother's room, Rae blushed when she
admitted that she'd just wanted to see what I was like because she'd
fallen in love with my mother and they wanted to live together as
soon they got out of the hospital.

"Does that sound okay? Is that okay with you? I want to ask you
for her hand. I want to marry her. If that's okay."

My mother was standing in the corner with her arms crossed,
nodding madly.

"Sure, if that's what you both want," I said, and in my head I
was thinking: *Wow, my mother is gay! Wow.* I was thinking: *This could*

be the answer to so many things, so many problems. I was thinking: *If she's gay and she never acted gay, maybe all her anger, all her rage, all her crazy, will lift away if she starts acting gay, maybe being with this odd but strangely charming person is all my mother really needs: someone sweet and non-male.* And most of all, I was thinking: *Maybe now she will get better.*

But my mother isn't actually gay. She's savvy and manipulative, and she's also intelligent, and sometimes she's sweet, too, and for some reason Rae saw the intelligent and sweet parts of her. Maybe she even saw the savvy and manipulative parts but didn't care. Because I believe Rae actually did love my mother, and in her own way I think maybe my mother loved Rae, too, though probably not sexually. In any case things did get a whole lot better after Rae came on the scene because Rae was not only loving and charming in a strictly schizophrenic sort of way but extremely wealthy as well. So wealthy, in fact, that for a good stretch of years—four or five—she paid for my mother to live at the height of luxury (at least when she wasn't in psychiatric hospitals), in a spacious and handsomely appointed apartment full of gourmet food and silk rugs and expensive furniture. During the same time period Rae sent my mother elaborate bouquets of flowers every week and, less frequently (but still pretty often), small but heavy boxes from top-notch jewelry stores. And this was a high point for my mother because, of course, life is just so much easier—particularly if you're sick or addicted or frightened or haunted—when you've got some money.

Rag, Rag, Rag

Tracy came out to stay with us for a few days, and the first thing on her agenda was to see our mother, so after we picked her up at the airport and dropped her bags at our apartment on Beacon Hill, she called McLean to plan the visit. She didn't stay on long. I could hear from her end of the conversation that things were tense. When she slammed down the receiver without saying good-bye, I asked what happened.

"She said she wants me to get ready for our visit."

"What's to get ready?"

"That's what I said. But she said 'curlers and makeup.' I said I wasn't going to do anything but get in the car and drive to the hospital, and she said, 'I don't want you to look like a *jerk*!'"

I tried to give Tracy a hug, but it just made her stiffer. "Do you want to punch a pillow?" I asked.

"No."

"Do you want to squish a banana?" There was a bowl of them right in front of us on the table. But she didn't laugh.

When we got to the hospital, Tracy sat next to our mother on her bed, David sat on a chair, and I sat on the arm of the chair. The first part of the visit consisted of our mother nagging Tracy about what she was going to do with her life because she'd recently dropped out of the University of Chicago. Tracy said she was thinking about getting a teaching degree at the University of Illinois, then moving to New York City to be closer to our father.

"Do you really just want to be a loser for the rest of your life?" said our mother. "Don't you have any ambition at all? Don't you realize what a *quality* mind you have? Why can't you just go back to the University of Chicago and get a real degree?" My mother can get a lot of words out of a single lungful of air, so without pausing for even a fraction of a second, she also added that she didn't like Tracy's eye makeup and that her shoes looked like clown shoes and when was she going to stop trying to hide behind her hair?

It seemed to me that Tracy was handling all of this pretty well. In fact, at one point it even looked like she was going to give our mother a kiss because slowly, very slowly, she reached toward her to brush her hair away from her face. But she didn't kiss her. Instead, she just stared at the pale, slightly bubbled, star-shaped scar on her neck.

"Ah. I knew this was coming. Satisfied now?"

"No," said Tracy. Then she put her hand up to the scar and touched it, like a blind person. Then she pinched it, hard. My mother yelped, and Tracy said, "Now I'm satisfied."

Rage

I wish I'd started practicing yoga in my twenties because if I had, I would have enjoyed my twenties a lot more. But I didn't. In my twenties I did other things. One of them was to write every day in a journal. Recently, I found this journal, and when I tried to read it, it was like looking at oil, if my eyes were water. I had to really concentrate simply in order to read a single sentence, and when I finally managed to do this a few times, I realized why all those words I'd written when I was twenty-three, twenty-four, twenty-five, repelled me so much. They were filled with *anger. I told long, boring stories about my anger, also a few interesting ones. One of the interesting ones concerned a woman I ran into on the T one day who claimed to have gone to Barnard with me, even though I had no memory of her.

"Are you still with that guy?" she asked. "That same guy?" I sensed in her curiosity a nasty streak, but she was beginning to click into memory, so I said yes.

"That's fucking amazing!" she said, so loudly that people all over the train looked at us. Then she asked, "Do you still fight all the time?"

"No," I said, as coldly as my shock would allow, although a more truthful answer might have been, *Not quite as much.*

In another entry I describe how I once fought with David when he had traveled to Mexico City to do some fieldwork for grad school. The plan had been for him to call me as soon as he arrived, but he got caught up with other things and didn't get in touch until two days later. When he finally called, I screamed so loudly, for so long, with such unbending fury, that I didn't hear the pounding at the door. It was only when someone started trying to bust it down that I went to see who was there.

"It's the police," came the answer, and indeed, when I opened the door, there were two nice young cops sincerely wanting to know if everything was okay, if I was all right. Snotty, tearful, exhausted, abashed, I explained that I'd been in a stupid argument with my stupid boyfriend on the stupid phone, but they insisted on searching the apartment to make sure I wasn't hiding anybody. I think they thought I was being hit and that maybe the person doing the hitting was counting on me to cover for them. I don't know. It was unclear. In any case it was only after they'd searched the whole place that they left, although not before helpfully suggesting that next time I might consider shutting the windows before I fought with my boyfriend.

The last story I read in that journal before stuffing it in a box and shoving the box into the back of a closet had to do with my mother's second hospitalization at McLean. This story was long and rambling—I apparently loved to ramble in my twenties. It began with me getting ready to go to a family therapy session with my mother and Mary Ann Frederickson when Rae called on my mother's behalf to ask that I bring along an extra-large bag of plain (not peanut) M&M's. But, she told me, it had to be a special kind of extra large bag of M&M's: a two-pound clear plastic bag filled with smaller, single-serving sized paper bags because for some reason M&M's in small paper bags tasted much, much better than M&M's in large plastic bags.

"Strange but true," said Rae. "Your mother told me."

So, before heading to family therapy, I rushed around town trying to find M&M's of the type Rae had described, and then I rushed to McLean. When I got there, I went not to Mary Ann Frederickson's office but to my mother's room because my mother said she no longer felt safe having family therapy in Mary Ann's office because the two of us always "ganged up" on her and at least in her room she had a *hometown advantage.*

It was awkward doing a therapy session with my mother lying in bed in her pajamas and me sitting at the foot of her bed and Mary Ann sitting in a chair at the side of her bed. But my mother was right—the invisible bond between Mary Ann and me was a lot weaker in her room. Things got even worse once I started talking about how upset I'd been when I was thirteen years old and my mother decided to stop paying for my ballet lessons simply because

I'd gotten a B+ in French. I was so distressed by this memory that I started crying. My mother said: "Come on. It's not like you were ever going to be a professional ballerina!" That made me mad, and it also made Mary Ann mad, but our anger didn't last long because my mother suddenly went stiff in her bed. Looking straight up at the ceiling, she flinched and cringed with her eyes wide open. Then she started whimpering and blocking imaginary blows. Mary Ann said, "Oh shit," and called in a nurse, who came bustling in and waved her hand in front of my mother's face.

"We lost her," she said. Then she explained that this kind of reaction sometimes happened if things got "too intense."

"Patients who've experienced a lot of trauma will sometimes slip back into some memory or other. That's where she is now."

It took the rest of the session, but the nurse finally succeeded in bringing my mother back to the present through a series of questions like *What's your name?* and *Who is the president of the United States of America?* Mary Ann and I were just about to leave when I remembered about the candy and handed the bag to my mother. She was sitting up in bed again, and when she took the big plastic bag full of small paper bags full of M&M's, she said, "Oh, goodie, you found them!"

"It wasn't easy," I said. Then I leaned down to give her a kiss, and she grabbed my shoulder. Very quietly, so that the nurse wouldn't hear, she whispered: "See? See what happens? That's why you shouldn't get mad at me."

Regency

My mother moved in as soon as she was released from the hospital. They wanted to live together like an actual married couple. This is why she bought two of everything (all on Rae's dime): two claw-foot mahogany bureaus inlaid with ebony, two scallop-shaped armchairs covered in slubbed silk, two wide-screen televisions. The apartment itself—twenty-four hundred square feet—was on the eighth floor of a luxury building called "the Regency," right across the street from the Boston Public Garden.

Unfortunately, because Rae was afraid of so many things, including urban settings and tall buildings and, especially, too much distance between herself and her psychiatrist (whom she saw daily), she never did make the move. It was all she could do, socially speaking, to have her limo driver bring her into Boston to visit my mother briefly, every other weekend. On alternate weekends she sent her driver to pick up my mother so they could eat together at her favorite steak house just a few blocks away from McLean.

Relief

"I know you don't believe me, but there might be terrible repercussions for you and David and the kids, so when I get down to New Jersey, don't call me. I'll contact you by mail. I just want to protect you, and believe me, you don't know what's going on with your phone. If I do call, act like you hate me. I'm just so sorry I ever moved up to Massachusetts. It was a fatal mistake. But I've finally forgiven you. And—this is *important*, Kimmy—I don't want your help. I don't want any help from you whatsoever. I can do this on my own. I *need* to do this on my own. And I know you have enough on your plate."

REM

I'd walked, with Oscar, our dog, across the Common to have tea with my mother because for a while that was something we tried to do. The doorman let me in; I took the hushed, mirrored elevator up to the eighth floor, then opened the door with the key she'd given me. I found her in bed, asleep, which was hardly a shock because she was almost always asleep when she lived at the Regency. I could tell she was having a bad dream from the noises she was making, but I didn't want to wake her up because I figured that might make things worse. So, I washed the dishes I found in the sink, and when I checked on her again, she was slowly rousing. I went back to the kitchen and made a pot of Earl Grey tea and arranged it, along with two cups and some chocolate wafer cookies, on a tray and brought the tray into her room.

"Did you have a bad dream?"

She nodded. I handed her a cookie. She took a one-atom nibble. She looked old (though, now that I think of it, she was younger than I am today).

"Do you want to talk about it?"

She shook her head. But then, after a while, she said, "It's a dream I've had for as long as I can remember—an awful dream." She patted the side of her bed so Oscar would jump up. He licked her face tenderly, and she let him do it for a long time. Then she said, "I love this dog."

After she drank some tea, she told me some more about her dream. In it, she said, she's always young, always a girl. "I'm at a beach, or maybe it's a pond, and there's a man there who's holding me down and pouring sand in my mouth so I can't breathe. I'm sure I'm going to die, and I try to scream, but the sand is in my throat, so I can't." Then she stopped talking, and her face crumpled. There were lines everywhere.

"What's the matter?"

"Every time," she said, "every time I wake up, I want to die. I want to kill myself."

"Do you feel that way now?" I asked, and she shrugged.

Rent-a-Tent

O——, Massachusetts, June 20, 1992

Too bad about the shrimp. Other than that, this is a great shot. Half a shrimp, actually, front and center, delicately clasped between my mother's thumb and forefinger. Her nails are extremely long and painted, if I remember right (the picture's black-and-white), a bright apricot color. On my wedding day she wore a pale-green suit, although here, in these distilled grays, her outfit looks as white as my dress. Around her neck is a long strand of pearls and a heavy chain on which hangs the tiny golden cuckoo clock my father bought for her, so many years ago, on a business trip to Switzerland. ("For some reason," he used to joke, "it just reminded me of her!") She's got me in a modified half nelson, her nose pressed into my cheek. In many of the pictures from that day, she's gripping me in highly dramatic ways like this. But I don't seem to mind; we're laughing. Our smiles, noses, and eyes line up—my mother's in profile, mine head-on: eye, eye, eye, half-a-nose, nose, half-a-smile, smile. We hold champagne flutes, and I wonder which one I'm on; I drank six in quick succession right after the ceremony—downed them like I was dying of thirst. How I managed not to fall over in those heels remains for me one of life's great mysteries.

Reruns

Boston, Massachusetts, 1994

On the glass-topped coffee table, there's a bottle of organic peach nectar and all three remote controls. On the floor is a striped toiletries bag, two massive flower bouquets from Rae, a Chinese cloisonné lamp, a jar of moisturizer, and the ever-handy dust-buster. She's sitting in an enormous, pink, super-plush armchair shaped like a huge puffy scallop shell. I suppose she wanted an objective view of herself because she wears glasses, no makeup, old sweats, and has made no attempt at smiling. Still, the mask is there: all hard edges. With this look my mother has intimidated many a shopkeeper, waitress, salesperson . . . She must have set the camera on top of the TV in order to take the picture, prompting me to wonder—is this a portrait of her watching TV? She certainly looks exactly like what she looks like when she does watch TV. I mean, she's doing exactly what she does when engrossed in some horror movie or old detective show—sticking her hand up into her hair, into a spot a few inches above her ear, where she "picks" one strand after another, teasing each one free from the rest, playing a little violin concerto on it, then plucking it out. A small pile forms on the floor. Thus, the dustbuster.

Resignation

The quality of elegance is the one my mother has always valued above all others, and when she was much younger, she seemed to me to physically embody it. But over the years, as she's lost more and more of her teeth, as her finger- and toenails have become warped with fungal infections, as her hair, now a light, pewter-gray, has assumed stranger and stranger shapes on account of her homemade haircuts and decades of trichotillomania, as her posture has become lopsided with age and whatever is going on with her inner ear, she looks not so much elegant as crazy.

The first time I understood that strangers, people on the street, saw her this way, I was in my midtwenties, working part-time at a bakery and part-time at a library. My mother had landed in the psychiatric ward of a city-run hospital. When she was on "good behavior," she was allowed outside for short periods of time during the day, so we'd arranged to meet for a cup of tea one afternoon at a café just a few of blocks away from the hospital and not far from the library where I worked.

It was a warm spring afternoon. Extraordinarily lucid. One of those days when everything—the air, the clouds, the cars and people and trees and everything, all of it—seems happy and relaxed and charged with sex or life or both. My mother was forty minutes late, but she's always late, so I wasn't worried. I sat at a table near the window and looked outside for a while, then I flipped through a magazine and read about a movie star's messy divorce. After that I looked up to find her crossing the street against the light. It was a complicated intersection, and as she navigated her way through it, she wore an expression of intense determination, glancing neither right nor left. An eighteen-wheeler shuddered to a halt in order to avoid hitting her, but when the driver blasted his horn, she didn't seem to notice, just kept marching across the street with that stern look still on her face, eyes fixed on the door of the café.

"I'm sorry I'm late!" she said when she reached my table. She explained that she'd had to wait in line for her meds because the nurse dispensing them had been completely disorganized and *so* passive-aggressive. I noticed that she'd dyed her eyebrows; they lay on her forehead like two small black caterpillars. She wore a Hermès scarf to hide the bald spots on her scalp, but the silk had ridden up to reveal two pale egg-shaped areas anyway, one on each side, and these looked so vulnerable that I reached across the table to tug the scarf down.

"It was a little crooked."

She came to this café often, and I noticed that she was careful to greet everyone who worked there in a friendly manner. One waitress returned her greeting with a gentleness that struck me as almost maternal, then furtively glanced at me.

"You dyed your eyebrows," I said.

"You like? Everybody says they make me look exotic. Oh, Kimmy, I'm so glad we could meet like this." She reached across the table and grabbed my hand. I told her I agreed about the eyebrows—they did look exotic. Then I complimented her outfit—a fluffy aquamarine jogging suit with pink piping and a French logo across the chest that Rae had bought for her. After we'd finished our coffee, we decided to get some ice cream at a shop down the street, and as we walked along the sidewalk, she put her hand in the crook of my elbow, and I gave it a gentle squeeze against my ribs. Suddenly it occurred to me that our fellow pedestrians seemed to be giving us an especially wide berth. Searching my mother's profile, I saw things there I had never noticed before—a childlike quality but also a kind of ingrained sadness. I looked closely but couldn't find a trace of the woman I'd known when I was growing up. The ghost of what she'd once been—quick, demanding, cruel, beautiful—seemed to have gone completely out of her. At the ice cream shop she ordered a vanilla malted, giving detailed instructions to the college kid behind the counter—*two shots of malt but only one scoop of ice cream, and fill the cup not quite all the way to the top.*

"I know how to do it," said the kid.

"Not for *me*," said my mother.

"I've done it for you before," said the boy, tonelessly.

"No, you haven't!"

He looked at his coworker, a girl in a ripped-up T-shirt with a little metal stick through her nose, and, without making even the slightest effort at discretion, rolled his young, arrogant eyes in an enormous arc.

Responsibility

It was 2:00 a.m. and I was tired. All I wanted was to climb back into bed, curl around David, and go to sleep again, and that's what I'd told the cop (except for the part about David).

My mother had been released from the city hospital a few days earlier. I figured she was safe and sound, reinstalled at the Regency, only now this cop was telling me she'd been arrested for DUI.

"Someone already posted bail, but she has no way of getting home tonight—no money for a cab, and she can't drive, obviously." He then explained my options: I could pick her up, or I could not pick her up. "Some guy named Ray" was supposedly going to send a limo to take her home in the morning, so it was really just about the one night.

"So, what do you say? You want to pick her up?"

"I don't want to do anything."

"I get that."

Something about the way he said these words made it seem like he really might, which is why I asked him if he thought was it wrong of me. I really wanted to know.

"In my experience," he said, "it rarely makes a difference what you do in this sort of situation with addicts of this type. You should probably do whatever you need to do for yourself."

The next day I told a friend, my best friend at the time, about this exchange.

"What a bad cop!" she said.

"No, really. He was a good cop."

We used to twin dress, not on purpose but just because we liked the same things and our budgets were similar. We were walking down Newbury Street, both wearing cropped green sweaters and black flats. Everything slightly different but essentially the same. We also liked the same books. The same movies. The same artists. The same makeup lines. The same recipes.

"Some things are just the way they are," said my friend. "Mothers are mothers, and daughters are daughters. It's nonnegotiable. You have responsibilities. I don't care what that cop said."

This friend, incidentally, had a needy but not a crazy or addicted mother. She had a mother who sent her care packages and who paid for her graduate school and who visited her once a month in order to cook stews and casseroles that she then packed in her daughter's freezer in single-serving-size plastic containers.

"You have an obligation," she insisted, "to take care of your mother, no matter what. It's just the way it is."

"But she keeps doing things like this. Like driving under the influence and getting arrested and fighting with everybody and trying to kill herself and calling just to yell at me, just to tell me I'm a terrible daughter. And actually, you know, I actually have other things to do. I actually have a life I should be living."

"But she's your mother!" said my friend, who at that moment, I realized, might not actually be my friend, despite her sweater.

Restoration

On my father's refrigerator is a sheet of paper with various inspirational quotes typed out on it. One of these refers to his favorite poem, by Walter de la Mare; it reads, "The Mermaid Is Here Today." One, lifted from an obscure movie directed by John Malkovich and having something to do, I suspect, with my father's tendency to fall for much younger women, says, "She's just a young girl, 62% water . . . and you could have been president." There are a lot of other quotes, all in different fonts and typefaces, but the one that my eye always lingers on longest, the one that makes me feel the solidity of the years behind us, is from the Bible. "I will restore to you," it promises my father every time he reaches for the skim milk, "the years that the locust hath eaten."

Robe

The desk clerk at the Regency caught up with me one day, just as I was about to punch the elevator button for the eighth floor, to ask if I could do something about my mother's behavior.

"It's getting stranger," he said. Then he described her leaving the building a few days earlier—a stormy February day with temperatures in the teens.

"I asked her where she was going, and she said she had to get some ice cream."

"That's basically all she eats," I told him. "Ben & Jerry's pistachio ice cream. Also peanut butter. Those are her two food groups."

My mother had told me all about the ice cream, so I told him about it too: Ben & Jerry's has many famous ice cream flavors, I explained, but pistachio is not one of them, and yet in my mother's opinion it is the very best flavor. Unfortunately, you can only get it at their retail stores, not in the supermarket, which is why she feels so lucky that there's a Ben & Jerry's right around the corner.

The clerk moved his white-gloved hand near his face, as if he were batting away an insect.

"The thing is," he said, "she was just wearing a robe."

"Just a robe?"

"Just a robe. It was fluttering around in the wind. All over the place."

I knew which robe he was talking about. A silky thing, voluminous and clingy at the same time. She'd made it herself in a moment of sartorial inspiration when I was still in college. She'd also made two somewhat lower-rent versions of the same robe for Tracy and me. Mine was entirely too large and made of polyester, with a print of white geometric geese on a navy ground. I'd thrown it out years ago. Tracy's, which was also huge, was made of a red tartan material. Our mother's robe was made of a rich turquoise-colored silk with a damask pattern of swirling peacock feathers. It fit perfectly.

"Well, I don't know what you expect me to do about it."

"Talk to her."

I shrugged. "What about?"

"Propriety."

I suddenly hated this man, with his fake-fancy accent. Something about the word *propriety* and the idea that seemed to be behind it—that my mother could suffer all she wanted in private—enraged me, so I didn't answer him, just gave him my best fuck-you smirk, pressed the elevator button, and let the doors slide silently between us.

Rocket Scientist

Boston, Massachusetts, 1996

Rae's arms are crossed over her heavy chest, one hand loosely gripping a roll of fat at her waist. Her hair—red, wiry, slightly gray at the temples—is a stiff helmet around her face. Her teeth are uneven and, like the thumb, index, and middle fingers of her right hand, stained from tobacco. Her eyes are brown and sweet, unguarded as a dog's. She's standing outside the little brick complex where she continued to live long after my mother had installed herself in the Regency.

They were "married" by this point. I put the word in quotes because their union was a gesture of such acute irony as to seem, at the time, nearly sincere—or maybe it was so sincere as to seem ironic. In any case I found it confusing. Unfortunately, this was long before gay marriage was legal in Massachusetts, so there were no official documents or procedures involved, which could have been useful, fiscally speaking, down the line. But their union did involve a ring: an enormous green garnet set with diamonds that my mother wore for years, even long after Rae was dead.

Rot

One day I came over to find her in bed, sleeping as usual, *Silence of the Lambs* playing on the TV, muted. She was making small, helpless sounds as she slept. I stood at her bedside for a while, watching. For some reason she struck me as incredibly textured. I know that sounds strange, but I just couldn't get over how detailed she was. Her skin was pale, her face shiny, every tiny pore apparent. Her lips were creased and slightly pursed, a filmy smear of peanut butter at one corner. Her hands, outside the covers, were ridged with blue veins. Her hair was thick and very dark, almost black, composed of strands that were, individually, also thick and very dark. The expression on her face seemed to me both worried and young, and I remember standing there for quite a while feeling maudlin about all of this before finally deciding I had to pee.

The master bathroom at the Regency apartment was a cavernous space covered in bisque-colored marble with a deep, claw-foot tub and a huge glassed-in shower stall. It had two towel heaters and two sinks, and one of these sinks, I noticed, was filled to the brim with pink water streaked with viscous threads of red. The other sink held a bloody washcloth and a pair of pliers. I stared at this bizarre still life just as I'd stared at my sleeping mother, mesmerized, almost paralyzed, not sure how to process the visual information in front of me. Eventually, I heard her stirring in the next room, and I pulled the pliers out of the sink and stomped up to her bedside.

"Oh, Kimmy," she said, "you're here." She patted the bed so Oscar would jump up on it.

"What are these?" I asked, holding up the pliers.

"Ah. I have this molar in the back, the way back, that's absolutely *killing* me. Of course, none of my dentists believe me. It's *filled* with rot, but they won't touch it, so I have to take it out myself, but I can't do it alone. That's why I'm so glad you're here! You're just what I need—somebody with a little upper body strength!"

Ruin

Eventually, her fiduciary said Rae couldn't afford to rent such a massive apartment for my mother alone, let alone fund her exorbitant tastes in furniture, clothes, and jewelry, so Rae's legal guardians cut off all financial support. Rather generously, I thought, they offered to buy my mother a small bungalow much closer to Rae.

"I laughed in their face," she said when she told me this story. "They want to shut me away in some crappy little house in some crappy little bedroom community—ha!"

"I don't know, Mom. A free house, no matter where it is, sounds like a pretty good deal to me."

"Trust me, Kimberli. They'll be sorry they messed with me!"

S

Salad

The yoga studio I go to every morning is two doors down from a Whole Foods, and when I stop by there after practice to pick up a few things, I notice someone who looks a lot like my mother sitting at one of the outdoor tables on the sidewalk. At first I figure this is just another doppelgänger and go inside to buy some almonds and eggs, but when I come back out, I see quite clearly that it actually is my mother sitting there. I know because for one thing she's wearing the blue lace sweater I gave her. For another she looks much more fragile than the women I usually imagine to be her. Even from the back, she looks nervous.

I can't decide whether I should stop and say hello, which might easily become a long and involved and probably embarrassing conversation (there are many people seated at nearby tables) or if I should keep going, which I know would be the easier but also the more cowardly option. I watch her eating a salad out of a large plastic box and reading something on her cell phone for a moment, then I walk over and say hello.

Squinting at me, she fumbles to remove her earbuds, then says: "Oh, my god, Kimmy, I didn't recognize you! I saw this *gorgeous* woman out of the corner of my eye, but I didn't know it was you, and then you were standing right there talking to me, and I thought, Who is this *gorgeous* woman, and what does she want? and I still didn't know it was you!"

Several people have by now looked up from their cell phones or salads or muffins or coffees to watch us, and I definitely hate them. I want them to stop looking—not at me but at my mother, who I realize is making an odd impression because she's speaking so loudly and everything about her seems too raw. I say that the salad she's eating—full of dried fruit and nuts and beans—looks healthy, and she says: "It is. It is." Then I ask if she's still planning on leaving in a few days, and she says: "I have to, honey. I need a radical change."

I say okay, and she reaches out to give my hand a squeeze.

"The sweater looks really good on you."

"Thank you. I really, really love it."

"I'm so glad." Then I lean down to give her a kiss goodbye, at which point she kind of grabs me, gently, by the shoulders and whispers, "You took all the good in me and none of the bad, you know that?"

Same

When I was still in college, during one of our weekly dinners at L'Osteria, my father told me the story of how he fell in love with my mother. We were sitting near the windows, which were actually a bank of French doors that sometimes stood open in the summer but that night were closed because the AC was on. The glass was beaded with condensation, and on the other side the blurry shapes of people and cars and bikes and dogs and children shifted along Second Avenue. I forget what prompted it, what we were talking about, but suddenly my father got very quiet. Peering into his glass of sparkling water, he shook his head and said, "Just thinking about all those years."

A little later, over a plate of *mozza en carrozza*, he told me that when he first saw my mother, he was only twelve years old and she was just ten—a long-legged, choppy-haired little girl. They were standing on line at a movie theater. She was ahead of him, and he thought she was beautiful, which is why he announced—loudly—to his friends that someday she was going to be his wife.

"The lesson?" he said, as if winding up for a joke. I smiled and put down my fork. "Be careful what you wish for!"

My mother tells a different story about how she fell in love with my father. They were in a car, the very car on the very night in which and on which I would enter, no matter how microscopically, the scene. My father was driving, and my mother, in the passenger seat, was wearing a white blanket around her shoulders.

"We were stopped at a red light, and your father caught my eye in the rearview mirror. He was such a handsome kid," she said. "He winked." We were talking long-distance, Boston to San Francisco, so I couldn't see her face, of course, but I could still picture the subtle twist of her mouth as she spoke because that's how she usually expresses irony, absurdity. "*One* wink," she said. "So stupid."

San Francisco

We moved there for no reason really, except that we were young enough and unencumbered enough to do it. We left our apartment on Beacon Hill, our friends, David's family, my mother. Just took off.

We lived there for five years, and they were really good years. One of the things we did while we were in San Francisco was get two more dogs—at which point, of course, we started walking around with three dogs instead of just Oscar, which was a little like walking around with a huge sign over our heads that said, "Go ahead, say something funny about our dogs." All three of them were small and sweet and goofy and troublesome, and one of them liked to sleep at the foot of our bed, and another one liked to sleep up by our faces, but Oscar was more austere and liked to sleep on the hardwood floor, though in the mornings he always jumped up too. Another thing we did in San Francisco was eat a lot of donuts because we lived five blocks away from what is, I suspect, the best donut shop in the world, Bob's on Polk Street. Many mornings—most, in fact—David and I walked the dogs down to Bob's to buy buttermilk crullers from Urmilla, the nice and talkative, but not too talkative, lady behind the counter. We'd get coffee too, then walk up to Lafayette Park, where we'd throw sticks and balls for the dogs in the empty tennis courts. San Francisco is where I got pregnant with Isabella, and it is where she was born. It is also where I learned what it is like to be not depressed, although at first I thought I just felt funny. For the first six months or so that we lived there, I simply didn't feel like myself. Eventually, I realized that this was because I was happy. And the longer I stayed happy, the more clearly I could see that I had been unhappy before, even though I'd never thought of myself as an unhappy person. But once I was living in San Francisco, with its gentle seasons and its generous distance from so many of the things that had caused my unhappiness, I was able to look at my life as it had progressed so far and see that depression had lain like a sheer black fabric over all of it—all but the bit that started in San Francisco because in San Francisco the fabric lifted. And yet the whole time we were living there, I kept telling myself that it was only temporary. I kept saying to myself and to David that we had to move back east. Had to had to had to had to had to had to. And every week or two, when I talked to my mother on the phone, I would say, casually, as if it were not really a question at all, "When we move back," and she would say, "Oh, Kimmy, how I look forward to that day."

And so, in this way, every day I spent in San Francisco felt a bit like marching toward a sentence. I didn't know what to call the sentence or how to stop the marching—I knew only that my time in that city where I was happy was meant to be finite. And as the years stretched on, something inside of me began insisting more and more vehemently that we move back east. David didn't understand why.

"We're happy here," he said. "If we go east, we might not be so happy."

I said, "My mother." I said, "Our daughter should know her family." And sometimes I said, "She should grow up with the seasons."

That's a romantic notion, of course—the bit about the seasons—and I leaned on it a lot, but in reality it was as if I'd put on blinders. I didn't care so much about the seasons as I did about the relentless voice inside of me that said *have to have to have to have to have to have to have to*. So I nudged and I nudged, and eventually

David gave his notice at his job, and we bought a vw camper van, and we told each other and all our friends that we were going on a fantastic adventure, driving back across the country, taking six weeks to do it, but somewhere deep inside of me, some other part of me started screaming *No!* At first, though, it screamed very softly, so it was easy to ignore.

Then, one day in June, after five years in our little apartment, with its pink silk curtains and its champagne crate window boxes, we packed up everything. There wasn't much because we'd lived so lightly in San Francisco, planning always to leave it. We shipped Isabella's crib and a few boxes of books and some clothes, and the rest we put in the back of our van, along with our dogs and a potted grapefruit tree that we'd grown from a seed, and then we started driving, only first we drove down to Big Sur and then farther south, to San Juan Bautista, just to say goodbye to those places one last time, then we drove back through the city to say goodbye to our friends. One night we had Indian pizza with our friends Katie and Steve, and I got drunk because by that point the small voice wasn't so small anymore, and I was starting to freak out. So I tried to shut it up by having a lot of beer. In the morning we said goodbye to Katie and Steve, and then we drove past our old apartment on Russian Hill, where we had lived those five excellent happy years. And as we idled outside for a minute, we could actually hear the building manager inside our old apartment because it was on the first floor and the kitchen window was open, and she was sighing as she looked through all of our now empty drawers—"So, so, so," she said. It was at that point that the voice took over my entire body. I started shaking as the black veil began moving back into place. At first it just went over my eyes. But as we drove out of the city, across the Bay Bridge, it kept descending, like a storm head. Suddenly, it was perfectly obvious that I'd been listening to the wrong voice, and that's when I screamed. It lasted a while. In a way it was more like a seizure than a scream. David had to pull over. After several minutes, when I could finally

speak again, I said: "This is a mistake. I don't want to go." But of
course it was too late.

Saving Grace

B——, Massachusetts, 1998

The transcript is balanced in the foliage behind the card, which is
attached by a purple ribbon to a bouquet of pale pink peonies and
green-veined calla lilies. In a stranger's block letters, the card reads:

DEAR MOM:

CONGRATULATIONS ON YOUR A'S.

LOVE,

KIM & DAVID

The main way Rae expressed love was through money, and even
though she was legally prohibited from doing so, she still snuck
my mother large cash infusions on a regular basis. These paid for
things like the last two classes my mother needed to complete
her BA (two decades after she'd started night school back in New
Jersey). Rae also paid for her rent, which is why she was able to
live in such a cute apartment even after she'd left the Regency.
The new place wasn't nearly as grand, but it was clean and cozy,
with a shining white kitchen, a bay window, a working fireplace,
and a spacious fire escape that she turned into a hanging garden
full of ferns and succulents. Only I didn't understand about the
money at the time. I had no idea that Rae was siphoning off her
cash allowance to my mother. I just figured my mother was making due somehow. Staying organized. I guess I didn't think about
it too hard. Just knocked on a lot of wood.

Scared

"Don't call me, I'll call you," she said right before she left. But
that was almost a week ago, which is why I touch her number on
the screen of my cell phone. When she picks up, she doesn't say

hello, just: "Thanks. That's terrific. Now they know *exactly* where I am. Good work." Then she hangs up.

For some reason, though, she doesn't seem to mind talking to Tracy. And Tracy talks to me. And Tracy says that our mother has been calling her from the highway because that's where she's been spending her days, walking along the edge, studying the wildflowers, especially the Queen Anne's lace, which is her favorite.

"I'm scared," says my sister.

Scrawled

The man my father once was is the reason the man my father is now finds it so hard to smile, I think. Because the man my father is now makes himself remember the man he once was, the slow, fat, angry man—the silent, drunk, and violent one. I know this because of something I once saw in a dresser drawer of his some nine or ten years ago. He'd broken his femur, and I was staying with him in New York City for a couple of weeks after he'd undergone a complex surgery involving pins and a metal cuff to put his leg back together. I'd come down on the train with Isabella, who was still in a stroller, in order to help out—walk his dog, do the shopping, pick up takeout, rent videos, bring out the trash.

Not long after I arrived, my father, still groggy on painkillers and lying in bed, told me I could find an envelope of cash to buy groceries in the top drawer of his dresser. But when I hunted around in the place he'd indicated, I couldn't find the money. He was half-asleep. I didn't want to bother him, so I just looked in the next drawer, even though it was immediately apparent that I shouldn't, since it was full of what were clearly personal effects. Still, I rummaged, curiosity guiding my hand, deeper and deeper into the papers, the old photos. When my fingers touched one particular photograph, I had the eerie sensation that there were suddenly three of us in the room: my father, me, and the man I'd grown up with. The photo showed my father in his early thirties. Behind his aviator glasses, his eyelids were half-shut, and behind his eyelids, his eyes were obviously swimming. Everything about the man was blurry. I don't mean that the picture was out of focus—it wasn't—but my father's expression, his whole mien, was. On a curled, yellowing bit of paper taped to the front of the photo he'd written two words: *Never Forget.*

Scrutiny

Eventually, she'd storm off in a rage (although not before removing a full-length mirror from my bedroom wall—a mirror she'd previously given me as a gift—and cramming it into the passenger seat of her car), but at the beginning of the visit, things were fine. I'd made us a pot of tea and brought out a plate of homemade cookies—hazelnut wafers shaped like oak leaves dipped in chocolate. This particular type of cookie happens to be a traditional Swedish recipe, and when I mentioned this to my mother, she said, "Oh, Swedish!" and made a fancy little flourish with her fingers. I made a similar flourish and said, "Yes! Swedish!"

Isabella was sitting near us on the floor under the table, playing with some plastic food—bananas, macaroons, long black eggplants. The dogs would have been somewhere nearby as well in that open, sunny space—the living room of our old apartment on Symphony Road in downtown Boston, the apartment we moved into after San Francisco. They would have been sleeping or scratching or drinking water from their bowl in the kitchen. Oscar, the largest and scruffiest, might have had his muzzle propped on my foot as my mother and I talked because he liked to do that.

"You're the only way this will ever get done," she said as she pushed a box full of old photographs across the table. "You're the only one who's together enough." She meant to put the pictures into albums. She wanted me to make three of them: one for her, one for Tracy, and one for me. I remember lifting the flaps of the box, peeking inside, and thinking, *So, I'm that person now—the repository, the in-between, the link, the keeper of family photographs.* It was, for a while, a vaguely satisfying idea, though within a matter of days it became perfectly clear that I wasn't a good repository at all. The problem was to a large extent a philosophical one. For example, I started wondering what, exactly, the role of a family photo album actually was, and I decided that at root it is a form of storytelling or at the very least an elaborate storytelling prompt, and this, naturally, led me to consider the sorts of stories that were attached to the photographs inside the box. For the most part these were pictures from my mother's childhood and my own, and when I imagined sitting on the couch next to Isabella, leafing through the pages of this hypothetical album, I knew that the only way to get around so many of these stories would be through the use of euphemisms, white lies, and silence. And while these are convenient verbal conventions under certain circumstances, I wondered: *would they be right?* I spent weeks scrutinizing this question from many angles, but in the end I still couldn't decide. There was, in particular, one photograph that bothered me more than all the others. This happened to be the very photograph that would almost certainly constitute the natural centerpiece of our family history (see *gesture*). But to include that photo in an album and at the same time evade or omit the stories connected to it would, I finally decided, be unfair or even worse. Not just a lie of omission but an actual injustice. And so I never made the albums. Instead, I keep the box under my desk, where it makes a decent footrest.

Selfish

She finally calls from wherever she is in New Jersey. I don't know because she refuses to say. Just tells me she's extremely sick and there's blood in her sputum and they won't give her any antibiotics because they're trying to kill her.

"But you probably think that's okay, though, right? Because you don't care, right? You don't really care about anything having to do with me."

"Oh, Mom."

"What's it like, *eh*, Kimberli?" Her voice sounds faint and sandpapery. "What's it like to be so *supremely* selfish? To care only for yourself? Your mother's homeless, sick, spitting up blood in her sputum, but you have other things to worry about, don't you? Other *things!*"

"Where are you, Mom?"

"It's really none of your business, is it? You and DMH."

Shrewd

Ry Cooder was blasting on the stereo. Isabella was pounding on a tiny toy piano. The dogs were fighting over a rawhide bone that my mother had bought for them. Her kitchen smelled of Lysol and the breaded chicken cutlets we had frying on the stove. I was slicing tomatoes and my mother was washing parsley when I said something that made her laugh. "Oh, Kimmy," she said, "you're so funny." Then she gave me a hug, and in return I touched her elbow, lightly, and she said, "You've always been like that!"

"Like what?"

"Like, love me but from afar." Flicking her fingers in a queenly sort of way, she added, "From over *there*."

Silk Couch

B——, Massachusetts, Thanksgiving 2000

Her hair is pushed away from her face in a sprayed-in-place but nevertheless charmingly windswept-looking arrangement. She seems relaxed, her smile easy, sincere. She's sitting at the dining table in her apartment (the smaller, more modest one), holding Isabella on her lap. Their cheeks touch.

In the foreground there are wine and water glasses, brass candlesticks, a bread basket, a gravy boat . . . In the background, lying next to each other on our mother's white silk couch, Tracy and I recuperate after having eaten way too much. I remember that particular bellyache—the meal had been a ruthless stuffing, an even more gluttonous than usual Thanksgiving pig-out. The old childhood formula of food = love was clearly at work, and that day I'd eaten seconds and thirds under the delusion that I could munch away my worries. My mother had managed to stay out of hospitals for a few years by that point and had lived simply—quietly and undramatically—in that small but graciously proportioned apartment. She still talked crazy and took way too many pills, but she was safe, and I just wanted her to stay that way. A slightly loopy but engaged grandmother. A story with a decent ending.

I'd eaten so much I actually worried, for a while, that something might tear. But by the time this photo was taken, I seem to have more or less recovered. Tracy looks cheerful too—laughing with her mouth closed, looking sidelong at our mother. Something about her expression makes me think she's on the brink of making a wisecrack. I'm scrunched down low, half-lost in a sea of throw pillows. Only my face is visible and one hand, which is raised, for some reason, in a peace sign.

Simpler

Rae didn't believe in exercise. She barely believed in moving. Over two hundred pounds, she spent most of her days hunched over a cheap black-and-white composition notebook in which she scrawled what she called her "equations." In reality these were made-up physics formulas combined with devastating memory fragments that obliquely referenced the sexual and psychological abuse she'd suffered as a child. Her favorite meal was the one she ate three or four times a week: sixteen ounces of rare prime rib from the steakhouse five blocks away from her group home. She took a limo there. The long and the short of it was that my mother's sorta-kinda-maybe-make-believe-maybe-real-I-never-could-tell-wife was a classic walking heart attack, and when the inevitable finally happened one cold January afternoon in 2001, my mother found herself homeless within the year.

For a while she stayed at a youth hostel a few blocks away from us in Boston. After that she found a roommate situation on the South Shore, but it didn't take long before she got kicked out. Then she went back to the youth hostel. They had a two-week limit, so every fourteen days she stayed with us for a few days, but she left pills everywhere, and when we found one in Isabella's bed, we told her she couldn't come back. Eventually, she found an old-school, hippie-style rooming house in western Massachusetts, and that lasted longer than expected—a month or even two. But after that she started living in her car.

Over the phone Tracy and I had many long and anxious strategy discussions. I thought we should wait things out: our mother had been unraveling ever since Rae had died, growing more and more agoraphobic, sleeping through most of the day, and seeming to be on a crazy mix of drugs again. I proposed we encourage her to commit herself to a hospital, which would then lead to a halfway house, and after that—hopefully—to some kind of subsidized housing. But Tracy said it made her too sad to think of doing this, which is why she invited her to drive out to Chicago and live with her.

"It's just simpler," she told me. "I have no kids. A low-maintenance boyfriend. I'm at work most of the time anyway. It'll be fine."

Sin

I've spent years trying to understand how a person could do the kinds of things my grandfather did to his children. I came close to real understanding only once. I don't remember the exact circumstances, but my mother was coming up the stairs, and I was fighting with her. Maybe she was dropping something off, or maybe she was picking something up. In any case I think she was on her way to Chicago.

Our Boston apartment was on the top floor of a four-story townhouse, and there was my mother, pounding up the stairs. She was mad, and I was panicky because I've always been terrified of her anger. I didn't want her in my home, yet there she was, getting closer every second. Boom! Boom! Boom! I couldn't possibly have heard each and every one of her footfalls on each and every one of those stairs, but I felt them . . . And the dogs did too. They started barking like crazy, so I shoved them into my study and shut the door. I told them to be quiet, but they kept barking because dogs, as everyone knows, are sensitive creatures; no doubt they read my alarm. Oscar, my favorite (yes, of the three, I had a favorite—Oscar smelled like woodsmoke, and we had him first; I couldn't help it), raised his bark to a series of high-pitched yelps. My nerves were expanding, unraveling. Blood in my ears. Senses closing down. What I did was kick him. He was a muscularly built dog, but small: just over twenty pounds. His eyes were brown and round, and when I kicked him, he looked up at me as his abdomen curled and his legs buckled. And then, immediately overwhelmed by a wave of self-loathing—black, absolute, nauseous—I kicked him again.

Do you see what I'm saying? There's a "because" in there. What I mean is this: because I kicked Oscar, I kicked Oscar again.

Slaughterhouse

"A Seven Hundred–Bed Adult In-Patient Facility." This is how the hospital my mother was recently committed to in New Jersey describes itself on its website. I found this site through a Google search, even though Tracy warned me not to look because these days even state-funded psychiatric hospitals have reviews online, and the Yelp reviews for this particular institution include such helpful suggestions and commentary as:

"Shut it down and burn it to hell."

"This is probably one of the worst of the worst."

"Patients there suffer at the hands of the staff and their military ways."

"A slaughterhouse."

"They profess to have a wellness and recovery care model but it has an abuse and death care model."

"No one wants to work there."

"Geriatric patients are treated badly."

"My grandmother was put in there for her 'own good,' and she never came out."

"I *told* you not to look," said Tracy.

Snow Day

The kids are playing a made-up game called "brainwaves." I can hear them from my study—a wooden platform that projects out over our living room.

"Legos," says Isaac.

"No!" says Isabella.

It's the third snow day this year. The house is a mess. I should water the plants. Do some laundry. The roads are so bad that David stayed home from the office. He's working on his laptop at the table, only not right now. Right now he's making a fire in the woodstove.

"Cake?" he suggests.

"You're not playing," Isabella tells him.

"Cake?" says Isaac."

"Think!" says Isabella.

I have two design clients breathing down my neck and should really be working on those projects. Then again, I should also do some yoga because the studio was closed this morning so I didn't get to practice and I always get a bit tetchy when I don't practice. The problem is, I don't feel like working, and I don't feel like doing yoga. I could clean the bathroom because the ring around the tub is getting a little hard to ignore. I could also feed the birds, who keep darting up to the empty feeder, then flying away again.

"Star Wars?" asks Isaac.

"I'm not going to play with you unless you listen to my brainwaves!" says Isabella.

When the phone rings, I know it's my mother. I don't know how I know, I just do. I always do. And even though I haven't spoken to her for weeks (the last time was a few days before she was admitted to the hospital), as soon as I pick up, she says she doesn't want to stay on long. She just has a favor to ask about her things in storage, especially the paperwork because—

I interrupt to ask how things are going, and she says, "Same old shit." I figure she's talking about DMH pursuing her even to New Jersey, but we don't get into it because all of a sudden she says she made a mistake and actually she doesn't feel like talking. Then she hangs up.

Now it's Isaac's turn. Isabella asks if he's thinking of Ninja weapons.

"No," he says, grinning.

"Hamburgers? Snow? Magic Markers?"

"Harry Potter!" I yell from my study.

Stitches

It didn't take long for her to start doing some crazy things in Chicago, but Tracy held out for ages. I'm talking about really inappropriate, boundary-crossing things. Bizarre things. For instance, once she sprayed insecticide in Tracy's face. Another time it was oven cleaner. Another time, on the highway, while Tracy was driving sixty-five miles an hour, she karate chopped her in the trachea because Tracy had said something she didn't like. There were other incidents more or less along the same lines. Some of them involved Tracy's friends and invasive, pushy phone calls in which my mother pretended to be Tracy. Some of them involved Tracy's employer and more phone calls in which my mother said things she hoped would get Tracy fired. Still other incidents involved Tracy's underwear, which my mother found, for some reason, necessary to repeatedly steal, wear, and hide no matter how many times my sister told her not to and no matter how many new pairs of underwear Tracy bought and squirreled away in secret places, such as inside the zippered cases of the decorative pillows she kept on her bed. There were also many arguments concerning bathroom usage, and these, I suspect, were pretty bad, judging from my own bathroom usage arguments with my mother, who can easily spend a stretch of three or four hours at a time in even a public bathroom. The turning point for Tracy involved her boyfriend, at whom my mother, in a fit of rage, threw a can opener—one of the heavy ones. He wound up with a gash on his forehead that needed seven stitches. It was at this point that my sister finally told her she had to leave. But my mother, who had lived in Chicago by then for nearly two years, sleeping in the good room, on the good mattress, didn't want to leave, mostly because she had nowhere else to go.

The eviction—which is what it turned into, ultimately—involved two policemen, one of whom called me that afternoon, hoping I might intervene long-distance.

"Could you please, please, tell your mother to get out of bed and get dressed?" he asked. She had stripped naked, which is one of her favorite techniques for dealing with law enforcement types.

"The trick with my mother," I told him (as if I knew), "is just to be really, really patient."

"We're trying!" said the cop, "but she keeps throwing things at us."

Tracy called me later that day. I couldn't understand a lot of what she was saying because her voice was garbled and squeaky, but eventually she calmed down enough for me to understand. "She's just sitting there. On the sidewalk. Just . . . picking her hair. I'm a terrible person. How could I do this? Kick my own mother out of my house?" Then she started sobbing. It went on for a long time, but after a while she stopped and we got off the phone. I called a couple of times after that for updates, and at both 8 p.m. and 10 p.m. Tracy said our mother was still sitting on the curb. But by the morning she was gone.

Within a week of the eviction, Tracy broke up with her boyfriend. Within two months she'd gained thirty pounds. Soon after that she gained thirty more.

Stricken

Because my mother didn't include me on her contact list, the hospital refuses to put my calls through to her, so it's been months since I've heard her voice when she finally calls "just to check in." She's been in the seven hundred–bed in-patient facility for ninety-one days.

"As you've no doubt gathered, I've been prevented from getting settled down here. I have no business being in this hospital, and everybody knows it. This place is for addicts. It's for convicts. My roommate is *actually* a convicted *matricide*. Do you know what that means? I'm living with a murderer." Then she says something about an assault and a guard, something about charges, but I don't think she's talking about her roommate anymore. When I ask her to clarify, she says never mind.

I get off the phone just as Isabella comes home from school. I had been in the middle of making cornmeal cookies when my mother called, so I study the recipe for a minute, trying to remember what I was doing.

"What's wrong?" Isabella asks as she pours herself some juice. "Nothing!"

"Then why do you look so . . . stricken?"

"What, this?" I say, exaggerating whatever I'm doing with my mouth. "Honey, I'm just concentrating. And smiling. I'm smiling."

Stunner

New York, New York, Christmas Eve 2001

I'm sitting on a couch, holding a glass of wine up high, away from Isabella. I have on my dressy gold-and-pearl seashell earrings, a black mesh top, dark slacks. Isabella is wearing a gray ribbed turtleneck and a velvet skirt printed with pink flowers. These are gifts from Grandpa Jake. They come from Saks and are quite chic, especially on a three-year-old. Isabella reaches toward me as I study her face. You can't see her green-gray eyes in this picture, but I can still find the strangely gilded image of myself floating in her pupils, an image not unlike the one my own eyes once reflected back at my mother.

I don't know if it was before or after this photo was snapped, but I remember asking my father that night if he thought my mother had been crazy the whole time I was growing up. His answer was as unequivocal as it was immediate: no.

"Of course she was addicted to Valium. And of course she made a few suicide attempts. But she wasn't crazy. Not like she is now. No way."

We'd driven down to New York to spend Christmas with my father and his girlfriend, Amanda. Amanda was sharp and snappy, and I wasn't at all sure I liked her. But she was about to do me a great favor.

We had this exchange over appetizers in my father's living room. Amanda, David, and I were drinking wine, my father a glass of sparkling water. I asked if he was sure about my mother, and he said of course he was sure, then reached for another stuffed mushroom, at which point Amanda put her wine glass on the coffee table kind of harshly and said: "Exactly how would you know the answer to that question, Jake? You were drunk the whole time!" And with that one sentence my whole childhood slipped instantly into clearer focus. It was, for lack of a better metaphor, a serious v-8 moment, a real head slapper. *Of course. He'd been drunk the whole time. I should have thought of that!*

T

Teeth

"The only thing my father ever did," my mother once told me, "the only thing that could be construed as the least bit fatherly, was he used insist that we kids take care of our teeth. 'Above all,' he used to say, 'you must brush your teeth!'"

Three-Unit Bridge

When she left Chicago, she started driving east toward Boston. Along the way there were many complications. Chief among these was a mishap involving a three-unit bridge—the kind a dentist puts in your mouth. Actually, I'm talking about half of a six-unit bridge that at some point during my mother's cleaning rituals cracked down the middle and as a result became so loose that when she took a swig of water, half of it got swept down her esophagus.

Three-unit bridges are weighty little constructions made of porcelain and gold. At the base, where they fit into the gumline, they are, as my mother described it, "sharp as razors." I don't think they are actually that sharp, but that the metal tapers to a very thin point is undoubtedly the case.

For a while, I remember hoping that the problem would somehow evaporate, as some of my mother's more exotic predicaments occasionally do. Her brain tumor, for instance, disappeared when her systemic bacterial infection started acting up. And her TMJ pain went away when her balance became an issue. She, herself, was convinced that the bridge was going to kill her. That she was bleeding internally and high up in the intestine was proved, she said, by the blackness of her stool.

Once she arrived on the outskirts of Boston, she stayed for a couple of weeks at a youth hostel that advertised itself on the internet as having an easy, laid-back, party-hearty atmosphere. After that, she lived in her car for several weeks while I, for my part—having refused her lodging for even a single night—entered a depression unlike any I'd ever known. This was deeper, more determined, almost businesslike at its darkest moments. There was even a stretch of time, shortly before I became pregnant with Isaac, when I occasionally found myself thinking about the mechanics of suicide in the same way I might consider the execution of a particularly complicated recipe. As in, technique, efficiency, clean-up.

Tornado

Isaac is going through a tornado phase. He often draws tornadoes and frequently finds creative ways to insert tornado references into everyday conversation. For example, on the playground today I overhear him explaining to a friend what's wrong with his grandmother this way: "It's like Mormor basically has a *tornado* in her brain!"

I can't imagine that the other child, a Chinese-American girl named Lucy, has any idea who or what a "mormor" might be, but she seems to understand the idea of what he's saying because she nods gravely and says, "That's really bad."

Trey's Place

New York, New York, ca. 2004

That's his favorite diner, Trey's Place, across the street, which puts us on 3rd Avenue. We're headed downtown. And here's a shocker (I'd never noticed this before, not in real life, only after looking at this picture): I'm nearly as tall as my father.

We're walking four dogs—my father, his 100-pound mutt named Roxy (half-wolfhound and half-lab and rather majestic in a lumbering sort of way), and me our three little scrappers. Chimmi, who's part Chihuahua, lags miserably behind, but Oscar and Inky are prancing right along. You can't see our faces—my father's and mine—because the picture was taken from behind, no doubt by David. Even so, it's clear we're talking and very involved in whatever it is we're saying. Our steps are synchronized: both our right legs are forward, our heels just touching the ground. My father's wearing a leather jacket and jeans, a T-shirt. The hand not holding Roxy's leash is hidden from view, but it's a pretty sure bet that he's holding a cup of coffee from Trey's—black, no sugar. We're just walking along. It's nothing special. But in a fire, I'd save this one.

Tug

After she'd come back from Chicago, we invited my mother over for dinner a couple times, but she declined. In fact, she seemed to be avoiding us. This meant I hadn't seen her in over two years when I ran into her in downtown B—. It was Memorial Day. I remember because Isabella had off from school and in the morning, she, David, and I took the dogs for a long walk in the woods, then went to our favorite farm stand. Among our purchases were strawberries and rhubarb, which Isabella and I had put in a pie later that afternoon. This is why I'd taken a walk to the small commercial center near our apartment: I wanted to buy a pint of vanilla icecream to top the pie for dessert.

When I emerged from the over-air-conditioned vault of the icecream store into a blast of early summer heat, I noticed a woman crossing the street with purposeful intent. She had heavy, pewter gray hair cut to her jawline and a determined expression on her face. She wore a white sleeveless shirt and a tan shoulder bag, and she looked thin and strong, and I thought: That looks like Mom, only German. And actually, it was my mother, although about the German part, I can't really say.

We talked for a while on the sidewalk. She held her hand over her mouth when she spoke because of having lost the bridge in the front, on the bottom. She told me she'd been trying to go to the pharmacy to pick up a prescription, but because it was Memorial Day, it had closed early. Then she said, "I recognized you by your carriage. From across the street, I knew it was you as soon as I saw you come out of that store."

It was very hot out and I found myself worrying about the ice cream in the brown paper bag I was holding. Although I wasn't crazy about the idea, I asked if she wanted to come home with me for dinner, but she said she couldn't.

"I can't bear for Isabella to see me this way." Then she took her hand away from her mouth and pulled down her lower lip, and I could see that she was right: what was there—six tiny yellowed nubs—looked like witch's teeth and would certainly have scared my daughter.

At that point, I started to cry, but fortunately I was wearing a pair of black sunglasses. I suggested we sit on a bench for a few minutes, so we did, and still I was worried about the ice-cream. We talked about my mother's housing options, which were few, and also about how she might speak without holding her hand over her mouth, but also without showing her bottom teeth, and she practiced doing this for a while so I could tell her when she got it right.

"Does this look okay?" she said, holding her lower lip very stiffly.

"It looks fine," I lied, because in reality it was obvious that she was missing a lot of teeth by the way her lip moved, and again, I started to cry, and again I was grateful for the fact that my sunglasses were so dark.

Eventually, I said that I needed to go since it was getting close to dinnertime, and she said, "Yes, you'd better. Your ice-cream is probably melting!" Then she told me that she, too, was hankering after some ice-cream. But she was worried she didn't have enough money for a cone, so I started digging in my pocket, at which point she stood up and said "No!" and started walking quickly away. I found some coins and ran after her, and we had a weird tug-of-war there in the middle of the sidewalk, with me trying to put the change in her hand and her trying to push the change away.

Turd

She lived in her car for six or seven weeks before finally checking herself into a city hospital. It was all part of a larger plan, she told me over the phone—she was just using them, the hospital, the doctors—to get what she really needed, what they should have been giving her anyway. Treatment. *Actual healing*. For instance, she was going to use this hospitalization to finally get her teeth fixed. But her doctors didn't see it the same way and as soon as she was admitted they put her on high doses of lithium and anti-psychotics. Pretty soon she reported that she was experiencing many unpleasant side effects from these drugs, including the sensation that her skin was turning itself inside-out, uncontrollable drooling, thinning hair, and rapid weight gain. But none of these things, I think, bothered her quite as much as the fact that the hospital had no immediate plans for dealing with the issue of the three-unit bridge.

David, Isabella, and I had been travelling in Greece on vacation when my mother first checked into the hospital, so it took me a while to visit. When I finally found a free afternoon to go see her, everything seemed to go wrong. I got lost on the way over and then, when I went to a grocery store to buy her some jellybeans (specially requested), I realized I'd forgotten my wallet and had to dig around in my purse for loose change. Then I couldn't find a parking space near the hospital, and, when I finally did, I didn't have any change left for the meter. I felt truly defeated by this last problem, which is why I put my forehead against the cool metal stump of the meter. Just then, a man walking by stopped to ask if I was okay. It was a beautiful summer day, and every second I spent within sight of that hospital felt like a penance, but I couldn't explain this to a perfect stranger, so I just shrugged, and he said, "Here," and put two hours worth of quarters in the meter for me. I figured my destiny was set.

The thing—probably the main thing—to remember about my mother is that she is, first and foremost, a drama queen. This is what I reminded myself when I saw her stumble out of her room with her hair in front of her face. She was wearing gray sweatpants, a green T-shirt and black platform flip-flops, and she was staggering the way a really hammy actor, trying to be subtle, might stagger in a movie where he's just gotten shot and has a long, agonizing death ahead of him.

It had been a few years since I'd been in a psychiatric hospital and I'd forgotten certain basics about visiting people there, like how the doors are locked, and how you get a suspicious once-over from the staff before they let you in, and how you have to register while somebody checks through everything you've brought for the patient, taking away plastic bags, pills, sharps, anything made of glass . . . But it was all coming back to me as I stood there in the hallway—not sure what to do with my hands, my feet—and waited for the guard to get my mother.

I figured she couldn't see me because her hair was hanging in front of her face like a curtain. The guard, who wore no expression, stopped my mother's progress when they got close to where I was standing, and although I'd called just before I'd left home to say I was coming, although I now said, not two feet away from her, "Hi, Mom. I got your *Jelly Bellies*," she still wondered aloud, as she fussed with her hair, *who* might have come to visit.

It took a long time and both hands for her to get her hair out of her eyes, but when she finally did, she said, "Oh, Kimmy! You look like a movie star!" Then she touched my hair and said, "People pay a lot of money for that color" and then she said, "Cute, cute, cute," touching the three plastic beads, borrowed from Isabella's extensive collection, that I'd put on a gold chain around my neck. These comments might have felt nice but I couldn't shake the sense that they were largely for show, for the sake of the nurse and the guard, who were standing nearby and whose vaguely appraising eyes I could feel traveling over me as my mother spoke. She then took my chin in her hand and asked the nurse, Nancy (according to the tag on her sweater), "Isn't she pretty?" Nancy nodded an expert mental health worker's nod, meaning there was no telling whether she agreed with my mother, intended merely to appease her, or simply wanted to save me embarrassment.

The guard then took us past a man wearing several hospital gowns doggedly rolling himself against a wall, and to a small room crowded with nine or ten vinyl-upholstered armchairs and a coffee table. The room had shatterproof glass walls and a shatterproof glass door, which he allowed us to close so that we could talk in private.

"Mostly they're nice here," my mother said after he left. "There's one guy I don't like. A real turd. But the others are okay. They like me. Can you believe that?" Her speech was slurred and slow because of the meds. I thought her tongue might have been swollen—it didn't seem to fit right in her mouth, and every so often a long, viscous strand of saliva would drop from her lower lip onto her lap. When the saliva happened to fall on one of her hands, she absently swiped at it as if she were shooing away a fly.

She'd been in the hospital for a few weeks at that point and had gained a surprising amount of weight since the last time I'd seen her. During that time, David, Isabella, and I had spent nearly a month in Greece, lying on beaches and eating late dinners of perfectly cooked fish and drinking enormous quantities of ouzo with friends and visiting islands of incredible beauty, and for this reason I was acutely aware of an intense sensation of guilt sparking electrically on and off inside of me as we spoke.

She asked to inspect my sunglasses, which I had tucked into the V-neck of my T-shirt. They were made of plastic the color of caramel and had green lenses and they were exactly the kind of thing my mother has always adored. In fact, the reason I'd wanted them in the first place was because they reminded me of her when we were both much younger. I handed them over and she examined them appreciatively.

"*Très cher. Non?*"

I said, "*très*" and explained, perhaps a little defensively, that they'd been a birthday present from David.

She shook her head and said, "You still have that man wrapped around your thumb." And then she said, "No!" and shook her head again, more vigorously. She said, "No, no, no, no, no!" and we both laughed and shook our heads and stamped our feet. When she finally caught her breath, she said, "*Finger!* You have him wrapped around your little *finger!*"

Then she told me to put the sunglasses on, so I put them on, and then she asked to wear them herself, so I gave them to her and I noticed that her posture instantly improved as she flipped back her hair and slid on the sunglasses—which are Chanel, and very glam—and she looked, for a minute, like her old self. With her mouth closed, I saw with relief that she was still beautiful.

One of the hospital attendants—the one she didn't like—came in with her dinner on a tray. This dinner included a pile of meat all smushed up because she said she couldn't chew regular food anymore on account of her teeth. There were also overcooked string beans and some mashed potatoes. But she skipped all of these things in favor of a strawberry mousse, and reminded the attendant, somewhat impatiently, that she'd asked him to bring her two butterscotch puddings and an apple crisp. She said, "Do you think you can do that?"

He was a young guy, maybe twenty-two, twenty-three. And as we waited for his answer, I realized that he probably didn't recognize— even though she was wearing my sunglasses, even though her mouth was closed—my mother's natural beauty.

Tweak

I could hear her in the background reminding her doctor to cover certain points, and I could hear the doctor telling her to calm down, that she'd be sure to get to all the things they'd discussed before placing the call in the first place. Then the doctor explained to me how the conversation was supposed to go: first she, my mother's psychopharmacologist, was going to tell me all the reasons why my mother needed to be on the particular drugs she was on at that particular time, at which point she would pass the phone to my mother, to whom I was then supposed to reiterate, with an appropriate infusion of daughterly concern, everything the doctor had just told me.

This woman spoke in clipped, almost metallic tones, saying she hoped I could talk "some sense" to my mother, who didn't want to take the anti-psychotics and lithium anymore, as she considered herself neither psychotic nor manic-depressive.

But things didn't unfold exactly the way the doctor had said they would, because in the middle of explaining how antipsychotic drugs are not used to treat psychosis exclusively, and how lithium can be thought of as merely an antidepressant, the woman's voice suddenly changed from that chilly, almost mechanical tone to a hoarse, even, you could say, desperate whisper, as she asked whether my mother had always been "like this."

"What do you mean? Like what?"

"Like—*crazy.*"

I knew enough about patient's rights to know that this question fell well outside the bounds of patient confidentiality, and I knew enough about my mother's pride to say, "I don't think my mother would want me to answer that," to which the doctor responded, "Don't worry. She's just stepped away."

She then explained that my mother had been insisting she'd never had a single psychological issue until she lost her job in 1990, and that her breakdown, at that time, had been completely out of the blue. But the doctor and her team had "serious doubts" about my mother's account, and, in her gravelly whisper, she told me that my mother's treatment would be significantly "tweaked" if I could help clear up this issue. And even though I could have, very easily, with one word, I couldn't quite bring myself to literally whisper behind my mother's back, which is why I told her, somewhat primly, that her question would no doubt be best discussed with her patient.

Twice

Isabella was in the passenger seat, Isaac in the back. It was raining and I was tired and for some reason Isabella and I were arguing.

Really digging into each other. I don't remember what we were fighting about, but do I remember feeling unappreciated in the mothering department. This was a couple of years ago; Isabella was in sixth grade. I figured she was probably taking something out on me—some middle school social drama—but I also knew that to say as much would only make things worse. In any case, I think it's safe to assume that my daughter and I were fighting about the issue of respect, because at the time we both felt we weren't getting enough of it from the other. Traffic was heavy and as we went back and forth, I could feel a certain phrase trying to rise up, trying to escape, trying desperately to make its way out of me. It was an urge, more than anything else, like the urge to scratch a rash, or eat a third slice of cake—I wanted, extremely badly, to do something I knew I shouldn't, and when my daughter finally said whatever it was that pushed one of my many buttons a little too hard, I gave into it and shouted, "Do me a favor, would you, and just *shut up!*"

Isaac, in the back seat, gasped. Isabella drew herself up very straight and after a moment said quietly, with great dignity, "That's *twice.*"

"Twice what?"

"That's *twice* in my life you've told me to shut up."

I knew this was meant as an accusation of the most serious kind. It was clear from her wounded tone and solemn facial expression that I had, in her eyes, just committed a parenting crime, and while I did on some level appreciate her point of view, I mostly felt like I'd just received a gold medal . . . My daughter had made it to twelve years of age and could still count on one hand—*two fingers*—the number of times I'd told her to shut up.

U

Ultrasound

After spending a few months in the city hospital, my mother was transferred to the psych ward of a nearby state hospital, which was a major step down. This place was huge and poorly lit. It looked and felt much more like a jail than a hospital, and it smelled like urine. The staff was barebones and largely Dominican, their English spotty. Once when I visited my mother there, I had to help the guard on duty fill out a form recording some of the things I'd brought her; *files* he spelled "fills" and *pens* "pins."

"They're sadists," my mother told me. "They don't get paid much, and they're mad about it. I don't blame them. It's hard working here."

Telephoning her at the state hospital was a serious drag because you had to call a pay phone in the hallway, and there was only about a fifty-fifty chance that someone would pick up. When they did, there was often a long period of negotiation.

"May I speak to Linda, please?"

"She's asleep."

"Could you check?"

"She's asleep."

"Maybe she woke up."

"She's asleep."

"How can you be sure?"

"She's asleep."

If and when my mother made it to the phone, our conversations were sometimes accompanied by screams in the background—long, unraveling wails that came from a woman of incredible stamina. She could keep it up for an entire twenty-minute conversation, but my mother never deigned to notice.

During the time she spent at this hospital, I became pregnant with Isaac. The day I got my first ultrasound, I called to tell her about the little pearl necklace of his spine, only we never got that far.

"I've been here six months," my mother said. She started crying. I said: "Don't worry, Mom. You just have to go through these next few steps. *Step-step-step.* You'll get there." I didn't know what I was talking about, but it seemed to help because she blew her nose and said I was probably right.

Useful

The ancient philosophical system of yoga teaches many useful things. For example, it teaches that the body consists of five *koshas*, meaning "layers" or "sheaths." These enclose the human soul, just as the layers of an onion enclose the onion or the petals of a rose enclose the rose. The outermost layer is called the *annamaya* kosha, which means the sheath made of food (*anna*). It is composed of bones, organs, and muscles. Beneath this is the *pranamaya* kosha, or the energetic covering of the soul, which is sometimes said to be made of breath. The *manomaya* kosha comes next. It concerns the mind and its processes. Beneath it lies the *vijnana-maya* kosha—normally defined as intuition. The fifth and innermost kosha is extremely small. Often it is said to be "no larger than a mustard seed." Despite this, the *anandamaya* kosha directs all the other koshas, although its influence can sometimes be difficult to perceive. This kosha is constant and invulnerable and it is made of pure joy. If we lose track of it, it is only because it has been obscured by confusion and disorder in the outer sheaths. The diligent practice of yoga, as I understand it, is one of the more efficient means for bringing equilibrium, steadiness, and strength to those sheaths and in this way allowing clearer access to the innermost kosha.

At the risk of being pedantic, I think there are a few points here worth stressing:

1. The anandamaya kosha is invulnerable.
2. Everyone has one.
3. It is made of pure joy.
4. Our access to it may be occluded, but it is never entirely obstructed.

There is one more extremely handy tip I've learned from yoga, which is that you can actually locate the anandamaya kosha quite easily, simply by closing your eyes and breathing softly while at the same time concentrating on the image of a tiny mustard seed floating just to the right of your heart.

V

Vanishing Point

A Suburban Street Somewhere in New Jersey, circa 1979

On a sidewalk bordered by velvety tracts of grass, a sidewalk that dwindles to a classic vanishing point, my mother stands towering over the camera. Whoever took this shot must have been crouching or else a child. The silhouettes of several trees splay down either side of the street. The quality of light in this Polaroid is bright and slightly pinkish. My mother holds her hand up to one side of her face. A bleached circle, one of those airborne sunspots, hovers in the upper-right corner. The fabric of her pants seems to luminesce—her legs look like two columns of marble glowing from within. Other than this, her form is indicated only by the bent angle of her arm, a glowing pouf of hair on one side of her head, the thin black band of her wristwatch. It must be a matter of habit, of knowing her features as well as I do, that I see her face here; in reality there's nothing but shadow.

Veggie Burgers

She claimed there was a rapist on the first floor of the halfway house she lived in after she was released from the state hospital. But upstairs, in the women's apartment, she got along pretty well with both of her roommates. I guess they didn't care too much about the little pieces of paper she taped all over the walls, near the sinks and light switches. One of these, affixed to the bathroom wall next to the jerry-rigged paper towel dispenser fashioned out of a bent clothes hanger (my mother's invention), read: "You MUST wash your hands BEFORE and AFTER touching ANYTHING else in the bathroom and dry them with a PAPER towel. This means AS SOON AS YOU COME IN AND AFTER YOU USE THE TOILET AND RIGHT BEFORE YOU LEAVE!!! (Plus use a fresh paper towel to turn off the light and open the door.)" There were many such pieces of paper scattered throughout the apartment, all giving detailed instructions about how to use things like the refrigerator, the microwave, and the oven while keeping them germ free, as well as many reminders scrawled on Post-its regarding the importance of flicking light switches on and off using your elbow, not your hand.

After she'd been living there for a few weeks, my mother invited us over for lunch. Isaac wasn't yet born, but I was extremely pregnant, and I remember that it was hard to get up the stairs because she'd stacked a small armory of cleaning supplies on them: boxes of extra-tall cans of Comet and Mr. Bubbles, multiple jugs of bleach and ammonia, industrial-size refills of Formula 409, Windex, and a job lot of that all-natural supposedly good-for-the-environment cleaning fluid they make from orange peel. The whole place smelled like manufactured orange zest.

Eventually, she'd move into her own apartment (see *hens' teeth*), but not before getting into an intractable argument with the landlord of the halfway house, who leased his property to DMH. The argument concerned several *serious health code violations* as well as *criminal abuses* taking place on the property, but in the beginning she seemed like a happy camper. It was a nice old Victorian, in decent shape, in a bedroom community about a half-hour from downtown Boston. Her room was large and sunny, with two oval bay windows. She'd asked for a fresh coat of paint and had received it: the walls were plum red, the trim creamy white. Scattered all over the floor near her bed were dozens of course catalogs and magazines about landscaping and gardening. We spent most of our visit that day outside, on the rounded porch structure off the kitchen. She had made a beautiful container garden out there (though some of the support systems she'd used to attach the heavy window boxes to the railings seemed a bit cavalier).

For lunch we ate frozen veggie burgers zapped in the microwave and a batch of tabouli that she'd made from scratch. The burgers were mushy, but the tabouli was delicious, and I remember feeling hopeful for a moment because it seemed like she was intent on making a fresh start. For example, she kept talking about how she wanted to go to graduate school to get a degree in landscape architecture. But over dessert I think she got confused because as she cut four pieces of frozen tiramisu out of a box, she told Isabella that she'd already been to Harvard and already had her degree, that she was, in fact, already working as a landscape architect and for this reason was "just like Daddy," only he was an architect of buildings and she was an architect of plants. Actually, the way she put it was that she was "on par" with David, because both of them were extremely lucky to have such *hard but interesting work*.

W

Well-Worn

NEW JERSEY:
Only the strong survive.
—*my favorite T-shirt*

What I'd Choose

I heard a woman on the radio the other day talking about how she'd once watched a movie in which one of the characters had to choose a single moment from his life to inhabit for all his afterlife—just one single experience to relive eternally. The woman explained that she was haunted by this question for months after watching the movie. Which moment would she choose? She studied the question carefully, from many angles, before deciding. In the end it took her years to make up her mind. As I listened to her speak, I naturally found myself pursuing a similar line of inquiry—only I was able to settle almost immediately on my answer.

In Maine, after dinner, if there's no pie, we make s'mores, roasting the marshmallows in the small firebox of the wood-burning stove on which we cook most of our meals. Isaac sits on my lap. Isabella perches close to the heat. David usually stands and orchestrates the ingredients—because there's a surprising amount of orchestration with s'mores. And as he orchestrates, he often speaks of the merits of cold chocolate, which he prefers. I like my chocolate slightly melted on a piece of foil on top of the stove. Isabella likes it either way, as does Isaac, just so long as there's a lot of it.

They take a long time—s'mores—because each marshmallow has to be individually roasted and the firebox is small. Or maybe they take a long time because they're sticky and chewy. They're also messy, of course—the chocolate gets everywhere, the marshmallow goo, the graham cracker crumbs, not to mention the milk that we drink with them, which always seems to spill. In short, everything seems to multiply on those nights we crowd around the stove.

Would-Be

The phone rings just as I'm on my way out of the house, and I sense that electric tug I feel whenever my mother calls. It's been so many months since I've heard her voice that I almost don't recognize it when I pick up. She's been in the seven hundred–bed in-patient facility for almost eight months at this point and, except for a couple of phone calls early on, entirely out of touch. I want to talk, I really do, but the timing is bad because I'm just on my way out of the house to pick up Isaac from soccer practice.

"Just give me one minute," she says. "I just need you to run a super short errand." She explains, and to my surprise it really does seem like a simple task. Not much of an errand at all, according to her usual standards. It involves only running over to her post office box, five blocks from my house, emptying it, and Express Mailing whatever is in it to her at the hospital. She says there is a very important document in the box, a legal form that she needs ASAP because they are having a hearing for her next week on account of some *trumped-up* charges about how she supposedly assaulted a mental health technician when *in actuality* it was the other way around.

"Basically, if I don't have the documents, I'm a goner. They'll commit me for good. I'll be doped up for the rest of my life in this place, and you'll never hear from me again."

The problem is that it's nearly four thirty, and the post office closes at five, and I'm already going to be late for Isaac. I explain all this to her—I tell her about soccer practice and the distance I need to cover just as rush hour is heating up; I also mention the other boy I've promised a ride to.

"The timing just doesn't work right now. I could do it tomorrow, tomorrow morning even, but not today."

"This is *crucial*, Kimberli. Crucial. Do you have any idea what I'm talking about? I'm talking about a lifetime commitment. I'm *talking* about the fact that they want to turn me into a zombie."

"I need more time, Mom. I need a heads up. I can't just jump when you say jump. You know it doesn't work that way. I need a warning. My life is busy. I can't do things when you ask—boom— just like that."

This is a discussion we've had many times before. It never goes well. So I am not surprised when she suddenly changes the topic to inform me, calmly, that I am a bitter person.

"I don't know why you have to say things like that. I am not a bitter person. I'm just a person in a hurry."

"No, Kimberli. You are a deeply bitter person. A deeply disappointed and bitter woman."

"Why am I disappointed?"

I would like to think that I ask this question in a facetious or rhetorical mode. Facetious/rhetorical is, in fact, the tone I attempt to adopt. But it is not the tone that comes out of my mouth. The tone that comes out of my mouth is closer to what I actually feel, which is worried. Because even if it means being late to pick up my son from soccer practice, I will pause long-distance to hear myself belittled, because for some reason I believe this belittling is necessary, believe that, on some level, my mother's words can tell me the truth about me.

"You're bitter because you're just a wannabe, would-be writer. You have no hope of ever becoming a *real* writer. You're bitter because you have no talent, and deep down you know that."

"Why do you do this?"

"Why are you so upset? I'm just being objective."

XYZ

Xmas

For years I've kept a very large jar of sun-dried tomatoes on my night-stand. On the bottom shelf of my nightstand, technically speaking, and behind some books, but still, it's there. David has asked me repeatedly to throw this jar away, but I've resisted, only put more books in front of it so that it's harder for him to see, because those sun-dried tomatoes are a great comfort to me. They were a Christmas present from my mother a few years ago, back when we still tried to get together on the holidays.

Isaac was little—just a year and a half old—the night we drove to her apartment for a late Christmas dinner. This was sometime in January because she'd been too sick or too depressed to get together on the actual holiday, but it still felt like Christmas because we were bringing presents and the car was filled with the scent of the cranberry orange cake I'd made earlier that day. When we got to her place, she told us she was going to jump in the shower *quick quick* and we should make ourselves at home until she got out. We waited forty minutes, picking at cheese and crackers. After she finally emerged and got dressed, we ate the roast chicken and steamed carrots she'd made ahead of time. Everything was salty and buttery, which is how my mother likes to cook, but it was good. After dessert we went into her living room to exchange gifts even though Isaac was already asleep.

I gave my mother a pair of leather gloves and a tea tin filled with her favorite cookies (shortbread made with saffron threads and vanilla sugar). David gave her a camel hair scarf. She gave David a handsome compact umbrella with a handle made of faux-tortoiseshell. Isaac got several children's books with pages made of heavy cardboard and Isabella a top-of-the-line Game Boy. Then she handed me a large and somewhat ornate jar of sun-dried tomatoes three years past their expiration date. The label was stained and torn, the oil cloudy, the lid of the jar dented. I nearly cried but stopped myself. Instead, I said it was late and started bundling Isaac's coat onto his floppy, sleeping arms. Although he was getting heavy, I held him just for the comfort of it while David helped Isabella lace up her boots. On the way home I stared out the passenger side window until I was sure Isabella was asleep, then I let the tears run wherever they wanted to—down my face, into my mouth. Every once in a while, David put his hand on my thigh.

"You should throw those out," he said later that night when he found me sitting at the kitchen table, staring at my gift. But I didn't. Instead, I put the jar on my nightstand—first next to our alarm clock, between a bottle of massage oil and a small, new agey figurine of a mother holding a baby that my doula gave me when Isaac was born. Later I shoved it behind my ever-growing pile of self-help books. It might sound strange, but for a long time those tomatoes were a powerful ally. Because whenever my mother called or stopped by to tell me something, such as I'm a sucky daughter or how she was having trouble extracting worms from her eye or she would never get rid of her bacterial infection if I didn't go to all her doctor appointments with her, I could simply lie down in the comfort of my own bed and inspect the jar slowly, at my leisure. It was like a magical guilt eraser and, at the same time, strangely calming, like a low-tech lava lamp.

But I'm ready now. I take the jar downstairs and hold it over the trashcan in the kitchen and look one last time at the brown tomatoes and slow yellow oil polluted by beige flakes of silt. Then I let it go.

Yet

Walking arm in arm down the stark, vinyl-tiled hallway of some hospital or another, I forget which, my mother stopped and turned to me. Pulling me close, she pressed her forehead against mine.

"This," she said, "is how you say 'I love you' in Irani."

Zigzag

The last time I saw her, the day before she left for New Jersey, it was late summer, early September. The kids were already in school. I was on my way to pick up Isaac, and at first I wasn't sure it was her coming toward me, about a block away, weaving this way and that on the sidewalk, wearing a baggy gray sweatshirt, baggy gray sweatpants, and a pair of flip-flops. As she veered back and forth, she picked at her hair. She was talking to herself.

When I was a kid, I thought of my mother as awesome—fascinating and frightening. I knew that people considered her beautiful, but I noticed all the bits of her, not just the ones that were aesthetically pleasing. I noticed the subtle hint of cellulite on her thighs, the almost three-dimensional gleam of her hair, the slightly crooked line of her upper lip, the shockingly large brown nipples of her breasts, the bumpy bones of her pinky fingers . . . That day in September, as she came closer and closer to me, lurching down the sidewalk with violent left-and-right motions, talking to herself, and somberly wagging her head in a way that made me think of Richard Nixon, I noticed all of her again. She seemed like a stranger but one I knew well, almost from a dream, and full of too many details—too many to keep straight. For instance, I noticed her teeth—broken and yellowed—and I noticed her smallness, because she has shrunken, and I noticed her skin, which was rough and pale and which hung from her cheekbones like worn fabric. There was no greeting, no embrace, when we finally got close enough to speak. She didn't change the timbre of her voice or start a new sentence, but suddenly it seemed clear that now she was talking to me, not herself, when she twisted her mouth sardonically to ask a rhetorical question about her phone service. Her eyes were more gray than green that day, and they were set on me but also not on me.

"Mom?" I said. "Mom, what are you saying? What are you talking about?" She shook her head and kept speaking, only I didn't understand anything she said because she was mumbling. Up close

I could see that something was really wrong with her eyes. They were floating: there and not there. Also, she'd plucked her eyebrows, and there were sores in them. Her eyelashes, too, seemed very thin, almost gone. "Mom, what are you doing?" I asked, but she just kept mumbling, so I put my hands on her shoulders and asked if she was okay, and she shouted: "Am I fucking okay? What do you think, you fucking *brat*? How could I be fucking okay? You have no fucking idea how un-fucking not-okay I am!"

Under my palms her shoulders felt bony and fragile, but I was mad, so I didn't pull her toward me to protect her from the staring strangers who kept passing us. Instead, I said, "Why did you do it?"

Most of the people walking by were parents, like me, on their way to pick up their kids from school. The crossing guard was there too—the one I always chat with but who today was careful to keep her back to me.

"Do *what?*" my mother shouted.

"You had a good situation. A nice apartment. You were safe. It was okay. Why did you throw it away?"

I thought she was going to tell me about DMH and Bill Gates and Medicaid, but instead her eyes stopped swimming and she actually looked at me. Something moved at the back of her pupils, something took shape. Then it was gone, and she threw my hands off. "You're talking like an ignoramus," she said.

"I just want you to be safe."

"You have no idea," she screamed. "No *idea*. You have a nice bed. A nice family."

I knew she couldn't see me. She was looking at me, but she saw something else. I understood this because I am used to it. But still it hurt, which is why I didn't simply nod, which is what I wish I'd done. Instead, I said, "It didn't need to be this way." And she said, "Yes, it fucking did."

&

Until the mid-nineteenth century the ampersand was considered the twenty-seventh letter of the alphabet. Not a letter like the other twenty-six—not a sound unit—but a word, *and*, represented by the graphic contraction of the letters *e* and *t*, or *et*: Latin for "and."

The opposite of *except, but, not*, closer to *yes* than to *no*, *and* opens the field, expands the view. It includes—brings together things and ideas and people and moods and realities to cover more than one possibility, a verbal umbrella:

I am happy and I am sad.

I am a mother and I am a daughter.

I have told a story and I have not touched it.

&

My mother spent nine months in the seven hundred–bed adult in-patient facility in New Jersey. I don't know what they did to her there. Or what she did. Maybe it was just a change in medication. But things are different now. For instance, she's reading books again, for the first time in decades. Also, she cooks meals for herself and speaks much less frequently about DMH and her teeth and her paperwork, and I haven't heard a single word of complaint about her new landlord. She lives somewhere in New Jersey, though she won't tell me exactly where. I think she is lonely, but she says otherwise, and I understand this to be an act of love, because she doesn't want me to worry, and also an act of pride.

We've gotten into a kind of groove with something new—texting. I send her pictures of the kids, my knitting projects, the birds at our feeder, our yard in the snow. And she sends me pictures of the food she makes—quiches and omelets and stews—and of her houseplants and of herself. Not weird pictures of herself, just innocuous selfies. One of these I even printed out because in it she looks lovely—old and careworn but still pretty and somehow a bit Swedish. We are, for the time being, friends, sort of. She says, in her texts, that I make her laugh, and I say, in my texts, that she makes me laugh, and both of these things are true.

It's strange, but good. The word *boon* comes to mind. Of course, it's all very long-distance, and maybe that's why it works. But I'm not so interested in why.

Often, when I get up in the mornings to go to yoga, it's still dark outside, and the first thing I do, even before I turn on the light above the stove and put the kettle on to boil, is find my cell phone and check to see what my mother has to say. Sometimes her texts are bright and cheerful. Sometimes they contain good advice, such as "those navel oranges are fabulous now" or "you can probably get some plants / baby trees for free from the national conifer society," and I take note. Other times her texts are far too long, and these I do not even scroll through because the point of a text is shortness and sweetness, and while it is much more difficult to do the whole pressure of speech thing in the form of a text message, it is not impossible. Sometimes my mother sends me ten or twenty texts before I have a chance to respond, and sometimes I don't get back to her for days because I'm too busy or because her texts are annoying or they somehow touch a nerve or simply because I feel trapped by them. But I do respond eventually because I've come to appreciate this fragile thread of words between us. I imagine it as a thin, thin strand of something precious and strange. Something that glints as it runs through the fabric of my life.

&

For my mother's birthday I bought her a candle that smelled like tomato vines and also a yoga mat and a microwavable bowl with a Japanese design on it. In addition, I sent a tin of her favorite cookies—saffron vanilla shortbread. For Christmas I made her more of the same cookies because she says she can't get enough of them and mailed a pair of colorful socks and another, slightly different microwavable bowl as well as a mystery novel. I sent these things to an address that she has told me is not the address where she actually lives. It is a strange address with a curiously long street number and a complicated apartment number, and although I have Google-mapped these numbers, I have failed to attach them to an actual building, and yet, through the eerie window of Google's "street view," I have at least seen that the general neighborhood is suburban and treeless and a little dilapidated but not terribly so. In any case my mother always gets the things I send. Recently, she told me that she likes to light the candle and read the novel while wearing the socks and nibbling on the cookies. Then, she said, she is *happy as a clam*. Then, she said, she is *in heaven*. And when she told me this, I, too, felt happy in a quiet, clam-like way.

&

I had a funny dream the other night in which I was brushing my hair when I found a gray strand. When I tried to pluck it out, it wouldn't budge. On closer inspection I could see why: it was attached, in a really complicated way, to several strands of brown. Disentangling the single gray hair proved a serious hassle, so I just yanked out the bunch of them. Looking at the clump in my hand, I realized that the thing in the middle wasn't a hair at all but some kind of fibrous root, which now fell easily away. About four inches long, as thick as a pencil, it was knobby and pale, like an underground tuber. I snapped it in half and watched as a beautiful, waxy white flower bloomed in my hand.

When I told David about this dream the next morning over breakfast, he said, "That's your book," meaning this one. I asked what possible connection a flower could have to these pages, and he said, "They both came out of your head!" And while I was secretly pleased by the comparison, I admit to feeling a little embarrassed by my own dreaming mind's Buddha-like aspirations.

Of course, it would be wonderful to grow a lotus like that— from your own head. But what I have grown is a something else. A glossary. A love letter. A reckoning. And this is it, I think. I think I'm done. I've made it through the alphabet, and the alphabet has made it through this material. These pages are something I've nurtured for years, and they are something I've torn out of myself, one line at a time. Writing them has been a difficult yoga, and I'll tell you a secret I learned along the way: there's something that lives next to memory that isn't quite memory, and there's something that lives next to love that isn't quite love, and there's something that lives next to hope that isn't. It's a muddy, leftover thing. And it's enough.

Acknowledgments

For giving me the metaphor I needed to stick with this project: Sven Birkerts. For their encouragement on early drafts: Alice Mattison, Tom Bissell, Gail Vita Hamburg, Steve Carr, and Louise Elving. For taking me on: Alicia Christensen and Tobias Wolff. For their heartening support: the Massachusetts Cultural Foundation, the Bread Loaf Writers Conference, the Edward Albee Foundation, the Key West Literary Seminars, the Boston Writers' Room, the Virginia Center for the Creative Arts, and the Ragdale Foundation. For their artistic example: Sara Egan, Beth Woodcome Platow, Julie Carr, Julia Werntz, and Pandelis Karayorgis. For their reading: Rita Zoey Chin and Lisa Gozashti. For their listening: Rebecca Drill and Nancy Cetlin. For their understanding: my mother, my sister, my father. For their teaching: Kate O'Donnell and Rich Ray. For their inspiration: Nina Carr and Jonah Carr. For his friendship, editorial eye, straight talk, and humor: James Carr. Thank you all.

In the American Lives Series

To order or obtain more information on these or other University of Nebraska Press titles, visit nebraskapress.unl.edu.